Democratizing Journalism through Mobile Media

Fueled by a distrust of big media and the development of mobile technologies, the resulting convergence of journalism praxis (professional to alternative), workflows (analogue to multipoint digital) and platforms (PC to mobile) results in a 24-hour always-on content cycle. The information revolution is a paradigm shift in the way we develop and consume information, in particular the type we call news. While many see this cultural shift as ruinous, Burum sees it as an opportunity to utilize the converging information flow to create a galvanizing and *common digital language* across spheres of communication: community, education and mainstream media. Embracing the *digital literacies* researched in this book will create an information bridge with which to traverse journalism's commercial precarity, the marginalization of some communities and the journalism school curricula.

> This book from one of the pioneers of mojo storytelling is an excellent introduction to the possibilities and potential of the smartphone through its intersection with journalism. Filled with personal experience, practical advice and theoretical reflection, Burum has produced an invaluable resource for teaching and research.
> —*Adrian Hadland, University of Stirling, UK*

Ivo Burum, PhD, is a sessional Lecturer in journalism at Deakin University, Australia. He runs Burum Media, a mojo and web TV consultancy that provides training for journalists, educators and remote communities internationally. He publishes regularly on mojo and blogs to www.smartmojo.com. He is the coauthor of *Mojo: The Mobile Journalism Handbook*.

T0372198

Routledge Research in Journalism

Democratizing Journalism through Mobile Media
The Mojo Revolution

Ivo Burum

Routledge
Taylor & Francis Group

LONDON AND NEW YORK

First published 2016 by Routledge

2 Park Square, Milton Park, Abingdon, Oxfordshire OX14 4RN
711 Third Avenue, New York, NY 10017

Routledge is an imprint of the Taylor & Francis Group, an informa business

First issued in paperback 2018

Copyright © 2016 Taylor & Francis

Library of Congress Cataloging-in-Publication Data

Names: Burum, Ivo, author.
Title: Democratizing journalism through mobile media: the mojo revolution / by Ivo Burum.
Description: New York; London: Routledge, 2016. | Series: Routledge research in journalism; 15 | Includes bibliographical references and index.
Identifiers: LCCN 2016001673
Subjects: LCSH: Citizen journalism—Social aspects. | Online journalism—Social aspects. | Mobile communication systems—Social aspects. | Digital media—Social aspects.
Classification: LCC PN4784.C615 B885 2016 | DDC 070.4/.33—dc23
LC record available at http://lccn.loc.gov/2016001673

ISBN: 978-1-138-64168-6 (hbk)
ISBN: 978-1-138-31971-4 (pbk)

Typeset in Sabon
by codeMantra

To my dear mum and dad, who never had the chance to finish school and who moved continents, leaving friends and family, to give us kids a chance. For my darling son Sam and all the stories he will tell.

Contents

List of Figures and Tables

Figures

Tables

Preface

Mojo, changing the world one story at a time.

Convergence and the proliferation of mobile technologies are resulting in unprecedented opportunities for citizens at grassroots levels, in particular those living in marginalized communities, to create and publish their own voice on a global stage. The same smart technologies and neo-journalistic literacies, also used by professional media, have potentially created a common digital language (CDL), between spheres of communication.

Based on Ivo Burum's PhD research and more than 30 years of television experience this book describes the degree to which citizens and professionals can be taught to tell and publish empowering digital stories using just a smartphone. It distinguishes between citizen witness and citizen journalism and introduces a perspective on the philosophies and pedagogy that underpin mobile journalism praxis. Using a case study approach, this is the first book to chronicle an investigation into the development and implementation of common mobile journalism (mojo) literacies across spheres of communication: community education and media.

This work introduces the framework behind the creation of a more empowering manifestation of user-generated content (UGC), which is called user-generated stories (UGS). The multimedia knowledge required to create UGS empowers citizens with digital skills that transform their alternative voice into a more mainstream form. The same skills provide teachers and students with challenge-based alternatives to traditional literacy programs. Mojo offers print journalists a nonthreatening digital storytelling toolkit, which they can use to help bridge their digital divide.

The primary case study, introduced in the book, investigates the accessibility and potential benefits of introducing digital tools and skills in remote indigenous communities, in outback Australia. Supplementary studies, conducted in Australia and China, investigate mojo's sustainability and relevance within the education sector. Further workshops, in Timor and the EU, describe mojo's adaptability and the impact of introducing multimedia tools to print journalists to create and publish digital stories.

A review of literature and a theoretical investigation locate the research in a theoretical investigation of the public sphere and Bourdieu's theories of habitus, capital and field. The introduction of UGS locates the research around a subfield of journalism commonly referred to as participatory.

An investigation of the media industry seeks to explore the shape of convergence and the 24/7 clickstream. In particular, the relationship between the mobile newsroom, citizen-generated content and the impact of social media, is discussed in the context of the development of digital news models and new revenue streams. Specifically, this is explored in the context of the dialectic between Fourth Estate ideals, which position the press as a sentinel promoting democratic principles, and its inadvertent role in limiting the discursive forum in which the public sphere exists, by delivering spoon-fed verified information.

The pedagogical examination of mojo praxis potentially provides a road map for teaching mojo storytelling skills across spheres of communication. These skills enable citizens to create politicized content and to participate in media's online strategies, including web TV. Essentially, the skills and technology discussed here, create a new bridge between alternative and more mainstream news creators.

Key aspects of research include relevant mobile technologies, the role of alternative citizen journalism, appropriate skills training to enable good journalism and the impact of producing and publishing personal online stories within and from communal environments. The book further explores the role of mojo in education and the impact of convergence, and in particular the mobile and social content creation stream, on the media industry.

In summary, the mojo discussed in this book provides a theoretical context that underpins a way of thinking and a method of making multimedia stories in the field. Mojo praxis requires multimedia, journalistic, camera, writing, edit, and publishing skills, making it a lot like a more accessible form of television production. Because mojo is based around accessible smart mobile technologies almost anyone, with the skill set and a smart device, is ready to mojo anywhere there is connectivity. Go mojo.

Acknowledgments

I would like to thank the teachers who helped on my journey, from knocking cars into shape, to doing the same with stories. In particular, I would like to thank my family for putting up with my wandering ways as I travelled the globe learning about storytelling from the people I met. I would like to thank Dr. Phillip Batty and Freda Glynn for letting me share their dream at CAAMA. Thank you to BIITE and Lynda McCaffrey, Queensland TAFE, Kristy Smith, John Bray, Poul Madsen, Geir Ruud, the staff and journalists at Ekstra Bladet, and other Scandinavian media, Emanual Braz and the staff at *The Dili Weekly*, Nottingham University in Ningbo, Dr. Adrian Hadland, my friend Ilicco Elia, Kate Day from Politico, Dr. Tony Dowmunt, Erik Sonstelie and the people at the IJ in Norway. In particular, I would like to thank Dr. Ron Goodrich for his early support, Robyn Ficnerski and Belinda Lee. To Associate Professor Joanne Williams for showing me how to make a graph, and my mojo colleague Dr. Stephen Quinn, who first saw the potential of this research. Thanks also to associate PhD supervisors Dr. Nina Weerakkody and Dr. Toija Cinque and to the unflappable Alison Caddick. To my journalism teacher John Avieson, whose kindness and skill helped a young panel beater begin his knockabout journey into journalism; and to Max Charlesworth, who made time to listen those many years ago. To my PhD supervisor, Associate Professor Martin Hirst, thank you for your support, for reading the material and for the comma safari. And to my editor, Felisa Salvago-Keyes from Routledge, thanks for being so patient. Finally, to those anonymous assessors who supported the thesis and those who assessed this book—thank you all!

1 Introduction

It is not the strongest of the species that survives, nor the most intelligent, but rather the one most adaptable to change.
—*Charles Darwin*

Overview

This research is an empirical study into the implementation of a set of multimedia skills and digital tools designed to help people become more adaptable to a convergent change process taking place across spheres or fields of communication: community, education and mainstream media. Using a case study approach, this research seeks to introduce and define the concept of user-generated stories (UGS). Whether they are short breaking news type stories or longer features, UGS can include narratives of luck, misfortune, hope and more, portraying the more personal color of life. They require a multimedia way of thinking that inter-laces audio, video, text, graphics and stills to create narrative and story bounce.

A multiplanar storytelling approach, required for creating UGS, relies on a set of neo-journalistic skills that include edit skills. Multimedia stories might (sometimes but not always) require more space on a page. They may need more screen time, which is enabled by the web's more elastic structure, but not necessarily by online editors, for whom news value can be a deciding factor.

An underlying rationale for this research is investigating a pedagogy for training citizens to create digital UGS, which enhance the possibility of creating grassroots journalism that's seen more as semiprofessional content that retains its alternative weight. This potentially creates a more meaningful or semiprofessional intersect and dialogue between alternative grassroots journalism and legacy media. Hence, this research contends that UGS skills can form a common digital language across spheres of communication, which can be an important step to generating a more effective public sphere, one with an informed, less marginalized dialogue (Habermas 1989; Calhoun 1992; Bourdieu 1989; Castells 2008; Volkmer 2012; Garnham 1992; McKee 2005; Hartley and McKee 2000; Fraser 1992; Meadows et al. 2010). This introduction works to contextualize the above-mentioned change possibilities within journalism and its subfields (Bourdieu 2005) through an action research lens (Wadsworth 2011; Yin 2003).

Social theorist Jurgen Habermas (2006: 412) believes the public sphere is "the normative bedrock of liberal democracies" that brings together the private autonomy of citizens and their inclusion in debates between state and society. Sociologist Pierre Bourdieu (1998) argues this debate is secured for a mass audience by cultural and symbolic logic, which is applied through the media and the journalistic field.

In the paperback edition of his book *We the Media*, author Dan Gillmor (2006) is amazed by "the growth of grassroots media," especially within media such as CNN[1] and BBC that "feature the work of citizen journalists" (2006: xiii). Gillmor is right: accessibility to computer and mobile technologies potentially creates opportunities for *citizen journalists* to infiltrate more mainstream media. In 2006, Gillmor saw this as a grassroots phenomenon, growing in strength and power. However, two years later, journalist Charles Feldman (2008), in his book *No Time To Think*, called the digital content stream a "tsunami" and a "potential disaster" (2008: x). Feldman was not so much referring to Gillmor's early bloggers, who were creating an alternative grassroots ecosphere, that was expanding what Castells (2009) called *network societies*, or journalists using blogging to connect with their audience. He was alluding to fragmented user-generated content (UGC) that results from social media and smartphone use, which has been described as "kludge" (Jenkins 2008: 17) and "gossip" (Keen 2006: 93). While referring to these shifts in communications as a modern revolution, Gillmor posits an important distinction that needs to be made between *communication tools* and *toolkits*. He tells us that technology has given us the "communications toolkit to allow anyone to become a journalist" (2006: xxiii). I believe this can be true only if definitions of toolkits include a complex set of journalistic skills, without which technological tools are not immediately toolkits. In recent times, even Internet evangelists such as Howard Rheingold (2012) have recognized this and moved from their technologically determinist positions to one that acknowledges a need for digital training.

The relevance of *We the Media* as a chronicle of the speedup of the Internet is invaluable. Released in a paperback edition just before the launch of the first iPhone, it describes a time where the Internet was idealistically seen as an opportunity for progress where "everyone from journalists to the people we cover, our sources, the audience must change their ways" (Gillmor 2006:xxiii). However, at the close of his book, with his optimism tempered by commercial reality, Gillmor laments, "The promise was freedom" (2006:209)—a freedom that Habermas had described as being rooted in,

> networks for wild flows of messages—news, reports, commentaries, talks, scenes and images, and shows and movies with an informative, polemical, educational, or entertaining content ... originating from various types of actors in civil society, that are selected and shaped by mass-media professionals. (2006: 415)

By 2006, this utopian view of convergence between technologies, platforms and suppliers was being derailed by what Gillmor calls "forces of centralization" by government, telecommunications and even the "pioneers who promised digital liberty" (2006a: 415). The research in this book finds added relevance in exploring the dialectic between media possibility and outcome, and in providing a model for a converging media sphere. This is crucial to understand if, as Gillmor (2010) suggests, citizens are to take control and make media serve us.

According to Feldman (2008), the *wild flow* of the convergence of platforms (PC to intimate handheld mobile communication) and workflows (analogue to multipoint digital), which result in 24-hour always-on content cycles, where information travels "faster than the speed of thought," can only lead to disaster. Conversely, author and media analyst, Robert McChesney, believes the converged anytime anywhere communication sphere has created a "critical juncture" (2007: 9) in our communications history. Here, McChesney adds, "Revolutionary new communication technology is undermining the existing systems of communications seen by many as discredited and illegitimate" (2007: 10). This distrust of media, partly fueled by their gatekeeping practices, that determine which news is covered and how (Shoemaker 2009; Hirst 2011; Bruns 2005), leaves the audience wondering, "How can media, facing essentially the same material reality, produce different versions of it?" (Shoemaker 2009: 2). As a result of bias, misrepresentation and hacking, audiences are seeking alternative and more dynamic media sources, which leads to shifts in revenue and results in layoffs at established media houses (Zaponne 2012; McChesney and Pickard 2011) and closures of newspapers internationally (Brook 2009; Dumpala 2009; McChesney and Pickard 2011; Hirst 2011). This has resulted in frantic trialing of new converged workflows, platforms and business models, including reader-funded soft and hard pay walls (Coscarelli 2012) and more outsourced *living* content (Entwistle 2012), to make the journalism business more viable and relevant.

Analysts like McChesney view what some call a potential disaster as a short window of opportunity to reposition communications into a more inclusive, participatory form (2007). This view is now shared by futurist Howard Rheingold, who, in *Net Smart* (2012), shifts from a position of technological optimism, where he said it was enough to be part of the switched-on *smart mob* (2002), to critical realism: "Right now and for a limited time we who use the Web have an opportunity to wield the architecture of participation to defend our freedom to create and consume digital media according to our own agendas" (Rheingold 2012: 2). However, his more tempered view suggests digital media will only further our social and political agendas if we learn to exert control over the medium (2012). He, like McChesney, believes smart mobs need to become *net smart* and create an articulated state where the message uses the medium to its fullest potential. Martin Hirst (2012) agrees, arguing the idea of a social media revolution is a myth of what Vincent Mosco (2004) calls the "promise of the sublime" (2004: 3). He describes this as a digital myth that's an entrance to another reality, rather than some organizing principle of change that spells the end of history, geography and politics (2004). In today's more developed digital sphere, Mosco, like Rheingold, observes that once past the point of believing technology will fix society, "people begin to consider the hard work of creating the social institutions to make the best … most democratic, use of the technology" (Mosco 2009: 1395). What is required, Mosco articulates, is a citizen sphere where the euphoria created by a *technology will fix everything* stage, is followed "by a period of genuine political debate" (2009: 1395). This post in New York University professor of journalism Jay Rosen's blog, "Press Think," describes this state from a citizen's view:

> The people formerly known as the audience wish to inform media people of our existence, and of a shift in power that goes with the platform shift you've all heard about. … Think of passengers on your ship who got a boat of their own … viewers who picked up a camera … who with modest effort can connect with each other and gain the means to speak—to the world. … The people formerly known as the audience are simply *the public* made realer, less fictional, more able, less predictable.
>
> (Cited in Rosen 2006)

As telling are Rosen's own concerns about the socialization of media: "Were we making something happen, because we decided it was good, or inviting citizens to fashion their own goods? And getting down to the nitty-gritty did public journalism work? How would we know if it did?" (Rosen 1999: 8). In 1993, when I developed Australia's first self-shot TV format, *Home Truths*, which gave 20 citizens—formerly members of the audience—an opportunity to tell their own stories on national TV and to become producers of UGC, I had the same self-doubts. But Jeff Lowrey, one of the participants, had no such concerns about his experience: "It's my opportunity as a single dad to get my message across that single dads do it just as hard as single mums" (cited in Burum 1994). Lowrey's experience was short-lived and his message was a one-off. In one sense, his exuberance is an example of Mosco's myth of the sublime, "that animate[s] individuals and societies by providing paths to transcendence that lift people out of the banality of everyday life" (2004: 3). However, Lowrey would argue his community perspective broadened his definition of journalism—hence its relevance to his and the wider world. In the YouTube age, this state of euphoric unpredictability, driven by the promise of "instantaneous worldwide communication, a genuine global village [in essence] a new sense of community and widespread popular empowerment" (Mosco 2004: 25), if still a myth, is hard to resist.

Twenty years after my first experience in self-shot television I am researching the possibility that a more complete set of skills, rather than a *broadcast opportunity*, will give citizens a more sustained voice, and professional journalists more relevant job prospects. Hence, my investigation into whether developing UGC to a more holistic, thought-out, mobile digital storytelling form called *mojo*—the production, editing and publication of complete UGS on a smartphone—can provide a countervailing force against a high level of social precarity[2] (Neilson and Rossiter 2005a, 2005b). The low level of employment, the lack of a political voice and no functioning press, drove the Arab Springers to revolution. This state is also common in many marginalized communities; in education, where teachers need to become digitally literate more than being technically adept; and in professional media, where digital immersion is required for job stability.

In this state of uncertainty, this research investigates the creation of UGS in three communities of practice where knowledge and resources are shared to enable production and publication (Wenger 2007). The case study communities are marginalized Indigenous people learning to bridge the digital divide, students learning to communicate with a global community, and print journalists learning digital skills to make them more employable. These three sectors of communications form a continuum along a spectrum of the public sphere, described as a "zone of communal engagement in which communicative rationality prevails" (Hadland 2008: 4), in a civil space that influences "a network for communicating information and points of view" (Habermas cited in Castells 2008: 78). With the right skill set and access to technologies, these spaces have the potential to support a digital communications language and praxis that could enable such groups to organize the public sphere more than any others before them (Castells 2008). Their shared UGS are published online where they have relevance and *use value* because they are developed stories. UGS circulate in new global knowledge economies extending the individual's and community's reach and power structures, beyond geographical limitations and even social media frenzy. In this environment content is created and potentially vetted collaboratively before being shared (Bruns and Schmidt 2011).

In 2013, according to Ilicco Elia, a mobile pioneer at Reuters, one key to any shared community strategy, or advantage, whether social, educational or business, is digital and more specifically, mobile. "Social media is nothing without mobile. If you had to wait to get to your computer to talk to people, they wouldn't do it, or if they did, it wouldn't be as intimate a relationship as you now have using mobile" (Elia 2012). Elia believes mobile provides a revolutionary modern-day campfire extended storytelling experience because "it enables you to take people on an anytime anywhere cross platform journey that creates the social in social media" (2012). But is this enough and does everyone have the same access? The simple answer is it's probably not and they don't—hence not everyone is able take the journey.

Even though the Internet is far more social and open to minority voices than print, television, or other broadcast media ever were, access to new digital media training and tools is still marked by inequalities and severe participation gaps (Wilson and Costanza-Chock 2009). Rosen's blogger may have *arrived*, but many citizens are still caught in a *digital divide*—the economic gap in opportunities to access communication technologies and learn skills that exist at different geographic and socioeconomic levels (Radoll 2002). The digital divide points to an irony in the current stage of the global information revolution: the contradiction between the promise of the sublime—cooperation and accessibility for all—and the realities of conflict among stakeholders. The reality suggests that many communities, especially those in remote or developing worlds, failed to create networks to empower people to employ digital communication technologies (Wilson 2005). But this is changing, and if we get the technology skills formula right, we may realize enhanced communication possibilities.

In 2007, just "10% of the world's population in developing countries were using the Internet, compared to almost 60% in the developed world" (ITU 2008 cited in Wilson and Costanza-Chock 2009). In 2013, this figure was 31 percent compared to 77 percent in the developed world. This ratio, and hence this research, is of particular relevance to Australia, a developed nation with almost 1200 discreet Indigenous communities, of which 865 have a population below 50 (Rennie et al. 2011: 17). However, we have not been able to provide these remote communities with generally available Internet communication terminal (ICT) access, or the training required to enable inhabitants to tell their own stories. This is vitally important because as Lisa Waller (2010: 19) points out, "senior Walpiri people from Yuendumu in Central Australia consider that because journalists don't listen to them or take an interest in issues they regard as important, their agendas and perspectives are not heard in public discussion of Indigenous affairs." Journalist Tony Koch's sobering advice that listening is the key to Indigenous reporting (cited in Waller 2010: 20) is critical. But perhaps even more relevant is providing training and technologies that enable a sustained and more holistic representation, as Waller suggests, of Indigenous people's own understandings of their world.

McChesney believes the accessibility of technologies and the anytime anywhere ability to communicate suggest "we are in the midst of a communication and information revolution" (2007: 3). He has no doubts it holds the "promise of allowing us to radically transcend the structural communication limitations for effective self-government and human happiness that have existed throughout human history" (McChesney 2007: 5). He believes that opportunities are so profound that in years to come we "will speak of this time as either a glorious new chapter in our communication history—where we democratized societies and revolutionized economies, or as a measure of something lost, or, for some, an opportunity they never had" (McChesney 2007: 5). In Australia, how this communication revolution impacts citizens and media will in part be determined by a series of government reviews that found a need for a more diverse media landscape that includes more local content. However, as media begins moving to occupy new online spaces (see AOL acquisition of the *Huffington Post*) and its reach and immediacy increases, it becomes even more critical for citizens to possess relevant skills to create grassroots user-generated perspectives. This is especially true if citizen journalism is to have an alternative power in a mainstream environment. Currently what is described as citizen journalism "emerges more as the latest incarnation of an existing 'discursive formation' rather than a transformative process" (Hall cited in Meadows 2013: 45).

Hence this book investigates a rationale and praxis for equipping communities, students and even journalists, with the skills and technologies to enable them to secure their own *transformative* voice in a new media landscape. In doing so it suggests that current shifts in communication technology, practice and pedagogy also create possibilities for a digital intersect across spheres of communication. This is a reality identified by many broadcasters, including the BBC, that is about to enter into a more socially equitable content-sourcing era, which, according to BBC director-general George Entwistle, will include more "public service content creation" (Entwistle 2012). This type of content may be stories and formats made using mobile digital storytelling skills and technologies.

Significance

This research arises out of a need to understand the opportunities that digital technologies and communication skills create for citizens to engage with public life at a local and extended level. The level to which content publication opportunities result in change will largely depend on access to education. Also key is whether communication scholars and students grasp the potential and whether media can adopt this change (McChesney 2007). The significance of the research in this book lies in its definition of a style and pedagogy for a more holistic digital storytelling form, which develops UGC into more relevant manifestations of the individual voice, called user-generated stories (UGS).

At a practical level, while drawing on a number of the author's past experiences in creating UGC formats for television (Burum 1994, 1999, 2003), this study extends the current knowledge base by introducing the new concepts of UGS and user-generated programs (UGP). Drawing on an action research case study examination of mobile journalism, the research road tests new technology and develops pedagogy around a model of communication loosely referred to as *participatory*, or *alternative journalism* (Atton and Hamilton 2008). It's driven by the current growth in mobile penetration to almost 7 billion handsets of which 2.5 billion are smartphones. Increased speeds, lower prices and seamless connectivity mean that more than 40 percent of new mobile users are going mobile only. Today about one-third of the world's population is walking around with more processing power in their pocket than the National Aeronautics and Space Administration (NASA) had when it landed a man on the moon (Kaku 2011). But, what are we doing with all this power?

Referred to as *gossip*, *kludge* and *churnalism*, much of the 157 million hours of UGC uploaded to YouTube in 2015 (Robertson 2014) was created by people using powerful technologies. In particular, the rise in popularity of YouTube, Facebook and Twitter—companies developed since 2005 that broker unstructured online content—is creating an unprecedented level of digital churn: 300 hours of footage uploaded to YouTube every minute— enough to fill the slates of 18,000 TV channels 24/7 for a year; 500 million tweets each day; more than 1.5 billion registered Facebook users; estimates that Google+ will grow to 5 billion users by 2020; the equivalent of 4 million years spent every month on social media; 20,000 new Apple apps created each month, with the app market estimated to be worth USD77 billion in 2017; and 100 percent of people owning a mobile in Japan making their next search for a purchase using that mobile (ABI 2013). Eighty-four percent of the people who log on to Facebook each day do it via mobile. Each of the 4 billion views on YouTube each day equates to $1 of annual revenue. Using social media and associated apps is now a way of life for billions of people, as is the use of mobile cameras to record life's sublime accidental witness moments.

But citizens need to learn to use the nascent technology—the current revolutionary shift in communications—to create long-term change. One recent example where mobile was used to ignite citizen witness moments and herald a call to action against repressive laws preventing a free press, was the Arab Spring. However, any lasting effect requires a sustainable change agent to subvert the fiefdoms that can often linger, even after seemingly successful change implementation. In essence, this means a media that has the potential to redefine journalism, taking account of its many forms and living up to its public sphere responsibilities.

With respect to press freedom, we are reminded by Kovach and Rosenstiel that "civilization has produced one idea more powerful than any other—the notion that people can govern themselves, and it has created a largely unarticulated theory of information to sustain that idea, called journalism" (2007: 193). The perceived view about journalism is that it perpetuates an environment where journalists report and citizens read results in "public opinion," which helps "connect the will of the people with public action" (Rosenberry 2010: 3). When this role of journalist, as intermediary between state and public,[3] goes missing, or is repressed, citizens take to the streets, as they did in Egypt in 2011. However, 12 months later, with the military in Egypt declaring absolute power, the Springers were back on the streets fighting for rights they thought they had won in 2011. This led one journalist to ask, "WTF happened to Egypt's socially led revolution?" (Shihab-Eldin 2012). The sad truth is that citizen witnesses, carrying smartphones and talking on social media, have not replaced media's watchdog role in any sustainable way.

Restriction of press freedom does not only occur with statist regimes. Internal gatekeeping practices can occur anywhere media is owned by a privileged few. In Australia, for example, one company with market capitalization of more than USD71 billion (combined) owned more than 70 percent of media in Australia. Hence, even in a democratic society, especially one where an individual controls the majority of media, it is critical for individuals to have an independent voice. In the wake of the *News of the World* scandal, the Australian federal government initiated a number of reviews to regulate media convergence, control and diversity: the Convergence Review (CR),[4] the Independent Inquiry into the Media and Media Regulation (MI),[5] and the Review of Australian Government Investment in the Indigenous Broadcasting and Media Sector (IBR).[6]

Common to all review findings is the view that Australians should be able to participate in a diverse mix of media services, including local content produced across multiplatforms and devices, which reflects our cultural identity (Boreham 2012; Stevens 2011; Finklestein 2011). Most relevant is that all three reviews found that training is integral to ensuring Australians benefit from convergence and the deployment of the National Broadband Network (NBN).[7] Hence, this research finds added significance in developing pedagogical models that transform user-generated citizen witness moments into more diverse journalistic UGS, which addresses recommendations made by the above reviews.

Citizen witness UGC can add unique voices to the communications mix by giving "audiences access to a virtually unlimited information bank." However, *accidental citizen witness* moments are "all too often fragmented, incomplete ... narrower ... addressing private concerns," rather than "building a more robust public sphere" (Rosenberry 2010: 4). The popularity of UGC is based on the assumption that where one comes from "affects the meaning and truth of what one says" (Alcoff 1991: 6). Hence it follows that the privileged person speaking for or on behalf of less privileged persons can reinforce "the oppression of the groups spoken for" (1991: 6–7). As individuals we speak to make sense of who we are in the context of the group, the community or even the revolution (see Chapter 2). Moreover, what can we do to minimize the oppressive nature of *speaking for*?

Mojo praxis is one set of tools that enables people to speak for themselves. This is particularly relevant in Indigenous society where spokespeople often take a national representative approach at the expense of the local. While manifold, the issues of *speaking for* can be mitigated by increasing the possibilities for dialogue based around skills in discursive spaces like classrooms and workplaces (Alcoff 1991). It has long been noted that existing communication technologies have the potential to produce these kinds of discursive interactions. Hence the aim of the training program, discussed in the book, is to maximize this potential by proposing sustainable techniques that create more discursive possibilities:

- A more confident and digitally literate Indigenous public sphere capable of producing local UGS;
- More inclusive student communication spheres using UGS to connect education with community and the professional sphere; and
- Skilled, digitally ready and employable print journalists.

This research tests my hypothesis that citizen, schoolyard and professional mobile journalists can use common digital literacies and technologies to create a common communications language bridge between their own voice and a more mainstream conversation. My research expanded from marginalized communities to include students and media to test this hypothesis. Journalism scholar Susan Forde points out that "even though the practices of alternative journalism are older than commercial professional journalism" (2011: ix), alternative citizen-generated media remains undervalued. I believe the unprecedented opportunity McChesney (2007) calls a *critical juncture*, the cultural shift that validates alternative journalism across spheres of communication, is real.

Curran argues that we need less conformity in journalism and acknowledgment of new communications technologies that sustain audience access to varied viewpoints (2007). I contend that this requires an approach that positions alternative and mobile journalism as a more defined subfield of journalism, so it's not regarded as just "anything that occurs outside the mainstream news media" (Hirst in Forde 2011: 3). My theory is based on a current reality, discussed at length in later chapters, that the developing online web TV environment will require a more complete citizen-generated content. As the BBC lowers the content gates (Entwistle 2012) and the *Huffington Post*/AOL rationalizes the closure of its Patch sites (Gahran 2013), media's reliance on community and education as suppliers of trained multimedia journalists is even more relevant. Hence a "neo-journalistic approach"[8] that advocates certain forms and values of past ways of doing journalism is required to enhance the participatory ideals of empowerment promised by the Internet.

However, unless citizens are trained to produce complete UGS, their UGC will continue to be subsumed by media as filler. This lessens the opportunity for creating cultural diversity at the source and a sustainable and effective public sphere. The generally held view is that diversity at source results in diversity of content, which generates diverse exposure (Napoli 1999). But this does not immediately occur as a result of UGC creation, which can be subsumed by media like CNN, and used as B roll[9] filler for their deep vertical content strands. In general, diversity arises out of opportunity, skills and recognition, which builds self-esteem and confidence (Hawkins and Catalano 1992; Meadows and Foxwell 2011). This encourages a more inquisitive view of the world, which researchers agree is essential even at school to encourage independent thinkers and civic-minded citizens (Clark and Monserrate 2011). Mojo training is part of a process of empowerment that engages citizens in a process of communication across a variety of platforms. As *Guardian* editor Allan Rusbridger points out, the possibility is here for all citizens to engage with media in an open journalism conversation (2010). What is needed is a participatory pedagogy that treats everyone as a co-creator (Freire 1970). I believe that mojo's neo-journalistic approach provides a framework that can transform participatory idealism into functional journalism.

Not Just Stringers—Keywords and Definitions

If the art of *storytelling* is one of the oldest forms of communication, *journalism* is one of its more industrial styles and *mobile* is a current delivery mode. Ask a journalist to define journalism and he or she will tell you the role of journalism remains what it has always been in a democracy—to provide information that citizens need to be free and self-governing. My research discusses a variety of forms of journalism and digital content creation:

- UGC—user-generated content, which is raw, generally freely available, is preferred by networks because it is easily packaged;
- UGS—user-generated stories—a term introduced to describe more developed multimedia content in neo-journalistic form (see p. XX). This term could also be user-generated journalism (UGJ), except that we are working with communities for whom the word *journalism* reeks with derision. Hence, UGS, a less threatening acronym, is used to encapsulate the work of professional journalism and the alternative journalism field. Moreover, we train citizens in principles of digital storytelling before we train them to make journalism;
- Alternative, participatory and citizen forms of journalism (Atton and Hamilton 2008; Forde 2011), which are based on citizens "playing an active role in the process of collecting, reporting, analysing, and disseminating news and information" (Bowman and Willis 2003);
- Civic journalism, which can be done by professionals and can be defined as the reason for doing the journalism—to be civic minded (Atton and Hamilton 2008); and
- Collaborative journalism, which can be done by professionals and citizens together and often focuses on a goal.

These various forms are discussed in the context of the neo-journalistic approach advocated in this research. Neo-journalism is market driven, to account for the need to develop digital platforms and story forms that hold audiences. These enable a multitude of actors with traditional and new skills to be involved in a new, more robust, public digital narrative. Neo-journalism suggests citizens can learn the skills to self-editorialize, on important public issues, as journalism seeks to redefine itself.

William Woo, director of the graduate program in Journalism at Stanford University, suggests,

> At its core, the functional definition of journalism is much like the functional definition of a duck. If it looks like journalism, acts like journalism, and produces the work of journalism, then it's journalism, and the people doing it are journalists. Whoever they are.
>
> (Cited in Kovach and Rosenstiel 2007)

Woo's functional definition, like Rosen's belief that "anything that broadens your horizon is journalism,"[10] makes journalism sound like the coyote in a Road Runner cartoon—wearing a different ACME disguise for each job. Perhaps as journalism struggles under the weight of commercial pressure to fulfill its political role, it has waddled into the jaws of its profession (Bruns 2005; Hirst 2011). In its ongoing struggle to fulfill its Fourth Estate role and transcend its commercial imperatives, journalism's ideals have, as Australian journalist and academic Julianne Schultz suggests, "taken a battering" (1998). As a result, journalism has, as Woo puts it, lost its way: "There is now a widespread and reasonable doubt that the contemporary news media cannot any longer adequately fulfill the historic role the press created for itself several hundred years ago" (Woo 2005: 1).

Woo expands his duck analogy by suggesting journalism is an activity that produces product made for an audience and intended for public benefit (2005). It is presumed that public benefit equates to public interest, "something being important for the public to know in order to make informed decisions" (Hirst 2011: 115). Hirst asks us to consider Michael Jackson's or Princess Diana's death. These were big news days, he says, "beyond the satisfaction of our curiosity" (2011: 115), and even without public benefit they still have news appeal years later. Hirst's observation suggests that we could add one more descriptor to Woo's definition, that of public interest. This broadens our definition to enable an investigation of current online content as a form of what Atton and Hamilton refer to as *alternative journalism* (2008), also called *citizen* and *participatory journalism* (Rosenberry 2010). Not withstanding the fascination with Diana's death, which falls in the realm of gossip, which is also created by journalists, I believe alternative journalism arises out of disenchantment with traditional news coverage, and generally represents the views of marginalized groups in society (Atton and Hamilton 2008; Gant 2007).

In another respect, alternative journalism is the product of current technological possibilities, in particular the Internet's cheap, accessible, many-to-many interactivity (Gant 2007). Its purpose may be to return journalism to "its status as an activity rather than a profession" (2007: 136), depending on the environment to which *it* is responding (Hirst 2011). In defining what *it* actually is, Bowman and Willis provide this observation about alternative (citizen or participatory) content creation: "the audience has taken on the roles of publisher, broadcaster, editor, content creator (writer, photographer, videographer, cartoonist), commentator, documentarian, knowledge manager (librarian), journaler and advertiser (buyer and seller)" (2003: 38). In short, as Rosen's blogger suggests, the audience is now the producer and doing alternative or participatory journalism, of sorts, presumably geared toward public benefit outcomes. But is it citizen journalism?

The term *citizen journalism* has been used to describe everything from the coverage of the Arab Spring to the first footage of the Hudson River plane crash to "perhaps the crown jewel of American citizen journalism—the famous Zapruder film" (Gant 2007: 139). Gillmor (2010) is in no doubt that Zapruder's film is an act of citizen journalism. However, a man watching a parade, who at best can be described as an accidental citizen witness, shot the film of Kennedy's assassination. Zapruder's film is the result of being *in the right spot at the right time*—a raw *citizen eyewitness* moment. It became newsworthy because Kennedy was assassinated. Is this journalism, or does journalism require Woo's qualifiers and an act of constructed journalism—orchestrated filming, editing, and a narration that structures raw content into a narrative form for public benefit and publication? While mobile technology makes us all potential Zapruders, does it make us all citizen journalists? Would it have made a difference if Zapruder shot establisher shots of the scene and vox-pops after the assassination? Or does the person shooting also have to structure the raw content in either an edit or a blog for it to become journalism? Does our constant connection to network nodes make a difference? It may. A real question we need to ask is not what is journalism, but where does the journalistic process begin? In the era of social media it might begin with citizen created UGC.

These issues raise questions about UGC: Is it a form of journalism, or does it depend on the way it is used? For instance, who was the journalist and who did the journalism in the reporting of the Hudson River plane crash? Was it the citizen who recorded the first *accidental* shots because he was in the right place at the right time? Was the first tweet journalism: "I just watched a plane crash into the Hudson river [*sic*] in Manhattan" (Beaumont 2009: 1), or does news need *some* structure around the information? Did the citizen on the ferry who tweeted what is said to be the first picture of the downed plane need to tweet more than "There's a plane in the Hudson" and "I'm on the ferry going to pick up the people. Crazy?" (Beaumont 2009: 1). Maybe it was the news agency that wrapped, integrated and voiced those early smartphone images into bulletins, or the structure of tweets on curating sites like Storify, or Facebook, that put the journalism around this newsworthy moment?

Using Woo's and Hirst's test, we can agree that the news agencies edited, narrated and published the raw pictures in their bulletins, causing the raw footage or stills to take on a newslike form. However, would anything change if the citizen recorded a sequence of shots, such as a wide shot, a close-up and cutaways, with an editing view or process in mind? This could make a great difference, especially if the cutaways[11] were shot so they could be used over specific story moments. The citizen, by choosing specific shots, is editorializing coverage in the same way a photojournalist does, and is probably creating the beginnings of a narrative or UGS—a more thought-out, structured representation of the event. While UGC fulfills a public interest test, the question of public benefit still remains.

The Arab Spring poses a slightly different conundrum. When 30-year-old Google executive Wael Ghonim spotted the picture of a dead man, Khaled Said, it was an accident. What he constructed next—a Facebook repository for photos, likes and comments—ignited a "politically galvanizing Internet" (Vargas 2012: 2) and can be regarded as an act of citizen journalism. His posts and links to websites were conscious acts of curation specifically published for public benefit. If this is an act of journalism, then were the Springers accidental witnesses or citizen journalists? Are their comments and likes on Facebook a form of alternative journalism?

Kate Bulkley writing in the *Guardian* newspaper, about the rise of citizen journalism, believes factual content creation has become hostage to new "immediate" technologies (2012). She provides an example of filmmaker Roger Graef's use of "citizen footage" "to supplement what he shoots himself" (2012). A number of questions arise. Is Graef's work citizen journalism, or is he merely curating citizen journalism or witness content to supplement mainstream work? Is Graef's citizen content, as UK TV's general manager of Factual believes, social media being used to provide free hybrid *amplification* around professional content and concept (2012) in the same way CNN uses raw citizen content from iReport?

While much of the literature on citizen journalism adopts a loose definition, this book discusses a narrower, more structured form, called *mobile journalism*, or *mojo*. I distinguish between *basic* UGC, which is recording and publishing of raw content (Quinn 2012), and the form I developed and called UGS, what Quinn has subsequently called "real mojo" (Quinn 2011: 68). This is recorded on mobile devices and produced to a broadcast-ready state (Burum 2012b) that is not as easily subsumed by media's deep verticals. Clay Shirky writes that becoming media active is about learning literacies, which "means not just knowing how to read that medium, but also knowing how to create in it" (Shirky cited in Gillmor 2010: ix). He says only then will we "understand the difference between good and bad uses" (Shirky cited in Gillmor 2010: ix). Use value is one of the considerations that distinguishes between UGC and UGS; the other is editorial empowerment at the source.

Summary

Current levels of online communication are in part due to opportunities that result from accessibility of new technologies and a sign of dissatisfaction with traditional mass communication forms. Citizens use social media to fuel a bourgeoning UGC sphere, create revolutions, protest financial and social inequality and provide entertainment, news, health and other advice. Moreover, digital convergence and mobile accessibility create unprecedented possibilities for a new online content currency, evidenced by the 4 billion views a day of YouTube. This is the equivalent of 240,000 feature films being uploaded online every week—that is more video content uploaded to YouTube in a month than the three major U.S. networks have produced in 60 years. Impossible to ignore, these numbers generate huge interest from media that is searching for new relevance and a viable business model.

In a comprehensive user participatory table in Singer et al. (2011), there is no mention of complete UGS and the user is primarily seen as commentator. However, in order to be "an equal citizen, equal consumer, equal member of the public," citizens need to "interact with the convergent environment" (Apperley 2011: 17). I contend real interaction needs to be purposeful and result in more than the creation of gossip, kludge or churn, and that for this to occur citizens "require access to digital media literacies as much as technical infrastructure" (Apperley 2011: 17). Real digital literacies enable a level of online participation so that citizens can enjoy the benefits of the digital economy by promoting opportunities for social inclusion, creative expression, innovation, collaboration and employment (Rheingold 1994). It ensures Bourke's democracy equation, resurrected by printing and Carlyle: "it matters not what rank he is … the requisite thing is that he have a tongue that others will listen to" (Tunney and Monaghan 2010: 5). This can only occur when citizens are empowered to produce and publish their own more structured journalism beyond their current witness moments.

Hence, in summary, this book investigates the following:

- Chapter 2 locates the research within current dialogue around alternative and participatory journalism and the use of UGC to create public voice, while introducing the more structured neo-journalist form of content called UGS. The theory section introduces the concept of capital while contextualizing the research within the work of Habermas and Bourdieu and an investigation of the public sphere and fields of communication situated within new global network societies.
- Chapter 3 provides a rationale and design for an empirical action research methodology to facilitate and focus investigation.
- Chapter 4 defines convergence and considers its impact on the media ecosphere to contextualize the possibilities of mojo and UGS.
- Chapter 5 considers the primary case study and discusses implementation, tools and outcomes, including quantitative data analysis.
- Chapter 6 introduces the supplementary case studies and contextualizes this research across fields of communication.
- Chapter 7 considers a detailed examination of the pedagogy around UGS, across community, education and media spheres.
- Chapter 8 provides an overview of some key points of mojo praxis.
- Chapter 9 considers outcomes and introduces future research possibilities.

Digital literacies can enable the type of inquiring minds that can, as Paolo Freire points out, fight against oppression for a more equitable and diverse society (1970). Forde (2011: 2) suggests that "alternative journalism takes very little account of mainstream journalistic practices and values." Mojo training provides competencies that enable us to question the role of journalism, to discern between Lippmann's spoon-fed view and Dewey's more reflexive purpose for it (Lippmann 2008; Singer et al. 2011). This is achieved through a pedagogy that uses technology to bridge school, community and professional communication spheres, and through job-ready digital skills and challenge-based transformative learning (Puentedura 2013) using multimodal contextual forms (Walsh 2011). Citizens have driven online digital migration around what is described as a digital Internet culture (Castells 2001), but more relevant than the culture is what people are doing with their screen-based technology (Deuze 2006). What we need is what Mark Deuze describes as active agents involved in a reflexive process of meaning making (2006), thereby increasing what Hermida (2011) refers to as "audience options." I contend that realizing extended meaning online—use value, relevance and sustainability—largely depends on the degree to which education embraces the opportunities and its responsibilities to create a digitally healthy citizenry, to countervail the impact of mainstream media's online migration.

Professor Oscar Westlund, talking specifically about the news industry, identifies the need to understand how the "sense making process" between different groups "during uncertain and challenging times [has] a bearing on the new" (2011: 2). Mojo praxis and UGS creation train citizens to embrace new digital technologies and storytelling in a meaningful way—something Ethan Zuckerman, the director of the Center for Civic Media at the Massachusetts Institute of Technology, believes is required if we are to transform the gossiplike nature of the current Internet (Zuckerman 2014). According to Maria Ressa, CEO of Rappler, this change can occur if we marry the discipline of old-school journalism with new workflows (Ressa 2014). This is the principle behind the neo-journalistic approach of mojo praxis.

I further contend that creating a common digital literacy between community, school and the professional media sphere can help make sense of society by facilitating a common dialogue for change. However, the form of training, the delivery model and the shape of publishing models are key considerations that need to be addressed before institutionalization of practices and beliefs shapes the medium in ways that underestimate its potential (Boczkowski 2004; Westlund 2011).

In summary, at the close of his book *We the Media*, Dan Gillmor says that he hopes he has helped us understand what this media shift is and where it is headed. I hope the research in this book is a road map on how to use a set of skills to transform the collision of old and new media into diverse local content at the source, based on a professional and universally accepted set of skills, wrapped in a new common digital language (CDL).

Notes

1. CNN's iReport citizen content portal is discussed later with respect to its use or abuse of content rights.
2. "Precarity" is used to describe the material and psychological state resulting from high levels of social unpredictability and low levels of labor security.
3. One of the fundamental Fourth Estate watchdog roles for journalism.

4. Glen Boreham, http://www.abc.net.au/mediawatch/transcripts/1339_convergence.pdf.

5. The Hon. R. Finkelstein QC, Report of the Independent Inquiry into the Media and Media Regulation, February 2012, http://www.abc.net.au/mediawatch/transcripts/1205_finkelstein.pdf.

6. Review of Australian Government Investment in the Indignous Media Sector, http://arts.gov.au/sites/default/files/pdfs/broadcasting-review.pdf.

7. The NBN is Australia's new optic fiber communications network.

8. See www.neo-journalism.org and Mark Deuze and Alfred Hermida.

9. B roll is footage that is used to cover edits, highlight points in an interview or introduce an on-camera person.

10. Rosen at the 2011 Melbourne Writers' Festival.

11. B roll and cover shots.

2 Story in the Age of Social Media
A Theoretical Perspective

> I think digital gives you a leg up ... and it's not just the size (or the cost) it's the difference between the pistol and the rifle.
> —*D.A. Pennebaker (cited in Stubbs 2002)*

Overview

This chapter continues a review of the literature commenced in Chapter 1 before locating the research in a theoretical investigation of the public sphere and Bourdieu's theories of habitus, capital and field. Moreover, this chapter elucidates the emerging literature around a new field of content creation called user-generated stories (UGS). This locates the research around a subfield of journalism commonly referred to as participatory, citizen or alternative (Atton and Hamilton 2008; Goode 2009; Lasica 2003; Gillmor 2006; Curran 2007).

Like a pistol, mobiles enable users to get in close to be part of the unfolding actuality. In fact, technical parameters demand close-quarter interaction between journalist and subject. But like any frontline action, it is imperative to know how to shoot. This empirical study of mobile journalism practice and the creation of UGS investigates the degree to which mobile digital technology and relevant storytelling skills can be employed to empower citizens to create a less representative[1] and more local voice in a more relevant public sphere. I contend the neo-journalistic form of UGS may assist in defining what has been referred to as citizen journalism's elastic boundaries (Lasica 2003), without limiting its alternative weight, as mainstream media attempt to own and define it (Goode 2009).

In 2004, realizing media was converging online, Arthur Sulzberger, publisher of the *New York Times*, announced the importance of having a convergent print–television–online strategy: "Broadband is bringing us all together [combining] all three elements. News is a 24–7 operation, and if you don't have the journalistic muscle in all three [platforms], you can't succeed in broadband" (cited in Quinn and Falk 2005). Seven years later, Rupert Murdoch's decision to split News Corp's publishing business off from its film and television assets (Economist 2012) shows that joining the convergent dots successfully is more difficult than Sulzberger had imagined.

Internationally, the closure of newspapers has been dramatic (Brook 2009; Dumpala 2009; McChesney and Pickard 2011; Hirst 2011). In Australia, convergence has resulted in large-scale layoffs as the media learns how to harness online business models that are becoming more reliant on social media and mobile communication (Huffington 2011; Jones 2011; Ruud 2012; Zaponne 2012). This new market reality can present citizens with unprecedented opportunities to create and use media as a *change agent* (Surowiecki 2009; Jenkins 2008; Gillmor 2006).

A recent example, the Arab Spring, provides a context within which to discuss social media's role in creating an alternate public sphere, where an effective free press did not exist. The Springers' use of social media demonstrated its short-term effectiveness as a wake-up alarm. However, studies on how people use communication artifacts (Boczkowski 2004; Hassenzahl 2003; Quinn 2012; Westlund 2011; Rogers 2003) support my thesis that technology best serves citizens when it is wrapped in *techne*. The high loss ratio of nonstructured user-generated content (UGC) post events like the Arab Spring (SalahEldeen and Nelson 2012) further supports this view. This suggests that social media risks losing its potency and important historical reference when used, as formless B roll,[2] to plug media's content stream.

Transforming raw UGC into more complete UGS begins an intellectual archival process in which one must consider "who says what to whom, in what channel, with what effect" (Lasswell 1948). Referred to as the Laswell maxim, this type of thought process encourages creators to think more about their content in cultural, social and economic terms. If the real importance of traditional or legacy media is its ability to lay an agenda for public discourse, how has this shifted with the mass audience fragmenting into anonymous and interpersonal communications? The process of understanding who says what, to whom, how and why becomes even more relevant. Finding this out can encourage what's been described as online clustering by like-minded individuals (Newman and Park 2003), around what Wenger (2001) calls functional and supportive *communities of practice*, and Castells (2009) calls *network societies*.

Media scholar Axel Bruns calls one output of this content creation state "produsage" (Bruns and Schmidt 2011: 3), which is made by "produsers" (producer and user). Bruns posits that produsage environments are based on open participation by a wide range of people; a revolving hierarchy based on meritocracy where participants "collaborate" on unfinished artifacts that are shaped and "improved" (Bruns and Schmidt 2011: 3) by the group. Bruns adds that because this type of society delivers a quality of work that can substitute for professional content, an industrial definition of what constitutes content and content production is "put on its head" (2011: 5). Currently, much of the online content produced and published by citizens is UGC. Described as gossip and kludge (Keen 2006; Jenkins 2008), it does not immediately replace professional work, nor is it necessarily constructed through a meritocratic process. Witness-type UGC can lack the editorial or political strategy that, for example, doing citizen journalism implies. It is, however, regarded as a form of journalism, when it inspires action or augments professional content streams and media involvement (Allan 2013). UGS are more developed forms of participatory or alternative journalism. Because they involve a personal and articulated process of construction, UGS potentially challenge what media scholars have described as media's gatekeeping practices (Bruns 2005; Shoemaker 2009; McKee 2005).

Because UGS are articulated, their immediate use value as B roll used for plugging holes in media's content strands—such as politics, classifieds, motoring, cooking or technology[3]—is diminished. However, UGS can be sold in the convergent market place like any other video, film or news story.[4] Therefore, more complete UGS have increased commercial value at the source, which increases as media's online involvement converges to more structured formats, such as web TV. A brief discussion of the use of social media and UGC in the Arab Spring provides an opportunity to discuss the impact of communications technology and social media as long-term change agents.

The Arab Spring: A Revolutionary Mobile Moment

On 25 January 2011, the day of the Egyptian uprisings in Tahrir Square, @FawazRashed tweeted, "We use Facebook to schedule the protests, Twitter to coordinate, and YouTube to tell the world" (Rashed 2011). The murder of Khaled Said, in Alexandria, lit a digital match across the Middle East. Six months later, Mohamed Bouazizi's act of self-immolation, in Tunisia, set off three months of horizontal uprisings that helped initiate the overthrow of governments in Tunisia, Egypt, Libya and Yemen. The world watched this unfold *text by text*, and 18 months later we are asking what went wrong (Shihab-Eldin 2012).

In 2010, Bouazizi, an unlicensed fruit vendor who was supporting his family on $140 per month, had unsuccessfully applied many times for a permit, but kept trading without one. On this day, like every other day, Bouazizi wheeled his cart 2 kilometers into town. But on this day a council inspector, a woman, "confiscated his scales, slapped him twice, spat on him and insulted his father" (Salt 2011: 22). Deprived of his income and shamed in public, Bouazizi went home, grabbed a can of petrol and set himself on fire. His cousin Ali filmed it on a mobile and then posted it on Facebook. What occurred over coming months had Middle East scholar Jeremy Salt saying there is "nothing in the history of the Middle East that stands as a precedent for this eruption of the human spirit" (Salt 2011). Salt is talking about the Arab Spring, which was engendered by years of repression, where statist regimes like Mubarak's devalued the public sphere, to a point where even the Arab bourgeoisie could not "gain enough economic weight to challenge the state" (Dodge 2012: 7).

The great paradox in journalism, as Hirst (2012) points out, is that news often happens when the press is absent. At least it did in an analogue news culture. Possibly the regime's great mistake in the Middle East was that it miscalculated the volume and speed with which mobile technologies generate instant viral content streams. The press, if not on the ground, can be present virtually. They aggregate, scrape and curate citizen witness texts, pictures and video moments, and upload them from the scene, to generate their stories. They use free UGC for news, and make meaning from it.

It is argued that deposing the regime in Egypt would not have been possible without social media, because in Egypt reporters could be jailed for up to five years for criticizing government[5] (Ghonim 2012). With government owning interests in newspapers and arresting reporters on the basis of national security, social media became a horizontal valve used to bypass censored communication structures (Mason 2012a). This new anatomy of mobile protest is described as an attempt to reclaim a public sphere through "2.0 revolution" (Lawson 2012). Citizens turned to social media to create "horizontal links using new technology" (Mason 2012a: 301). This arguably turned the streets into "parliaments, negotiating tables and battlegrounds" (El-Ghobashy 2012: 23) that ignited and galvanized a collective action, which citizens had possibly been preparing since the Damascus spring.[6]

Hirst reminds us that "one tweet does not a revolution make" because revolutions "are made in the streets and not in cyberspace" (2012: 1). Data from the "Arab Social Media Report" by the Dubai School of Government supports this. It lists penetration and usage of some new media services in the region, in spring 2011, as very low Facebook had a penetration rate of 22.49 percent in Tunisia and 7.66 percent in Egypt. Twitter was 0.34 percent in Tunisia and 0.15 percent in Egypt (Sabadello 2012).

Notwithstanding this, protests were identified "with Facebook" and "tech-savvy middle classes" and "involved significant participation by the urban poor," using Facebook decoys "to enable the real demonstrations organized via word-of-mouth" (Stein 2012: 23). It became a crowd-sourced manifestation that could provide a news item with the dynamics to enable it to connect with Western audiences. Westlund (2012) observes digital habitats stimulate ubiquitous, participatory media landscapes. Technology impacts how journalists work and how much time they spend in the field observing what they report (Pavlik 2000). In the case of the Arab Spring, digital technology did this and much more. Social media was used as first-stage momentum to enable meetings to overthrow dictators like Mubarak. It broke the "barrier of fear" (Stein 2012: 23), which is probably the revolution's real legacy.

However, even after Egyptians created a revolt aimed at delivering a more participatory public sphere, they found "themselves living under an even more tyrannical and authoritarian military dictatorship" (Shihab-Eldin 2012). In the weeks following Mohammed Morsi's June 2012 proclamation as Egypt's president journalists were being arrested in the region (Mansour 2013). The revolution might have occurred, but as Eric Goldstein from

Human Rights Watch points out, "the laws that Mubarak used to put journalists in prison to control the media are still there" (cited in Dutton 2012). The report published by the Committee to Protect Journalists (Mansour 2013) documents at least 78 assaults against journalists from August 2012 until Morsi's fall on 3 July 2013. If this was the result of a social media revolution, then we can assume the outcome was a few tweets short of a complete narrative. In light of this, apart from showcasing a frustrating potential of nascent technologies to mobilize and inform, what were the gains made by social media following the Arab Spring?

While the Internet is one of the defining opportunities of our time, its use as a revolutionary crowd sourcing tool (Quinn 2013; Surowiecki 2009; Shirky 2008) or as a means of auditing the crowd (Sabadello 2012), is determined by its level of accessibility and the freedom of the prevailing public sphere. The danger with any patchwork of movements that join horizontally is that they can lack the long-term structures required for sustainability (Stein 2012). Consequently, they risk losing the focus of their shared revolutionary story (Lawson 2012). This is compounded by the fact that their technologically horizontal online world can take on "various asymmetrical characteristics" (Goode 2009: 1302). While we are seeing what Grunig describes as a two-way symmetric model of communication (cited in Pavlik 2000: 235), I do not adhere to the view that "no one group dominates the process of persuasion" (2000: 236). The curatorial practices of media editors rank UGC in order of its appeal, which may exclude international coverage. They also rank that coverage according to its perceived use value. Bloggers like Ghonim also create vertical editorialized forms as they did with Springer content. In one sense, blogging collectives and media take the place of Bruns's produser cooperatives and decide the fate of raw social media content. But these forms of gatekeeping mean that citizen witness moments created a *source* risk being marginalized at *exposure*, and their message risks being lost.

Sustained democracy requires freedom of expression and the protection of an effective public sphere supported by a free press. Without this, it can be argued, revolutions like the Arab Spring only pave the way for another repressive state (Mansour 2013). Once reporters have soaked up the ambient journalism (Hermida 2010a) of revolution and moved on, one question remains: How can new media be used to do more than initiate revolutionary moments, which, as Sabadello suggests, "is the 'sexy' part that media usually focuses on" (2012: 18). How can it be used to build civil society with heterogeneous visions of a democratic public sphere? In our networked communications sphere, this is an issue that concerns us all.

Horizontal and Vertical Scaffolds

The ability to express one's views in the public sphere is fundamental to any civil society. The progressive dialectic[7] between news and the public lost its way as the adversarial, or conflict model, of journalism gave way to trading and government subsidy models, which rely on suppliers of prepackaged news, and results in a compromised Fourth Estate (Lewis et al. 2008). Audiences began looking elsewhere, including to alternative online sources, for a less mediated view. However, as philosopher Susan Buck-Morss observes, in her analysis of 9/11, the speed with which 9/11 images were linked to one image—the American flag and "the nation under attack" (2001: 13)—reduces alternative online media to a flattened singular message. This happened in 2011, to millions of Springer tweets and UGC, when media subsumed and homogenized it to one strand captioned as "the Arab Spring revolution." Fairfax Media's head of training, Colin McKinnon (2012), refers to these content strands as "deep verticals," a term that describes specialist publications built around vertical delivery, structure and editorial strategies.

Vertical content structures are systems used to flatten asymmetrical individual content into a branded media by focusing publication practically— up the chain from less to more experienced editors; thematically—flattening content to fit a style; and editorially—to fit an upward referral model. Moreover, while vertical structure and editorial flattening can showcase citizen witness UGC, it is also a form of gatekeeping. This occurs because media and journalists prefer one type of content, or form of story, to another. Bruns calls this "gatewatching" (2005: 2), where media watch online websites like they once watched the wires. They curate, repackage, editorialize and subsume the raw UGC and the tweets. This is why the iReport contributor agreement gives CNN rights to use iReports in any program. Geir Ruud, former digital editor and chief of Danish tabloid *Ekstra Bladet*, believes gatewatching is part of media's filtration role, "as there is no filter in social media ... Facebook and Twitter is [sic] taking a strong position, but they don't edit stuff, that's our role and our future" (2012). Ruud believes journalism could have played this curating, verification or gatewatching role much more during the Arab Spring.

In an online world, with growing contributor pools, vertical filtering usually begins when raw content hits structural nodes and editorial curatorial frameworks. In today's network society this presents an interesting conundrum. A lack of vertical structure enables sweeping horizontal communication, where according to Ingrid Volkmer, citizenry can exist in parallel with strong *tribal* collectives (2012: 1). According to Volkmer, this world provides a global "generative frame of unity within which diversity can take place" (Featherstone cited in Volkmer 2012: 1). This suggests a trend to a diffused definition of the diversity principle based on access and localism (Napoli and Karppinen 2013). The diversity equation, discussed earlier, has been conceptualized to promote and preserve a diverse array of ideas, viewpoints and content options from source through to exposure (Hitchens 2006; Horwitz 2005). In Volkmer's *space* "the public (and its opinion) is no longer a substantial element of the political system of a society, but has turned into a more or less autonomous global public sphere," a space between "the state and an extrasocietal global community" or "world citizenship" (2012: 1). However, unlike the meritocratic hierarchy, which theoretically exists in Bruns's produsage community, Volkmer's autonomous public sphere, with its asymmetrical interpretations of individualism, may not have the skills, time, politicized will or frame of reference to create and shape its own diverse and sustained influence.

Volkmer (2012: 1) cites CNN's *World Report* as an example of a structure that creates and shapes an "extra societal communication sphere" that gives form to the concept of world citizenship. Notwithstanding that CNN's *World Report* contains professionally produced stories, it can be argued that it is an example of targeting transnational audiences by extending political news beyond borders. It can also be argued this happened with Arab Spring UGC when professionals edited it into their stories and into the vertical structures of news operations, like the *World Report*. However, once UGC is uploaded to a central portal like a website, it changes form, is editorialized and risks losing its diverse character as it succumbs to the vertical content structures of a publishing process. Although potential to make one's own story is diminished when raw UGC is uploaded and used as B roll, it is increased when UGC becomes UGS at source. What CNN has shown is that more complete stories can be formatted into programs like *World Report*. Notwithstanding *World Report's* status as a CNN program, its use of complete citizen UGS increases the probability of the citizen's view remaining intact when published. Retaining a grassroots form, as alternative content moves from locally made to globally exposed, is key to maintaining a diverse voice. However, this will only occur if a fourth equation exits: linguistic diversity. This is impacted by access and skill, which can determine the level of locally produced content (Napoli and Karppinen 2013). The skills needed to produce UGS result in more determined linguistic control, a critical step to creating a diverse public sphere. UGS creation requires and enables something Jürgen Habermas refers to as "willful control over technical practice," a process that is also defined by "goals of efficiency and productivity" (cited in Bourdieu 1990: 337). This conscious process is one of the factors that occurs in the transformation of citizen witness UGC into citizen journalism, or UGS. This form will become increasingly valuable as media moves more into more formed web TV.

For example, the new director general of BBC confirms that what lies in store for BBC "is more distribution of our services via the internet" (Entwistle 2012). He believes BBC will enter more into "public service content creation" (2012). This shift of ambition from "live output, to living output," made to embrace public and private sector production, "abandon(s) Fortress BBC once and for all," and "social recommendation and other forms of curation [will] play a much more influential role" (2012). BBC's greater reliance on audience recommendation and curation will involve a redefinition of acceptable content, with a greater regard for user content. Hence, I believe the next phase of content development will include

- UGS that are used as interstitials and as story content for a broad range of in-house and "public service" formats; and

- User-generated programs (UGP) that curate UGS around a thematic produced by groups identified by networks like BBC, such as art councils, community radio and community-generated online programming, which meets network editorial and technical standards.

BBC is not alone in its thinking. ABC has been experimenting with this since 1994.[8] The *Guardian* is currently embracing citizen content as a main driver of its news, along with the *Huffington Post* and *Ekstra Bladet*, whose daily ebLive enables citizen conversations with a vertical form and agenda. These initiatives and formats, while commercially driven, potentially empower a new global public sphere by growing cultural and social capital. This is required to build grassroots comment into a viable and *acceptable* element of a new, more inclusive global communications sphere, which is discussed next.

Sphere between the Nobility and the Public

> The enjoyment of free speech presupposes not merely the physical ability to speak but to be heard, a condition without which speaking to some effect is not possible.
> —*Talal Asad*

Freedom of speech is the most basic of human rights and one that determines the degree of democracy in any nation. Without it, the public sphere is replaced by statist regimes that quash the public's voice, a right that media scholar Mark Deuze (2006) identifies as a cornerstone of democracy. The notions of *public* and *free speech* have been intertwined since the public's right to speak was defended in England in the 17th century. Milton's *A Speech for the Liberty of Unlicensed Printing* (1644) and the Lockean theory of individual liberties (*Second Treatise of Government*, 1690), a precursor to the Bill of Rights, outlined the individual's right to conscience and their property (cited in Muhlmann 2010: 44). The Age of Enlightenment (Rousseau, Voltaire, and Kant) in the late 17th and 18th centuries popularized or journalized the thoughts (philosophies) of Locke and his confreres. Enlightenment philosophies provided ideas to undermine the existing social and political structures. One of those was a more participatory approach to freedom of speech. While Locke had a view that freedom of speech should exist but be limited in its publication (2010: 47), Kant notes freedom of speech is important to democracy precisely because it results in a "new sociability" and an "interchange of varied points of view," a more participatory social and political dynamic "that constituted the public" (2010: 47).

Freedom of speech as an absolute right is an ideal that even the French revolutionaries wanted to limit by law (2010: 61). This view is based on the assumption that "liberty in conflict with the general will, was not a true liberty" (2010: 65), because it may be at odds even with the press. Muhlmann argues journalism, seen as a profession and business, "imposes biased and distorted points of view" compared to those that would freely circulate in a public space "not controlled by the media" (2010: 12). Yet, at the time of the bourgeois revolution, journalism was also the sentinel of free ideals, its role being to provide a reasoned and balanced lens through which to view society and the state. When this avenue no longer exists, when the public sphere chokes and journalists are thrown into jail, citizens plan a sometimes clandestine use of social media to express their anger.

Of relevance here is Jurgen Habermas's sociological study of the public sphere as an enlightened space where the media play a central role providing information necessary for citizens to make informed choices (1989). Habermas's thesis has its roots in 17th-century Paris, with its small-scale bourgeois public sphere of cafes and small political journals challenging the principle of divine or autocratic rule by the aristocracy. It has been argued that his model remains underdeveloped (Dahlgren and Sparks 1991; Benson 2009), one major flaw being that a bourgeois public sphere was exactly that, a class of emerging industrialists motivated by their own capitalist and political interests. Hence this research, which explores the creation of a more inclusive and globally discursive space, includes a discussion of the work of social theorist Pierre Bourdieu, in particular his concepts of "cultural capital," "habitus" and the journalistic field (Benson 2009; Dahlgren and Sparks 1991). These concepts provide a mechanism for examining the two forms of power (economic and cultural) that Bourdieu sees as impacting modern media (Swartz 1997). A study of Bourdieu is also relevant because his sociology, which emerges from a broad interdisciplinary background, fits an empirical mode of investigative research (Benson 2006). This wider approach to the public sphere is important when discussing the dialectic embedded in media practice, in particular the use of language (now also image and sound) to develop meaning and identity, and the role of agency[9] (one's ability to act individually) in undertaking journalistic interventions (Bauder 2010).

The emergence of network societies is shifting communications offshore, or more correctly, off planet. It has ushered in a new global communications sphere defined by instant messaging, social media and mobile communication. Accordingly, the notion of a public sphere as a space for debate of public affairs is shifting from the nation–state to a global sphere increasingly built around communication networks. Notwithstanding this shift, the nation–state is still occupying a beachhead, with transnational companies restricting what may and may not be heard or seen: for example, Google's banning of the film *The Innocence of Muslims*,[10] the Chinese government instituting the great firewall,[11] or the Gutnik defamation case, which tests the globalization of media, setting precedents that ascribe geographic and nation–state principles to legal arbitration around issues of cyber law.[12]

As Asad points out, it is not only about being able to speak, but also about having the power "to be heard" (Dole 2012: 94). An effective public sphere enables the freedom for citizens to have a local voice, something new technologies potentially facilitate in marginalized communities (Husband 2000 cited in Waller 2010). Creating this shift is part of my motivation for investigating how mobile technologies and skills can be used to create complete UGS to infuse a less culturally homogenized and a more diverse and democratic *public sphere*.

Habermas's Not So Public Sphere

Habermas's most quoted work, *The Structural Transformation of the Public Sphere* (1989), is a sociological study in public opinion built around a study of the bourgeoisie. The study has roots in explorations by Durkheim (1893), whose examination into what holds individuals together in social institutions revealed two types of social integration: the mechanical and the organic (Shortell 2012). This thesis forms the basis of Durkheim's differentiation theory, which describes a society with specialized functions requiring specialist social mechanisms (cited in Hallin and Mancinin 2004: 77). Durkheim further argued that the survival of society could only be based on overarching principles such as human rights, democracy and inclusive citizenship, which requires "an even greater role for an independent and effective media" (Hadland 2008: 3). This underpins Habermas's research into "publicness," in particular, a realm of social life where the public organizes itself in a sphere that enables its members to share informed opinions (1989). Without this, the state cannot enact its responsibility to its subjects to provide, as Dewey (2012) suggests, crucial democratic debate in public affairs, which contributes to the individual's self-respect. When the state fails in its public role, this debate often moves indoors. Seyla Benhabib extends the definition of the public sphere to include a "private dining room ... in which dissidents meet," or even a forest if it is the "object or location of an action in concert" (1992: 78). Benhabib believes these locations take on a mantel of publicness and become public spaces by virtue of the discourse that takes place there. This occurred in the Middle East during the Arab Spring, creating what Benhabib describes as sites of "common action coordinated through speech and persuasion" (1992: 78). These indoor meeting areas, also found in Kosovo[13] and in Sarajevo,[14] formed an underground or *revolutionary* public sphere where citizens and media met to debate change possibilities in a society choked by statist regimes or war.

Habermas's public sphere sat outside the official economy as a theatre of debate, allowing only some citizens to "be critical of the state" (Fraser 1992: 110). This frame of reference, the free market liberal public sphere, which "supposes that social equality is not a necessary condition for participatory parity in public spheres" (Fraser 1992: 121), suggests a flawed concept. Fraser argues that a conception of a public sphere that excludes women and also has racist and property implications supposes that the public sphere is bereft of gender and culture, yet inclusion that is not based on social or cultural discrimination is a key function of an effective public sphere (Fraser 1992). What is needed is a more democratic expansion of "the discursive space" (Fraser 1992: 194) into a transformative sphere of consciousness that facilitates action. It was not until the mid-18th century, when the aristocracy almost bankrupted France, that the bourgeoisie realized it needed the workers. Their joined efforts in February 1848 to overthrow the monarchy resulted in the first real attempt to reach beyond the public sphere's flaws to a more normative state (Calhoun 1992).

The continued commercialization of the public sphere in the late 19th century led to the emergence of additional publics, which Habermas says led to "new relationships of power between owners and wage earners" (1989: 124). This signaled the sphere's "fragmentation and decline" (Fraser 1992: 122), and one of the first institutions affected was the press. The public sphere became even narrower as industrialists came to own the presses. Commercial pressures constrained press freedom, forcing it to work in a sphere of limited consensus.[15] In a society where the public sphere was shaped by the interests of capitalist merchants who invested in mass media (Kuhn 2011), the result was a decline in effective political journalism, narrowed political debate around commercial imperatives and reporting without "its independent critical edge" (Benson 2009: 177). This suggests that liberal theories of empowerment that rely in part on technological deterministic free market views are unrealistic because "market-driven development and commercial media systems by themselves are incapable of fostering democratic communication systems or assuring universal access to telecommunications for diverse people and ideas" (Johnson cited in Rennie 2001: 66). Indeed, as Garnham points out, the main attraction of a free press market model is that it "removes the weight of conscious social choice" (Garnham 1986: 51), in other words a public sphere that envisioned consent under domination (Rennie 2001).

Habermas's theories, even his more modern position that describes the public sphere as a "network of communicating ideas and points of view, which filter and synthesize diverse streams of communication" (1996: 330), are based on "face to face argument and mediated communication" (Gripsrud et al. 2010). His is a single analogue space where freedom of assembly is thought to guarantee access to communication. In the new global environment where a more fragmented individualized content replaces mass communication, we are forced to rethink the "relationship between communications and politics and the nature of citizenship in the modern world" (Garnham 1992: 362). Jay Rosen states that what is required in an effective public sphere is for the public "to be in discussion with itself" (1999: 63). While it is argued this may be occurring online, the degree to which the discussion is of public benefit depends, as Fraser points out, on the relevance of the discursive nature of the sphere (Fraser 1992).

Hannah Arendt observes that the transformation of private or public space into a public sphere is an "action" or an "exercise of thought," which she defines as a form of "storytelling," with the express purpose to "orient the mind in the future" (Benhabib 1992: 76). In modern society informative storytelling was largely regarded as the role of the media. When media is censored or fails to tell its story, as happened in Egypt (El-Ghobashy 2012: 22) and in South Africa, when media was accused of inciting violence through its headlines (Hadland 2008), the public sphere becomes choked. Historically, the lack of a public sphere, or the existence of a heavily mediated one, as occurs in many Indigenous communities (Hartley and McKee 2000), has led to alternative community or underground communication: the Paris Commune (1871), where workers' rights were championed; the Russian Revolution (1917), where the Bolsheviks deposed the tsars and formed what would later be known as the Soviet Union; the shadow Kosovo Assembly (1991), where parallel underground Albanian schools, clinics, and hospitals existed; the rise of organizations like the Central Australian Aboriginal Media Association (1980) to champion Indigenous rights in Australia; and the Moqattam slum city of Cairo (2011), where a lack of food turned the *zabaleen*[16] into potential revolutionaries (Mason 2012b). These examples demonstrate that any investigation of the public sphere needs to move beyond Habermas's narrow view of landowners and capitalists who challenged feudal systems for their own vested interests (Benson 2009). It needs to include all the forms of alternative and community media functioning as a "resource that facilitates cultural citizenship in ways that differentiate it from other media" (Meadows et al. 2010: 167). This, Meadows (2005) says, can play a significant role in framing Indigenous issues.

Habermas makes an important contribution by indirectly demonstrating the need for links between civil society and the media. But his narrow view marginalizes the important role and rights of ordinary citizens. He argues for media "self-regulation" by a media that "operates within its own normative code" (Habermas 2006: 419), and argues that this is necessary for the media to play its neutral role. However, this view fails to imagine how media might avoid commercial colonization, in order to act as a force for what he later called "communicative action" (Benson 2009: 181); or how it will best enable the potential of digital technology to empower citizens and communities. This is not surprising given that Habermas's media exists within a bourgeois public sphere where any self-regulating philosophy is impacted by its commercial and class interests. Calhoun suggests that what is required is an investigation of the public sphere as a "socially organized field with characteristic lines of division, relationships of force, and other constitutive features" (1992: 38). In his later work, Habermas acknowledges this and suggests a broader, more politicized approach that includes personal relationships and broader communities. He called this the "life world," where agents achieve "free or ideal speech" through a process of "communicative action" (cited in Benson 2009: 177; Habermas and McCarthy 1987).

Communicative action also sits at the heart of Pierre Bourdieu's sociological interest, which posits a more inclusive public sphere that empowers a "modern form of enlightened citizen" (cited in Benson and Neveu 2005: 9). Here, human existence is essentially *relational* and therefore *conflictual*, influenced by what he calls "habitus," with its emphasis on how "cultural capital" shapes action.

Bourdieu's Habitual, Cultural Fields of Practice

Habermas's public sphere is a finite space occupied by a commercially motivated bourgeoisie comprising a very small section of the public—2.5 percent of the population. Bourdieu believes in a broader concept of commercialization, based on the codified protection of a diverse set of *fields*, which can enable public sphere ideals that embrace the wider social, cultural and economic resources, needed to promote its relevance and autonomy (Benson 2009).

Bourdieu's sociology emerges from a broad interdisciplinary background, including the ethnography of peasant life and sociological analysis of artisans and consumers, science and religion. His field theory (Bourdieu 2005), and in particular the journalistic field, provides an alternative perspective on the public sphere. Bourdieu sees "journalism [as] a microcosm with its own laws, defined both by its position in the world and by the attractions and repulsions to which it is subject from other such microcosms" (Bourdieu 1998: 39), or fields. Field theory is an empirical form of investigation that describes the discursive autonomy within these cultural spaces of society, which allows for multiple perspectives that arise from within fields (scientific, artistic, religious, business, trade union, legislative, judicial, party political). Fields are one component of Bourdieu's conception of social practice. Bourdieu's practice model is shown in Figure 2.1: [habitus plus capital] plus field = practice (Bourdieu 1984: 101).

Figure 2.1 Bourdieu's practice equation.

Fields are "defined through their mutual relationships" (Bourdieu 1984: 101), such as symbolic power. Power results from and enables discourse among internal and external agents acting in and on a field. In media this relationship is "reflected in a dialectic between journalistic reporting and social political structures" within which discursive events are shaped by situations, institutions and social structures (Bauder 2010). Bourdieu argues that fields possess some autonomy from external forces, which they get from an internal set of laws (1998). These laws, or rules, enable decision making and resolution of problems and for agents to engage in power relations between fields (Bourdieu 1984).

In the media context, the power that the journalist field once wielded has been partly eroded by the current disruption in the media business model. This, according to Sparrow (1999), is one way new journalistic rules were, and are developed, "as the outcome of organizational dynamics in conditions of uncertainty" (cited in Benson 2006: 188). This suggests the potential exists for current organization and technological convergence to cause a shift in power and create a new set of rules that map a new way of working within, and between, subfields of journalism.

Bourdieu argues that a rigorous and productive discussion of power, which must be anchored to a broader view about *social life*, requires a theory of society. His theory is based on a logic that "structures must intersect at some point with the beliefs and practices of individual(s)" (Gaventa and Pettit 2012: 1). This intersect occurs within and between fields and is in part determined by what Bourdieu (1990) calls habitus, the socialized norms that guide behavior and practice. To more completely understand the homologous aspects of the journalistic field and how it interrelates with other fields, we need first explore Bourdieu's concept of habitus.

Habitus

Bourdieu believes human action or behavior is regulated by habit and is the "product of obedience to rules" (Bourdieu 1990a: 65 cited in Swartz 2002: 61). He suggests these rules are initially obtained unconsciously "through osmosis or repetition," which he calls habitus, or "the way society becomes deposited in persons" (Gaventa and Pettit 2012: 1). Bourdieu argues habitus is created through a social or group interaction "without any conscious concentration" (Bourdieu 1984: 170). While habitus aims to explain the societal impact on lived experience, it also raises a number of questions. The notion that habitus deposits social knowledge, culture and practice through osmosis presupposes that citizens lack reflectivity, surviving by mastering actions, relations and practices learned from their social field (Wacquant 2005: 316 cited in Navarro 2006). Experience suggests that even in the most mundane situations, social life is rarely only osmotic.

Research for this book undertaken in marginalized communities in Australia, Timor-Leste and China (discussed later) demonstrates that individuals can function within their own ethical and political dimensions, but also those that are outside the cultural template of their own habitus. Anthropological studies by Gellner show that tribespeople, whose lives are orchestrated by cultural mores, can reflect upon themselves (cited in Archer 2007). In traditional Indigenous cultures, for example, habitus determines that much of what happens does so on the basis of group consensus. Using an osmotic process of predictive occurrence called *cultural lore*, communities can influence how an individual develops. Micronesian islanders relied on ancient training systems to provide the relative objectivity required to choose their master navigator. Sociologist Margaret Archer suggests that "internal conversations mediate the role that objective structural or cultural powers play in influencing social action" (Archer 2007: 5). In other words, you can choose to act and how to act. In my experience, individuals can demonstrate emancipated thought beyond habitual norms, for example, through nontraditional education, a desire to work outside the community, leaving a lucrative job to become a poor student, or a desire to experience something "beyond," for example, being a master navigator. This is called agency.

Archer is highly critical of the concept of habitus, implying that it ignores the "dialectical confrontation between *habitus* and the place one inhabits in a geographic space" (2007: 5), that it alone defines the rules by which society exists. Archer believes the constraining and enabling effects of social contexts on individuals are mediated by an individual's own reflectivity. Bourdieu posits "that the responses of the habitus may be accompanied by a strategic calculation tending to perform in a conscious mode the operation that the habitus performs" (1990: 53). However, Archer says that individual responses are more than just strategic and that "internal conversations mediate the role that objective structural or cultural powers play in influencing social action and are thus indispensable to explaining social outcomes" (2007: 5). In the social sciences the debate about whether reflectivity can circumvent the impact of habitus is over whether *structure* or *agency* shapes human behavior—agency being the capacity of individuals to act independently and structure being the habitual forces of society that limit choice and opportunity (2007: 5). Here the mechanism for change is quantifiable, but the degree of actual change is based on the tension between structure and agency that Mosco (2004) calls mutual constitution.

The above tension poses an interesting dialectic in journalism: How does one achieve the reflectivity often associated with subjectivism and still maintain objectivity? John Dewey addresses this in *The Public and Its Problems* (Barker 2008) when he rebuts Walter Lippmann's (Dewey 2012) treatise on the role of journalism in democracy. Lippmann's view is that journalism amounted to repackaging expert information to elicit emotive responses from readers, the supposition being that the public was incapable of thought, and that internal conversations do not exist. Dewey refuted this, saying politics is the right and responsibility of each individual, achieved through interaction mediated and facilitated through journalism. His is a model where members of society are accountable for their actions precisely because, as agents, they exist in a more inclusive public sphere that enables them to make choices to improve knowledge (2008). This notion of accountability to the craft and a eudemonic responsibility to the group sits at the core of mojo studies and praxis. The aim is to provide citizens tools so they can learn to be more discerning of the political possibilities and the responsibilities of being able to upload millions of hours of content.

One explanation of the unprecedented level of citizen-generated online content is that it is a result of internal conversations, a search for contact and knowledge in the individual's relationship between family and society, two of the primary interlocutors affecting habitus, which Archer suggests extends to school friends or workmates and is used to reinforce the subject within the community when they first move away from home. One view of the level of online UGC is that it can be seen as a first attempt by citizens to, as Archers suggests, "initiate their own inner dialogues and to use self-talk to establish their personal agendas of problems and preoccupations" (2007: 271). Archer argues mental activities such as thinking, clarifying and especially imagination are ways "people extend their horizons" (2007: 272). While not replaced, family, friends and spouses are superseded temporarily as interlocutors by unknown webmasters and other *onliners* seeking contact in new social global communities. Bourdieu's use of Durkheim's descriptor of an "ensemble of invisible relations [existing in] a space of positions external to each other and defined by their proximity to, neighborhood with, or distance from each other" (1989: 16) describes the online space.

Bourdieu (2005) did not apply habitus to the specifics of the journalistic field. However, we can see how journalists' and editors' own habitus, such as standards, journalistic integrity, selection and verification, impacts their work. The journalist's *gut feeling* that distinguishes a go-story from an almost-ran and identifies newsworthiness is a habitual characteristic of the journalistic field. The final factor that impacts Bourdieu's practice equation (Figure 2.1), which is inextricably associated with the reflectivity required to grow fields and extend one's habitus and to circumvent control of the state, is *capital*.

Capital

If habitus is a template for a structuring structure that governs the principles of social division (Bourdieu 1984), then capital is its *power source*, which generates practice and results from practice. Capital is an enabling agent of change, which occurs within and transports agents across fields (Bauder 2010). In economic terms, capital is the use value that results from the mental and physical capabilities existent in human beings (Swartz 2002). Bourdieu (1996) further distinguishes between cultural and social capital. *Cultural capital* explains the different opportunities people have as a result of education, family attitudes and societal pressures. *Social capital* is derived from the relationships and infrastructures within a society that enable durable networks and membership in social groups. *Economic capital* is the sum outcome of cultural and social capital (1867). And the relationship between *habitus*, *capital* and *field* provides the cultural capital that enables agency.

Ironically, while access to capital is first based on habitus, capital works to perpetuate or transcend habitus. In more restrictive and or marginalized societies, cultural lore, a lack of education or a nonexistent public sphere can suppress or limit knowledge transfer, which results in existing opportunity structures benefiting a controlling group (Benson and Neveu 2005; Bourdieu 1986). In the digital era, the potential exists to circumvent these negative forces by making cultural capital—the knowledge, creation and distribution of information—more accessible. This potentially creates a less marginalized more local voice in a potentially more diverse public sphere. This sphere, with multiple sources that can create diverse content with broad exposure, is a first test of diversity (Swartz 1997).

In theory, the divergence equation in Figure 2.2 suggests that an input of diverse cultural media capital can generate diverse content. In practice, case studies conducted for this research show this model also requires specific *social capital* within *established fields* of power to sustain it. Napoli (1999) points out that variety can refer to the number of outlets, and diversity refers to the number of choices possible in terms of content or ownership decisions. In Chapter 5, it's argued that even variety of ownership doesn't guarantee diverse content without an input of relevant cultural capital.

Figure 2.2 Diversity equation.

In remote Indigenous communities and in the developing world in particular, cultural capital, such as the digital literacies required to mojo, needs to be introduced in stages. Traditional cultural capital (lore, craft, art, custom, family) is sourced from within, often from elders and family members. It's generally introduced at predetermined stages (milestones) governed by custom (see case study in Chapter 5). The introduction of nontraditional cultural capital, such as digital story (mojo) skills, can happen via the education field (Western knowledge), the media field (information) or the political field (policy). Without the right balance, a technology-rich environment can re-create existing marginalization. This occurred with Imparja television,[17] where the transmission of Western media via satellite TV bombarded Indigenous people with Western programing. This became a staple diet and subsumed the potential for creating diverse grassroots content.

Western electronic media, including news, has become one of the major influencers of cultural capital in remote Indigenous communities in Australia. This results in a highly mediated and increasingly marginalized Indigenous public space. Local issues are increasingly lost to a more national perspective. One reason this sphere, made up of faceless representatives speaking for community, has flourished, is due to a cultural reliance on "we," especially when dealing with local issues. This form of cultural gatekeeping, together with gatekeeping practices of media and even Indigenous-owned media, compounds marginalization at the local community level.

One fundamental requirement for human culture is interaction: "for an intelligence to function there must be another intelligence" (Lotman cited in Hartley 2009: 133). In fact, the recognition of the existence of dual parallel cultures, "a pair of mutually untranslatable languages," is the minimal prerequisite for "generating new messages" (Lotman cited in Hartley 2009: 134). However, as Eric Michaels (1986, 1989) found in his participatory journalism experiments, perpetuating local language to counteract gatekeeping practices, even internal ones, requires reflectivity on the part of the message makers. Bombardment by global Western media works against enabling time to reflect on one's owns environment—unless it can generate an interest in counteracting the media assault. This requires literacies and tools.

In any concentrated media landscape, especially Australia's, standards that promote reflectivity and an alternative independent cultural voice are essential. Meadows et al. (2010) found that when broadcasters monitor their own standards and alternative media is marginalized, the transformation from citizens to consumers is accelerated. This results in "narrowing the range of public sphere debate" (Meadows et al. 2010: 177). This argument was made about Imparja and is again being made, 20 years later, about NITV.[18] Standards alone do not guarantee the best level of alternative content, just as a high level of alternative content doesn't guarantee a focus on diverse local issues. This results from an input of cultural capital—in the form of training—to understand the issues and to enable the creation of local content that creates a focus of positive change and marginalizes the impact of media's centralizing policies and practices. Relevant cultural capital enables the reflectivity, which creates awareness and praxis scaffolds, to empower local participation in a new politicized and more professional and marketable alternative journalism field.

Fields

The third conceptual tool for testing Bourdieu's practice equation is the spatial metaphor he calls "field" (2005). The production of cultural discourse, such as the alternative media discussed here, is marked by a struggle for distinction within and between journalism fields. Bourdieu says the structure and characteristics of agents within a field and the level of interaction between fields distinguishes a field from other fields. Hence, Bourdieu conceives fields as being relational, as "configuration[s] of objective relations between positions" (Bourdieu and Wacquant 1992: 97), situated in "a determinate place in social space" (1992: 214). Cultural capital supports social capital and shifting levels of power as fields interact. This enables agents to alter their positions, status and power over the field and that field's power over fields (Bourdieu and Wacquant 1992: 96). Field theory—the epistemology of field—supports agency.

Change within or between fields is impacted by what Bourdieu calls doxa, or what we know without knowing (Bourdieu 1985). Doxa limits social relations that regulate change by suggesting individuals are subject to incorporated mental structures and boundaries restricting more individual and deliberate cultural consumption (Crossley 2004). Hence a doxic state, where interests of dominant groups achieve a taken-for-granted status, requires an input of cultural capital for change to occur (Bourdieu 1984). As an agent's capital within a field grows, so does its power within and between fields. This occurs by reputation—the result of actions—within and across field–subfield relationships, and is true for the three communication fields (community, education and media) explored in this study.

Mojo praxis is an example of using *cultural capital*—communication tools and knowledge—to overcome *doxa* influences so *agents* can transcend relational positions within their and other *fields*. This role is extended when mojos work with local media organizations and their work enters a journalistic field. In the education field, student mobile journalists transcend doxa influences that presuppose their position as servile vessels, which is regarded as a first step to meaningful education (Crossley 2004). In media, mojo skills enable journalists to be more relational within the journalism and participant citizen content creation fields. This new, more diverse expression of *power* located in more *specialized subfields* of journalism becomes part of the broader information ecosphere in a changing *communication (literary) field*.

A need to articulate journalism along a generalist–specialist continuum reflects various media publics (audiences), media houses and journalist proclivities. For example, in reporting on the Indigenous sphere, journalists will generally see it as a specialist role in concert to their other duties, as either a health, political or sports reporter. The Indigenous reporting space is generally limited and is heavily impacted by economic rationalism and time constraints, which results in Indigenous issues traditionally being reported by rote. This underlines the importance of having Indigenous journalists report on this subfield, rather than non-Indigenous specialists. It is hoped they won't acquiesce to editorial gatekeeping practices, a trend seen among early career specialists described as the "process through which the social reality transmitted by the news media is constructed" (Marchetti 2005: 65).

Hence, a local Indigenous mojo field can potentially serve to enable accurate local reportage by creating a specialized local journalistic subfield of Indigenous reporting. It is hoped that mojos are less likely to become what Marchetti refers to as transitory figures in the subfield (2005) because, as Hirst (2011) observes, alternative journalism revolves more around cultural capital than money. But it can only occur in any meaningful manner if the inputs lead to sustainable outcomes.

One of the major aims of this research is to investigate a cultural practice bridge—a *common digital language*—of common digital literacies and a professional approach to the creation and development of UGC to UGS. In the schoolyard this language creates a student journalism subfield where schoolyard mojos provide an alternative perspective on student life. This occurs when students interact with the wider community and build student citizenship ideals. Mojo creates a bridge between local news outlets, community and education, especially in tertiary institutions, where journalism education has an emerging subfield called multimedia journalism.

The mojo skill set works across all fields of communication to increase confidence among agents who are recognized for their growing reputation as mobile journalists. Community mojos claim local media jobs; students report on the relationship between school and community and even break news stories (Burum 2012b). This prepares students with the skills needed for a career in journalism's converged space. Mojo literacies enable print journalists to stay in work and be able to interact professionally with the global media sphere.

Moreover, as citizen audiences become online producers of diverse content, communication shifts from a controlled analogue public sphere principally defined geographically by the nation–state, to one more defined globally and expressed in network societies (Castells 2009). This study argues that a redefined journalistic field that encourages and trains a new breed of journalist to provide a countervailing voice is critical to democracy. The degree to which citizens can use global networks to create local voices will largely depend on access to technology and skills that enable them to create empowering UGS. Mojos with multimedia skills, working in a journalistic field, across network societies, producing publishable quality alternative journalism, can potentially counteract the gatekeeping practices of large media by enabling a global public sphere with a more diverse politicized frame.

A Global Network Noise

> Freedom of the press is guaranteed only to those who own one.
> —*A.J. Liebling, American press critic, 1904–1963*

One of the major obstacles in creating a new concept of journalism "stronger than either of the original concepts" (Merrill 1993: 12) is the dialectic between the ideals and the profession of journalism. This clash underpins the ideology of a local voice and a nonrepresented media,[19] the type that defines network societies. What is needed, as Merrill (1993: 12) points out, is to be able to separate the "wheat from the chaff" and form "compatible strains of wheat into new but similar hybrids." Merrill (1993) suggests that the basic principle of this dialectic is to let opposites clash and wait for the winners to form a new group. As discussed earlier, this might result in organizational dynamics and rules, but I believe we also need relevant training during the transformation phase. The aim of mojo praxis is to provide the training and to find and unite compatible story narratives and people into more relevant hybrid forms called UGS, created in communities of practice.

This ideology has always been important in shaping the public sphere and promoting a civic society where citizens articulate their autonomous views in order to influence political institutions (Castells 2008). Professor

Manuel Castells defines network societies as social structures built around grids of "digitally processed information and communication technologies" (2009: 24). The nature of networks is to search for structural links and reject others, thereby creating an "us and them situation" (2009: 25). As a result, network societies create a potential for the global to overwhelm the local, "unless the local becomes connected to the global as a node in alternative global networks constructed by social movements" (2009: 26). This is in effect what happened with certain Arab Springer networks, for instance, Ghonim's page. Castells argues that another feature of the network society is an overarching network culture with its own values and beliefs, resulting in a duality—a commonality and a singularity (2009). However, rather than being a converged public sphere, as McKee (2005) suggests, the network society's lack of form and focus can result in a trivialized, commercialized, fragmented space, without a politicized perspective. Arguably, the current network space suffers from all three issues.

In a network society, Bourdieu's core concept of habitus—his template for interaction with society—receives an input of fragmented cultural capital, from a much larger global family who do not really know each other. Tweets and other UGC are structured in, for example, Storify, where they're augmented by millions and subsumed and editorialized by media. Network societies have been described as largely delivering versions of online noise (McKee 2005; Keen 2006; Jenkins 2008). However, Archer (2007) doesn't see this as all bad. Her analytical dualistic approach posits that without people, there would be no structure. Hence, she argues that internal conversations, in whatever form, generate important patterns of social mobility (2007). In other words, the effects of associations (like those created online) will depend on how they are interpreted and how individuals relate them to their own subjectively defined concerns.

In a 1980 interview with protégé Loïc Wacquant, Bourdieu said, "I write so that people, and first of all those people who are entitled to speak, spokespersons, can no longer produce … noise that has all the appearances of music" (cited in Blumenkranz et al. 2013). This was the role of the press that we lost trust in, that Merrill (1993: 12) says was "sterile without obligations to people." Citizens found alternatives in network societies, where individual citizens can be their own spokespersons; all that was needed was a language to enable people to be reflective about possibilities. Mojo skills encourage reflectivity that helps transform noise to narrative. Theoretically, these skills can enable citizens to use network societies to take advantage of what Robert McChesney (2007) sees as a once-in-a-lifetime opportunity to create a paradigm shift in global democracy, education and governance.

In summary, one-third of the world's population is connected online. The 4 billion hours of video watched on Google's YouTube each month is uploaded at a rate of 300 hours every minute. More than 990 million daily users on Facebook who log on via mobile deliver 1.13 trillion likes in a media frenzy that is basically a creation of copycat content. Notwithstanding

Archer's observation that copycat content, or internal conversation, has its own place, what may be required is a more politically reflective alternative media sphere—one that is conceived as a politically active voice, based on ideologies and supported by skills, which is enabled by mobile journalism.

However, finding a balance between autonomy and heteronomy within the field requires clarification. Habermas advocated a "self-regulating media system" that operates "in accordance with its own normative code" (Habermas 2006: 419). Bourdieu favors a more autonomous *journalistic field*, that is, a space in which journalistic excellence is defined according to journalistic criteria, not by profit maximizing or political agendas (Bourdieu 1998). The empirical reality suggests that journalists, like other professionals, struggle to maintain their autonomy from economic and political pressures. A balance is found in the dialectic that exists between their role of serving society (their real masters), business (who pay their bills) and journalists (who judge their skill). The collision of these opposing forces and values is where real change can occur. In this convergence of three opposing tunes, Hegel (cited in Spencer and Krauze 2012) believes moments begin to be synthesized and thesis converges with an opposing force, before forming a new paradigm. In discussing the dialectic in convergence, it's suggested that technology can alter the "meaning of words" because "embedded in every tool is an ideological bias, a predisposition to construct the world ... to amplify one's sense of skills or attitude more loudly that another" (Postman in Hirst and Harrison 2007). Yet the producers of the antithesis, the bricolage of citizen-generated online content that's causing journalistic anxiety, are yet to fully realize the potential of the opportunity, which McChesney (2007) concludes is a brief window of opportunity, in communications history, to create a more diverse public sphere.

Habermas asks journalism to keep an open door to civil society, yet his public sphere consisted of a select bourgeoisie with a closed view about journalism's role as an interlocutor between state and society. Hirst describes this as a "historically situated contradiction within the bourgeois model of both journalism and the public sphere" that contributed to "alternative journalism" (2011: 125). He says today this occurs as a result of news media functioning within what Daniel Hallin calls "spheres of consensus and limited controversy" (cited in Hirst 2011: 126), which limit the effectiveness of the public sphere as a facilitator of interactions between state and society. "If citizens, civil society, or the state fail to fulfill the demands of this interaction, or if the channels of communication between two or more of the key components of the process are blocked, the whole system of representation and decision making comes to a stalemate," says Castells (2008: 79). There is no doubt the journalistic field as watchdog suffers from its responsibilities to its commercial masters, a relationship that eats into its ability to take the position required to address other experts or politicians. When the autonomous becomes heteronomous, society is left without an arbiter to act on its behalf. In this situation, "the news media functions to dampen, if not destroy, any enthusiasm the proletariat might have for revolution" (Bourdieu in Hirst 2009: 5). This, according to McChesney, is when de-politicization occurs, "especially amongst the poor and working class" (2001). This results from a decreased ability of nationally based political systems to manage problems.

One early public manifestation of this, the proliferation of citizen-generated UGC, occurred in the Arab Spring. Here a breakdown in public trust and the journalistic field's inability to act led to an explosion of social media that became elevated as news-type content. In a revolution, one place the dialectic plays out is between media that favor the regime in power and those against it. In the context of such a split, and the low level of credible media interest and reporting before the Arab uprisings, citizen media accounted for much of the instant documentation of the events in Tunisia, Egypt, Yemen and Libya. Sharek[20] received more than 1,000 camera phone videos of the Cairo uprising against Mubarak (2001). James Curran (1991) argues that citizens need "a democratic media to enable them to contribute to public debate and have an input in the framing of public policy." Without this, society will resort to extreme revolutionary measures, like the Arab Spring, to effect change. Marx and Engels suggest revolutionary acts occur when social actors are caught in a cycle of tensions between the economic base of a culture and the ideas and value systems of that culture, that has reached crisis point (cited in Ferree et al. 2002: 297). This occurred in the Arab Spring because of a failing statist economy and because there were no intermediate associations, like a free press, arbitrating between state and society. This failing economy caused the regimes to become vulnerable, which enabled "revolutionary pressures to emerge during 2011" (Vargas 2012).

Since 1987, researchers have been advocating that a sphere where citizens "are addressed as a conversational partner and are encouraged [by the media] to join the talk rather than sit passively as spectators before a discussion conducted by journalists and [political] experts" (Lawson 2012: 13) is essential to building a healthy public sphere. Today open journalism and social justice programs at the *Guardian* are creating bridges and resulting in citizen stories developed in conjunction with the newspaper (see Chapter 8). The hope is that a new cooperative media discourse will reduce apathy and encourage political engagement by citizens in a more inclusive public sphere. But as John Gaventa (2002) argues, people often do not rise to challenge even decisions that are contrary to their own interests, because they perceive they have no voice. "How people perceive themselves as citizens, and how (or indeed, whether) they are recognized by others, is likely to have a significant impact on how they act to claim their citizenship rights in the first place" (Carey 1987: 14). Moreover, the argument that public participation alone transforms individuals into engaged citizens implies that (1) media content should first and foremost encourage empowerment, (2) participation is available to all and (3) all citizens have skills to enable participation. The real issue is how we mobilize people's consciousness to believe change is possible and to act in their own interests. One answer is through an active and free press, the other is by mobilizing citizen journalism ideals, skills and practices within the education sphere and within communities to create a "community public sphere" (Gaventa 2002: 5).

In conclusion, Rosen recently revised Liebling's remark to account for the Internet age: "Freedom of the press belongs to those who own one, and blogging means anyone can own one" (Meadows et al. 2010: 178). The reality is that until everyone knows how to blog and has the resources to blog, Rosen's comment suggests he has fallen victim to a digital sublime. Therefore, I would add *and with appropriate training, citizens will be able to produce and publish relevant news and information to benefit others*. Hence, this research explores what digitally equipped and trained citizen mobile journalists might do with an idea if they only knew *what* to do with it:

> When what results from these efforts is of a quality [in both depth and breadth] that enables it to substitute for, replace, and even undermine the business model of long-established industrial products, even though precariously it relies on volunteer contributions, and when their volunteering efforts make it possible for some contributors to find semi- or fully professional employment in their field, then conventional industrial logic is put on its head.
>
> (Rosen cited in Bruns 2008: 1)

Volunteer contributors are not yet replacing professional news gathering. But professional journalists are now using mobile journalism technology and skills to create UGS. Students have used mojo to win national digital story awards, and some of the citizen mojo participants in this study have seen their UGS appear on the evening news of a national broadcaster; others have found jobs as journalists within their communities. However, just as no one speaks or writes academic English as a first language (Bourdieu and Passeron 1994: 8), creating mobile digital UGS is a learned craft. A relevant community sphere relies on contestation with the mainstream public sphere; however, this will be most effective when citizens have the appropriate multimedia skills to create their own UGS (Ewart et al. 2007). Hence the next chapter, designed to explain how to undertake this form of research, describes the methodology used to create and test the effectiveness of the mojo skills program, its technology and its digital language.

Notes

1. In this research, "representative" is predominantly used to denote that the one represents the many, that is, where one voice purports to represent the wishes of a constituency.
2. B roll coverage is a most important cover shot element that enables expansion, compression, highlight and introduction of interviews and within stories.

3. Media's specialist niche publications that surround UGC with a high level of structure and editorial prefer raw footage that enables them to add their stars' voiceovers and use them to color their own stories cheaply.
4. News stories and feature pieces acquired by companies like Journeyman are on-sold, creating income for the creator.
5. Even though freedom of speech is guaranteed in the Egyptian constitution.
6. Members of the 2000 Syrian revolt against declining standards of living and oppression met in private houses (salons) to discuss reform mobilized around a number of demands expressed in the "Manifest 99," a document signed by prominent intellectuals.
7. Dialectic study established by scholars like Socrates and Hegel and members of Frankfurt School investigates discursive process, its context and the agency.
8. *Home Truths* was a self-shot format that developed UGS, to UGS and UGP.
9. An individual's capacity to act individually and make his or her own choices.
10. Blocking this film in Libya and Egypt because it lampooned Mohammad was a defining act by a transnational that operates on a bias in favor of free global expression.
11. Policed by up to 50,000 officers, the firewall blocks content through restricting Internet protocol (IP) routers, URL and Domain Name System (DNS) filtering and redirection and connection resets.
12. Gutnik (2001), from Australia, sued the Dow Jones News Corporation, from the United States, for defamation over an article published in one of their subscribed publications. Gutnik's victory in having the case heard in Australia, where he resides and where defamation laws are some of the toughest in the world, signals warning bells for online publishing.
13. Before the Kosovo War, citizens had an underground mirror of their normal society where they schooled their young, healed their sick and planned their future.
14. Oslobodenje staff operated out of a makeshift newsroom in an underground bomb shelter.
15. See footnote 10—a sphere of communication defined by subjectivity and the business of media.
16. The Zabaleen is a group of between 50,000 and 70,000 people who live in seven settlements around the garbage dump areas of Cairo.
17. Imparja in Alice Spring was the first Indigenous television station in Australia.
18. See submissions to the Indigenous Broadcast Review.
19. Where individuals are empowered to create their own grassroots voice.
20. Al Jazeera's citizen media service.

3 Defining an Action Research Context and Methodologies

> That which does not kill us makes us stronger.
> —*Friedrich Nietzsche*

Overview

This chapter describes a mixed-method participatory action research mode for investigating mobile journalism. Case study workshops are used to investigate the development of a practical approach to teaching people to create user-generated stories (UGS). Investigating the user experience of people learning mobile journalism (mojo) praxis across community is supplemented by data from implementing mojo in the educational and professional communication spheres. This multifaceted approach explores:

- The potential of using mobile technology to train citizens to push local content out from marginalized groups;
- Mobile journalism as a curriculum device across education for increasing engagement, digital literacy skills and employment prospects; and
- The application of mobile technology and digital journalism skills to create more responsive, relevant and employable journalists.

Like most case study research, the mojo workshops were designed to empirically investigate the introduction of a story-focused form of mobile journalism required to create UGS. As Gilgun (2010) identifies, the aim of this type of investigation is to develop new knowledge by testing assumptions in training praxis, pedagogy and philosophies. Immersive qualitative research is a mode of study that adopts an interpretive approach to data by investigating elements within their context and considering the subjective meanings that people bring to their situation (Clough and Nutbrown 2006). Hence the methodology is designed to explore the creation of mojo skills within new communities of practice, with participants who "have had [or are having] the same life experiences or significant life events" (Weerakkody 2009: 53). The case study workshops investigate groups engaging in a process of collective learning.

The primary case study workshop, NT Mojo, is an Indigenous study in remote communities. The supplementary workshops, in secondary and tertiary education in Australia and media in Timor, Denmark and Australia, were designed to further develop mojo praxis and pedagogy with students and print journalists. More specifically, the study investigates my contention that a digital partnership, built on a common digital language, which creates collaborations between community, education and the media profession, is made possible by common pedagogy and technologies.

Interdisciplinary mass communication arts and practice-based research, such as this, often focuses on empowerment and the observable (Lottridge and Moore 2009: 150). Arts-based research[1] is a response to the increased role print and broadcast media has had in society (Jensen 2012). It has raised complex questions about how to evaluate the quality of research and even whether distinctions exist between *art* and *research* (Wadsworth 2011). However, as the physical sciences begin to accept that the natural world works not so much through cause and effect as through relationships and connections (McNiff and Whitehead 2006), we begin to understand the value of arts and practice-based research—where outcomes are more than research in books.

Moreover, the relevance of this study is enhanced by the shift from singular reproduction in the hands of the rich, arty or religious, to a more egalitarian reproduction using digital tools. As Walter Benjamin described, theoretically this "emancipates the work of art from its parasitical dependence on ritual ... to be based on another practice, politics" (Jensen 2012: 7). Jensen uses this to describe the *always-on state—editing curatorial and change capacity—made possible by mobile digital devices.* This potentially creates a state of global choice and control, a sense of being able to be "virtually present in a literally absent world" (2012: 8). With the right skills, this could result in a more political voice and engagement with public events and issues in a new global public communications sphere.

Unlike art where you have senders (artists) and receivers (audience), the digital media sphere consists of networks of asynchronous media. These media enable a mass of people to be both sender and receiver, to "raise and answer questions, one on one and collectively—synchronously and asynchronously—introducing new forms of interpretation and interaction, as they become eyeballs for one another" (Jensen 2012: 8). It is this key concept of interactivity—eyeballing the world—that begins to clarify the relationship between *communication* and *action*, and the resulting power shifts, particularly in what has been described as today's communications-driven network society (Castells 2009). Also, it is the study's relationship between *technology* and its impact on communication in action that underpins the action research approach of this investigation.

Design

The purpose of a theoretical framework is "to move the research ... into the realm of the explanatory [not] for it to be a straightjacket into which the data is stuffed and bound" (Anfara and Mertz 2006: 68). Yet qualitative research prefers inductive approaches and necessarily encompasses a wide range of research strategies and methods (including data), embracing the perspectives of both researchers and participants (Haseman 2006). Hence, qualitative research around immersive media practice (such as that described in this book) often begins in written form (abstract to sell the concept and describe the process as research), but is often presented using some other method, such as video or training manuals. In keeping with usual qualitative practice, this is a work-based action research (practitioner-led research) project. The investigator undertakes data-driven action research in training participants that leads to publication of artifacts, process documentation and results (Dick 2000). While qualitative research such as this relies on the observation, capture and interpretation of behaviors (Haseman 2006), my mixed-method approach includes quantitative data to more clearly articulate results.

In line with mixed-method approaches, this investigation is also seen as work based, as it impacts a number of workplace environments. While this research is not immediately about supposed good or bad practice, success often relies on eliminating what could be called bad practice. Moreover, as in traditional work-based research, the aim of this study is to arrive at observations and recommendations that are capable of being implemented in further development of the format or style (Hart 2005).

In this study, as *practitioner-researcher*, the workshop structure and training was based on 20 years of the researcher's own experience in pioneering self-shot television production (an early form of UGC). In doing so, the researcher was able to compare proven training methodologies against new digital mobile technologies, workflows and associated praxis. The final stage of any work-based approach involves a report evaluating what has been learned, what has worked and what has not. The structure and output of this study follow the traditional work-based action research style, described in Table 3.1.

Table 3. 1 Research structure

Stage	Description
Creative work practice	Action research and immersion into communities to use the researcher's existing skill sets to create case-study workshops to train mojos and undertake investigation.
Creative capital output	The artifacts of this research are: – UGS workshops—further developed through new knowledge learned from running workshops – lesson plans—developed specifically for digital storytelling across the three abovementioned spheres – comprehensive training manuals—developed from self-shot formats and rewritten to focus on digital storytelling skill sets and further developed during mojo workshops – short training videos and manuals for schools and media – editing knowledge used to create UGS – technology application—knowledge about various hardware and software to create UGS – iBook on *How To Mojo* – two documentaries describing the workshop process – mojos UGS (videos)
Exegesis	The collation of information including the findings and recommendations provided in this work-based report format (Hart 2005).

Action research is a postmodernist model that situates the researcher as a participant, "an active democrat prepared to make statements about what your work is about and how it can best serve the interest of others" (McNiff and Whitehead 2006: 65). Action research enables practitioners to investigate and evaluate their work as trainers and agents of research that's developed on the job (McNiff and Whitehead 2006). In the course of research, professional practice is developed, which potentially assists your organization and the receiving community (Dick 2000). This influences theories that may be based on many years of nonacademic practice-led investigation. The opportunity to investigate those theories and past praxis enables the practitioner to become researcher and show how he or she has contributed to new practices and how these and associated data sets can inform new theory. Producing artifacts such as documentaries, which describe the research, sees the researcher as developing performing artists (Dick 2000). As McKernan (1988) describes, it is self-reflective problem solving, which enables practitioners to better understand and solve pressing problems in social settings. In *The Reflective Practitioner*, Schön observes that:

> practitioners themselves often reveal a capacity for reflection on their intuitive knowing in the midst of action and sometimes use this capacity to cope with the unique, uncertain, and conflicted situation of practice ... an analysis of the distinctive structure of reflection-in-action is susceptible to a kind of rigor that is both like and unlike the rigor of scholarly research and controlled experiment. (1983: viii)

However, the conclusions reached by practitioners involved in action research are rarely neutral: "different people prioritize different values. ... Evaluation processes are always politically constituted and involve the exercise of power" (McNiff and Whitehead 2006: 69). One reason for this is because practitioners bring years of world experience to bear on research. Sometimes this is seen as a shortcoming of action research, for instance, by academics occupying the high ground of research, who Schön (1983) calls professional elites. Practitioners, on the other hand, working in the research swamplands, create practical knowledge that is useful, but not seen as "real theory." The irony is that "the research produced in the swamps is generally most useful for ordinary people" (McNiff and Whitehead 2006: 17), because it presents in accessible language something professional elites can keep as obscure. This is why anthropological research, which can use a combination of field, laboratory and theoretical study, often produces culturally exciting books. This is also a reason why documentaries describing this research were produced.

Schön maintains that action researchers create knowledge through investigating their practice and present theories in the same academic forms as the professional elite. McNiff sees action research as providing a necessary flattening of that elite topology because "many people working in higher education now perceive themselves as practitioners in a workplace with the responsibility of supporting other people in workplaces" (McNiff and Whitehead 2006: 18). Hence Whitehead argues that using action research to investigate self-study enables practitioners to create supportive and "democratic communities of practice committed to a scholarship of educational enquiry" (2006: 18). Indeed, Zuber-Skerritt and Perry (2002) suggest that an action research approach assumes a core action research cycle leading to a thesis action research cycle. Adopted in this investigation, this process involves evaluating and adapting action research during research to adjust for findings (2002).

In action research the degree to which researchers are able to embed themselves into the community determines the degree to which research becomes a social *participatory* process, where structures are understood and the community and researcher work in sync to produce critical knowledge, aimed at social transformation. A major perceived difference between the two forms of research is that "*participatory researchers* assume they will be resisted by vested interests from above, whereas action researchers are often consultants hired by the powerful" (Herr and Anderson 2005: 16). However, it is often difficult to do participatory research without having been invited, and being a consultant does not immediately exclude one from being involved in participatory research. Indeed, action research can often adopt a participatory approach. Immersion helps research participants to trust the researcher to shift the power flow and guide them into the horizontal information sphere—sending and receiving communication. It is argued this is critical to increasing the "autonomy of the communicating subjects" (Castells 2009: 5).

Unlike Haseman (2006), who suggests many action-based researchers do not begin their research with a problem, this is exactly why this research was instigated. The aim was to investigate, develop and provide an intervention to deal with problems caused by marginalization through media. Traditional observational research frowns on intervention, whereas action research demands some form of intervention. Zuber-Skerritt and Perry (2002) observe that action leads to developing thesis stages. Herr and Anderson provide a list of intervention milestones they call a "spiral of action cycles" (2005: 5). Figure 3.1 demonstrates how these mirror the design steps of the NT Mojo case study workshop.

Each subsequent cycle in the action research spiral increases the researcher's knowledge of the original question, in other words, each change brought about by action or intervention. For example, the difference between the way a workshop participant uses a smartphone camera before and after a workshop adds to understanding of the user experience. This occurs in a cyclic or spiral process that alternates between action and reflection and leads to refinement of existing theory, new theory about practice and a solution to the problem. Change is achieved through a greater understanding and new levels of literacy. This will be discussed in Chapter 5.

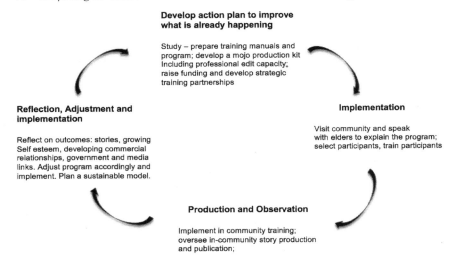

Develop action plan to improve
what is already happening

Study – prepare training manuals and
program; develop a mojo production kit
Including professional edit capacity;
raise funding and develop strategic
training partnerships

Reflection, Adjustment and
implementation

Reflect on outcomes: stories, growing
Self esteem, developing commercial
relationships, government and media
links. Adjust program accordingly and
implement. Plan a sustainable model.

Implementation

Visit community and speak
with elders to explain the program;
select participants, train participants

Production and Observation

Implement in community training;
oversee in-community story production
and publication;

Figure 3.1 Mojo case study spiral action cycle.

Because the media landscape is changing very rapidly, one concern was maintaining currency. This is why the primary focus of this study is on the story element of mojo rather than shifting technology. Hence, this study also develops a framework around which to investigate pedagogy about the transference of knowledge required to create UGS.

A Methodology for Case Study Workshops

Case studies are generally seen as "the preferred strategy when *how and why* questions are being posed [and] when the focus is on some contemporary phenomenon within some real-life environment" (Yin 2003: 1). In this case, real-life experience centers on introducing mobile journalism, or mojo skills and technologies, across spheres of communication.

The primary workshop, NT Mojo, investigates the potential of Indigenous people to acquire and use basic journalism skills and mobile technology to create locally produced content from remote communities. A secondary consideration is whether mobile journalism skills will increase literacy and hence engagement levels where, for example, citizens living in remote communities apply for and secure community-based media jobs. Research demonstrates that the strength of Australian community radio and television is that it can have a positive impact on the well-being of audiences. According to Meadows and Foxwell, this results in a type of empowering social glue that creates a sense of belonging that binds the community and has a "positive impact on individuals in terms of their perceptions of social well-being" (2011: 4). Research indicates that community-based media can assist in managing an individual's state of mind and assist with social isolation by providing a view of a "positive future" (Meadows et al. 2009, 2011).

This is said to be because community journalism is "closer to the complex 'local talk' narratives at community level that play a crucial role in creating public consciousness, contributing to public sphere debate and more broadly the democratic process" (Meadows et al. 2009: 158). Basically, community broadcasting has given communities an opportunity to say "we are here" (Meadows and Foxwell 2011: 13). While it has immediate well-being attributes, such journalism has wider democratic implications. It creates what has been called a "series of local public spheres or a community public sphere ... for local level public discussion and debate for those whose voices were typically marginalised or non-existent in mainstream media" (Forde et al. 2002 in Ewart et al. 2007: 181). This research investigates whether this also impacts positively on the content creators working at a local level.

While undertaking the NT Mojo study, it became apparent that the role of institutions and educators will be instrumental to achieving mojo sustainability. Hence a number of supplementary workshops were run in schools to test application and develop pedagogy for delivering better-trained and more aware student citizens. Workshops run at the tertiary level were designed to investigate whether journalism school students were receiving job-ready journalism training and whether mojo was a relevant skill. Hirst and Treadwell (2011) have identified the need to graduate digitally trained journalists, and ask whether "educators should be teaching software and application in classrooms"? Using Storify,[2] for example, to contain pieces of digital content and craft story, is an example of the technical supporting the creative. Many journalism schools are only just training students to create complete digital UGS. Until very recently, journalism schools did not see it as part of the journalism toolkit, and neither did their teachers (Hermida 2010b). One reason for the lack of attention by journalism schools was that print media still saw social and mobile as a citizen tool. There is still a fear among journalists, and in particular interns, that if they used mobile in newsrooms, they would be less professional. A number of journalism graduates who I worked with in Denmark and who had not been exposed to digital felt that using mobile to create news was amateur. In fact, much of the online video scraped from the Internet, by in-house journalists, is UGC shot on mobile-type devices.

Training journalism students to mojo is only relevant if mojo is relevant to media. Hence, this research also scoped mojo's use value as a tool for upskilling print journalists and delivering content for online news and more formed web TV. The media workshops identify the key technical and political implications of implementing mojo pedagogy and practices in media and described the degree to which trained journalists were willing to become *digital immigrants*.

Study, Size, Scope and Language

The decision regarding the number of participants in the investigation is a reflection of the study's purpose, and in this case, also the remote environment. Samples for qualitative studies are generally much smaller than those used in quantitative studies, and as little as 10 subjects may be sufficient (Attran et al. 2005). The NT Mojo case study workshop was comprised of 11 participants. Ritchie et al. (2003) suggest that as a study proceeds, more data (more subjects in a study) does not necessarily lead to more information. This is primarily because in qualitative research the view is that one occurrence is potentially as useful as many in understanding the process behind a research topic (Mason 2010).

Hence, as a general rule, the sample size of qualitative studies should "follow the concept of saturation and cease when the collection of new data does not shed any further light on the issue under investigation" (Mason 2010: 2). Mason further suggests that a small study making modest claims might achieve saturation quicker than a study aiming to describe a process that spans disciplines. Running workshops across multiple environments, such as occurred with the supplementary studies, produced the *socio-specific* results and a more useful conclusion.

Geography is a determinant that impacts the participant's views of a study. For example, initial training, held at Batchelor Institute for Indigenous Training and Education (BIITE), was difficult for trainees who were away from their families and community. The impact of location on the study is discussed in detail in Chapter 5.

Other factors impacting the workshops related to the need for a fully articulated training proposal for ethics approval. This was particularly the case for the Indigenous workshops, which required certain technical safeguards and cultural protocols.[3] Restrictive government practices and bans on Google and YouTube impacted the workshops held at a journalism school at Nottingham University, in Ningbo, China.

Language played a part in the implementation of the Indigenous and Timorese workshops. Indigenous participants struggled with language, making it necessary to extend workshops. In some instances, Timorese participants required a translator, which slowed workshops. Details of these factors are provided in the full description of the case studies in Chapters 5 and 6.

Ethics Procedure, Collecting Evidence and Analysis

Data was collected in many forms, including video. Hence an important consideration was that participants would be identified in their own videos. Ethics applications to run case study workshops were made to the national ethics committee. Explanatory statements and a set of comprehensive guidelines ensured that all involved knew what we were about to do and why. The design methodology addressed three concerns identified by Waller (2010): (1) consultation, (2) respect and Indigenous involvement and (3) outcome benefits. These and other ethical issues, which are crucial to practice-based research, are discussed in Chapter 5.

Permissions

In each instance permissions were sought to run the workshop and report on the findings from the community, school, university or media organization. All case study candidates were informed that participation was voluntary and that confidentiality of data would be maintained, but they would be identified on camera, for which their consent was required and obtained. Participants were informed that they would be identified as journalists on camera in videos and in written material, as this was an aspect of investigation. The national ethics committee approved these requirements and all participants agreed to being named and shown on camera. Care was taken to ensure that participants did not feel threatened by the program or the group dynamic. It is understood that the method and psychology of working with individuals within groups often relies on pairing (choosing) participants to better facilitate discussion (Fontana and Frey 2000: 663). What is not often realized is that a group dynamic is never fully understood until a pairing is made. Research design needs to account for this shifting state that I call "organic group dynamics."

Collecting Evidence

Case study research expert Robert Yin argues that no one form of evidence "has a complete advantage over all others," and case studies will want to "use as many sources as possible" (Yin 2003: 101). In fact, Yin suggests that research evidence can come from as many as 11 sources. In this research seven were used:

1   *Direct observation*: The case study workshops occurred on location, providing an opportunity to observe how participants dealt with the technical, journalistic and social aspects of mojo work in real time. Direct observation forms a part of action research, and as much of the investigation explored the manner of skill implementation, understanding training methodologies was important. Carr and Kemmis (2004) identify that the things that action researchers research and aim to improve are often their own educational practices and the situations in which they practice. This is primarily because their teaching modalities are their own and hence subjective. This occurred where mojo modalities were transferred from television training and developed for use across a number of environments. In this instance development occurs when the trainer, or researcher, observes their performance and gauges this against retention of knowledge, the psychological state of workshop participants and outcomes. "The interpretive researcher aims to understand practices and situations by seeking their significance in the idea of actors" (2004: 180). In doing this, the participants are observed directly, as is the emerging dialectic between trainee and trainer.

2 *Documentation*: News articles and books written about the use of the media and Indigenous media development are included in the research. Government reviews such as the Indigenous Broadcast Review (2010) and the Wilmot report (1984) were included.

3 *Interviews*: Semistructured interviews were used. We live in an interview society (Atkinson and Silverman 1997), where the interview is "as much a product of social dynamic as it is a product of accurate accounts and replies, [it] has become a routine, almost unnoticed, part of everyday life" (Fontana and Frey 2000: 647). Yin (2003) suggests interviews can remain conversational and still focus on research imperatives.

Interviews with traditional Indigenous people are much easier today because exposure to Western media even in the most remote communities means they are aware of the structure of interviews. In reality, and certainly in a participatory action research environment, the interview becomes "a discourse between two or more speakers" with meanings "contextually grounded by interviewer and respondent" (Schwandt 1997). Fontana and Fey further develop this concept:

> Researchers are not invisible, neutral entities, rather, they are part of the interactions they seek to study and influence those interactions. There is a growing realization that interviewers are not the mythical, neutral tools envisioned by survey research … interviews are seen as negotiated accomplishments of both interviewers and respondents that are shaped by the contexts and situations in which they take place. (2000: 663)

Moreover, this statement implies certain types of interviews are better suited to particular situations. Hence the interview style varied to reflect an understanding of the interviewee and his or her environment. As described by Yin, interviews were "guided conversations rather than structured queries … likely to be fluid rather than rigid" (2003: 106). I first experienced this in 1990 when interviewing remote Indigenous people for the ABC TV documentary *Benny and the Dreamers* (Burum 1992). In that film Indigenous people preferred to be interviewed with another community member sitting behind them, to the left or right, who would corroborate they were telling the true story. Indigenous people are more reflexive in face-to-face situations, so interviews were conducted with all participants of the NT Mojo workshop before and after the workshop. Interviews were also conducted with a number of teachers, key experts in mobile journalism and the media around their field of expertise and the impact of digital and social media on their working environment. Interviews were primarily used in the making of documentary, but also to act as an archive for the case study findings. Interviews were conducted with professionals working in online media and Indigenous media. Interviews are discussed further in Chapter 5.

4 *Surveys*: Surveys are a form of interview used, in this case, to elicit more specific information about participants' use of technology and their views on the relevance of the training. Where possible, participants were asked to complete a set of survey questions about their use of mobile phones and social media. These were designed to help participants think more about aspects of the workshops. Students in primary school worked with teachers to complete their questionnaires. Some journalism students and journalist participants chose not to complete their questionnaires due to time constraints. Surveys are part of a mixed-method approach that provides a level of quantitative data about prior exposure, experience and use of technology. Surveys were also helpful when working with students and journalists, who didn't have time to be interviewed.

5 *Video*: Documentary film such as *Satellite Dreaming* (1991), about Indigenous use of media, was used to provide a historical underpinning of the need for, and the development of, Indigenous media.

6 *Physical artifacts*: Artifacts included videos made by the mojos and the training manuals and videos used to impart the mojo skill set.

7 *Data*: Various data that included a quantitative representation of findings was used.

A Methodology for Choosing Technology

A concept of user well-being, especially one that relates to self-confidence and empowerment, has become an important consideration in research. Hence, the mojo kit was designed with the user experience in mind. User research is often bound by an investigation into well-being and two distinct philosophies: *hedonism* and *eudemonism* (Ryan and Deci 2001). Hedonism reflects a view that "well-being consists of pleasure or happiness," whereas eudemonism posits that it lies in the "actualization of human potential" (2001: 143).

They intersect when technologies, like smartphones, which deliver a high degree of *hedonistic* user pleasure, are used to achieve *eudemonic* outcomes (Ryan and Deci 2001). The basic premise here is that *perceived ease of use* and *perceived usefulness* combine to influence behavioral intention, which in turn affects how the system is used. My contention is that once beyond the subjective hedonic phase, of seeing mojo tools as icons that provide immediate pleasure, newly acquired skills can be used to enter a new moral activity based on an ethical approach designed for communal good. I contend that this requires a more objective approach to personal stories, which can help alternative journalists to, as Forde (2011) suggests, appeal to wider audiences, make a modest living and grow the outlet, in essence, to create saleable alternative journalism, based on a definition of objectivity that rejects neutrality, in favor of "the quest for truth" (2011: 118). These are important issues when alternative journalism is considered in a broader context than community grassroots, or citizen witness media.

Hassenzahl's model of user experience is one method for understanding the relationship between technology and the user that acknowledges subjective impact in varying situations (Hassenzahl 2003). The framework described below is based on the assumption that product character can be described as a *pragmatic* and *hedonic* experience and measured against intended *function* and *stimulation*. The major components of the framework as they apply to this study of the application of mobile technology are as follows:

- *Product features*: The iPhone's functionality, creating a user-friendliness enabling practical and theoretical components of training to be tuned specifically for each workshop environment.
- *Pragmatic attributes*: The iPhone's variable and seamless connectivity between platforms (cellular and WiFi), spheres of communication and training workshops delivering real-world skill sets that lead to job opportunities.
- Hedonic attributes
  - *Stimulation*: Positive user responses to the style and brand of technology, the workshop's ability to empower personal growth and development of skills leading to job-ready expectation and self-esteem;
  - *Identification*: The expression of self and a user's value to their community through artifact use and skill application defined by being in possession of a new tool symbolizing participation, which has a social value; and
  - *Evocation*: The product's ability to provoke memories and inspire people to talk about important past events, relationships, ideas or stories.
- *Consequence*: An ethical judgment holding that the value of the device, and hence the act performed, lies in its capacity to produce positive outcomes—that is, benefits to the mojo and the community
  - *Emotional*: Self-esteem, pride in achievement, in being a useful community member and being able to personalize content ideas into a broadly accessible form;
  - *Personal*: Growing confidence, desire to embark on further training and engagement, and enhanced job prospects; and
  - *Communal*: Immediate and purposeful role in the community (local, work or extended) as message maker, and sustainable role as teacher as skills are retaught by the mojo to others in a local environment.

The premise is that any truth or meaning imbued in technology and training "comes into existence in and out of our engagement with the realities in our world" (Crotty 2003: 149), or through a *community of practice*.

In the remote Indigenous context, user experience can be viewed as a consequence of interaction impacting the user's internal state (lore, predispositions, expectations, needs, motivation, mood, digital literacy and so on), the characteristics of the designed system (e.g., complexity, purpose, usability, functionality and beauty), the social and cultural context within which the interaction occurs and feedback from that and external environments.

A qualitative approach to assessment of these appraisals can occur where the researcher is able to create an environment in which participants are encouraged to describe emotional reactions during interaction with a product. Referred to as the thinking-aloud method (Mahlke 2008), this suited the study's more reflective digital storytelling environment. An example is the emotional outpourings from mojos in the making of the NT Mojo video. Thinking *aloud*, in the context of Indigenous culture, is like talking aloud or telling stories to a community group. The Micronesian master mariner[4] navigates between islands to enable social, educational and cultural inclusion. Like them, our mojos became intercommunity pilots, *way finders* in a virtual sea of interconnecting digital nodes, a reflection encouraged by the interactive nature of the iPhone.

Moreover, understanding the user experience helps shape pedagogical outcomes by helping define the style of use of tools of the trade—the type of hardware and the praxis—to determine the practical and hedonic nature of any program. The length of courses, the type of equipment and the outcomes can all be impacted by the way the user perceives the experience at its outset. Chapters 5 and 6 explore in greater detail four stages of user experience: innovation—the technology or delivery; communication—the structure of the workshops; time—taken for the innovation to be adopted; and community—across three distinct user groups.

Publication

In a broader context, because initial responses to events and circumstances usually result in hedonic responses that are subjective and often last only a moment, having participants record, construct and publish their stories—potentially turning *a personal citizen witness moment* into a more *eudemonic act of citizen journalism*—is critical to shifting the focus from individual to community perspectives. Table 3.2 outlines how, in the context of this study, publication was intended to occur in three ways: artifacts, content and product. Creating online exposure is a key component not only because publishing content is a politicized act and needs a distribution vehicle, but also because seeing stories on a bigger public canvas provides greater incentive to "get it right." In 1981, in self-shot video workshops run at an inner-city high school in west Melbourne, publishing stories was a vital component in getting students to try harder. In students' minds, publication equated to television, which meant creating content of a quality

Table 3.2 Publication elements

Genre	Definition	Example of publication
Artifact	The result of the research design activity—case studies; review of literature	– Training workbooks and other material – Lesson plans – Research findings in the exegesis – Scholarly publications – Conference presentations
Content	UGS contain the output of the mojos exposure to and their use of the artifacts and the result of recording and editing on iPhones, iPods or iPads	– UGC is formed into UGS that are constructed and published on the web and constitute mojo content—complete story packages developed and produced by mojos
Product	The recognition of mojo content in its various forms as commodified and monetized capital	– Mojo UGS on television and web – Mojos skills used to create news stories for broadcast – Mojo created government messaging – Mojo UGS screened at film festivals in competition – Mojo practices become part of various curriculum – Mojo work assisting development of edit App on sale through the iTunes App store – Mojo production kit developed for use in the case studies – Mojo documentary on mainstream TV
Capital	Mojos being employed for their skills	– New levels of cultural capital exhibited by mojos engaged in mobile journalism praxis

that others would watch. One of the participants in the NT Mojo project observes, "My grandfather has seen the story on video and the web, but he's always more proud to see community stuff on TV." For students, publication is validation of their link with the community and provides added incentive to do more. For journalists, publication is fundamental to doing journalism and a key to adoptability. The relevance of publication is further discussed in Chapters 5 and 6.

Pedagogy, Creating Digital Literacy in a Mobile Environment

The problem with learning through "trial and error," which is often the way when early adopters move from one device to the next, is that they are never there long enough to get a complete sense of possibilities. Hence in mobile environments, learning is often equated with home screen functionality, calling and sending text and pictures online. What this methodology encourages is a more digitally literate user, with a more holistic view of the potential of acquiring knowledge, which takes years to filter and learn to communicate (Palmer and Raffensperger 2011). Rheingold says powerful pocket-sized multimedia studios and global information networks can mislead us if we don't learn how to exert mental control in relation to always being switched on (2012). It is as much about realizing the potential as it is about not being misled.

Although media and educational institutions have been slow to incorporate digital storytelling literacies, practical know-how with basic training is available to those who want it, and who figure out how to find it. A key to online success will be increasing social capital, including developing an online tool sense, in virtual communities, by curating information before it becomes overbearing (Rheingold 2012). To achieve this level of traction, digital pedagogies need to be relevant across multiple locations and spheres of communication (Puentedura 2013). This creates a need for a common digital content creation and publishing language (CDL) in a multimodal literacy program (Walsh 2011), taught at primary school, developed at secondary, implemented with work practices in mind at the tertiary level, and used by professionals. An examination of these possibilities is presented in Chapter 6.

Effectiveness, Outcomes and Translation

A key element of the methodology is what I call the "value-add back end." In academic terms, this is the translation phase of the study. Discussed in Chapter 5, the effectiveness of workshops can be measured against real outcomes in the translation phase. This phase investigates the effectiveness of the program: the balance between technology and training material across communication spheres. A major aim of the research is to develop pedagogy that balances the relationship between technology, the user and the various spheres of implementation. Expressed in his book *Understanding Media: The Extensions of Man*, Marshall McLuhan calls this relationship the *techne* (1964). While we are accustomed to "splitting and dividing all things as a means of control," McLuhan believes "the personal and social consequences of any medium, that is any extension of ourselves, results from the new scale that is introduced into our affairs by each extension of our selves or by any new technology" (1964: 23). In essence his 1964 postmodern trope, that the "medium is the message," is consistent with this belief that a techne relationship exists and impacts our lives, although this is seemingly inconsistent with his latter view that "electric media could conceivably usher in the millennium, but it also holds the potential for realizing the Anti-Christ" (McLuhan 1969: 22). If McLuhan means that an untrained user will be unwieldy and not realize the potential of the techne, then his trope holds true.

McLuhan contends all media can work to break the balance that existed in society before electronic media when the senses purposed life. For him, it seems, technological innovations are "extensions of human abilities and senses that alter this sensory balance—an alteration that, in turn, inexorably reshapes the society that created the technology" (Rogaway 1994: 1). This certainly can be true of mobile technology, which has been transformed into a media-rich platform that makes disseminating information, entertainment and news possible, on the move and from anywhere (Westlund 2013). In the online age, one manifestation of this is new virtual mobile tribalism, something McLuhan also predicted and which is founded in what are described as online colonies or network societies (Rheingold 1994; Castells 2009) made possible by new technologies. It is a movement that is changing how, for example, people access news with some legacy media predicting that mobile news consumption will "surpass that of personal computers in a few years" (Seale cited in Westlund 2013: 8).

As users become more prolific content creators, another layer of investigation is needed about the skill set required to capitalize on relationships created with the techne. More specifically, this relationship can be expressed as the balance between practical skills and what Lee Duffield refers to as "a study of contexts" (2011: 1). In a pedagogical sense, this is an evaluation of what Ruben Puentedura calls the translation phase (2012): the balance in training between mechanical job-ready skills and theoretical capacity. In a journalistic context, that is training in ethics, style, legal aspects, narrative construction and writing. In some instances case study workshops become a window into a translation phase:

- In a community translation can occur when skills create recognition that results in job offers, or a desire to embark on further training.
- Within education the translation phase provides new opportunities for introducing pedagogy that enables new forms of literacy training across multiple curriculum areas, and the creation of intercurricular spin-offs. Teachers see that the skill sets can translate into a willingness to learn new skills and engage with community.
- In the professional sphere training enables a rational integration into digital content and complete story delivery to create a more employable digital journalist.

In summary, Nina Weerakkody (2009) identifies this type of social research as political research, which she defines as studies located in a politicized context. The research reflects this definition because much of it is focused on marginalized Indigenous voices, subjugated student populations and journalists without digital storytelling skills. The aim of the project after undertaking workshops, was that participants in each sphere create UGS uniquely related to their experience:

- Community mojos provide grassroots perspective on local issues.
- Student mojos create content relevant to their local community and become more citizen-minded.
- Professional journalists trained to participate in a new style of digital storytelling intersect more with citizen journalism.

Hence the research explores sustainable mojo pedagogies in the three identified spheres (community, education and media). More specifically, it investigates a common digital language that bridges these spheres of communication. Hence the research validity—efficacy of design against desired outcomes—needs to be discussed from an internal and an external perspective. The internal validity addresses the correctness of the design, in particular

- Creation of workable unambiguous training methods. This occurred through a training manual whose validity was tested and verified over many years of use in a citizen television environment.
- Obtaining permissions. Ethical clearances were required to enable the study and confirm the study was relevant.
- Realization of outcomes. The study scopes (1) methods of training and (2) sustainable mobile journalism pedagogies; long-term outcomes were not factored into this study, although a number of long-term outcomes were realized and are discussed as part of the evaluation phase in Chapter 5.
- Flexibility to modify the study. When it became evident that sustainability could be achieved in the education sector and that media required the same digital training program, the duration of training was altered.

External validation of this research was made possible by deploying the workshops across differing spheres of communication in Australia and internationally. What began as a study in marginalized communities was extended to the education and professional spheres. Running the workshops with different demographic groups and in a variety of cultures confirmed the common visual language translator aspect of training. This enabled a triangulation of practices delivering results from various perspectives across interdisciplinary spheres of communication. The impact of convergence on the three spheres discussed above and what is required for users to capitalize on change, beyond a rudimentary use of smart devices, is discussed next in Chapter 4.

Notes

1. Includes humanities-based research.
2. Storify is a social network service that lets the user create stories using social media.
3. See guidelines in Appendix C.
4. Based on an oral culture, Micronesian navigators are chosen through a process of learning and a process of selection that begins at a young age.

4 Convergence at Click Speed

> The newspaper is in all its literalness the bible of democracy, the book
> out of which a people determines its conduct.
> —*Walter Lippmann*

Overview

The research presented here scopes the shape of a common digital language, a bridge across converging spheres of communication and a praxis that transforms raw user-generated content (UGC) into more complete user-generated stories (UGS). Hence this chapter seeks to explore the shape of convergence, in particular the development of digital news models, new praxis and new technologies. Understanding this provides a road map to an online connect for citizens, schools and journalists wishing to participate in online digital media publication.

Lippmann's quote above does not so much refer to Fourth Estate ideals, which position the press as a sentinel promoting democratic principles, as it does to the press acting as preacher or prophet. He sees the newspaper as a bible by which to mold lives, which limits the discursive forum in which the public sphere exists, to one delivering spoon-fed information (Dewey 2012). Lippmann acknowledges the importance of public opinion formed through collectives with political interests whose role is to manipulate the masses. Hence his desire for a press to maintain freedom of opinion and in particular to distinguish between errors, illusion and misrepresentation (Lippmann 2008). When media converges online, it changes and redefines the shape of the public sphere from a controllable national space to one existing in a global network society. As more citizens begin to create content on billions of devices converging online, the public sphere becomes more difficult to define. Also difficult to rationalize is the role of the press as sole purveyor of credible information and sentinel of truth and democracy.

> Not everything or everyone is globalized, but the global networks that
> structure the planet affect everything and everyone.
> (Castells 2008: 81)

The introduction of technology has always signaled a convergence phase in communication. In 1746, the invention of the telegraph, known today as the Victorian Internet, enabled the first real-time wired point-to-point electronic communication across borders (Standage 1998). The wireless enabled the next communications shift to one of mass distribution and heralded a new era in entertainment, propaganda and journalism (Starkey and Crisell 2009). In the 20th century news became bigger business and the monopolization of news created a new tension between those who championed journalism ideals and tabloid businessmen like Randolph Hearst. Television, which killed the illustrated newspaper and reinvented the way news and information were communicated, was the next major change (Hirst and Harrison 2007: 89). The news platform aspect of the Internet developed in two stages: the takeoff years from 1995 to 1996, and the period 2005–6 prompted by "wireless technology and the upsurge in user generated news" (O'Donnell et al. 2012: 15).

As early as 2001 Sue Tapsall found that journalists felt the Internet was a useful tool, but concluded journalists felt "powerless to maintain news quality in the face of technological change and media commercialization" (cited in O'Donnell et al. 2012: 15). The issues were workload and a fear that quality public benefit journalism was at risk as news converged online and became more defined by the 24-hour news cycle and UGC. This is seen as one of the major challenges to quality investigative journalism. Only three years earlier, in 1998, journalists at the Australian Broadcasting Corporation expressed the same concerns when the national broadcaster began its shift to digital and multiskilling.

Pavlik and McIntosh (2014) describe convergence as technological—the rise of digital media and online communication networks; economic—the merging of Internet and telecommunications companies with traditional media companies; and cultural—the values, beliefs and practices shared by a group of people. Table 4.1 is a representation of Quinn and Filak's more elaborate convergence descriptor, with my suggestions added around impact of convergence. The two descriptions provide the vocabulary needed to discuss convergence (2005: 4).

Quinn and Filak question whether "editorial managers are adopting it [convergence], to save money or to do better journalism," and conclude "the two issues go hand in hand" (2005: 4). I believe that, depending on the definition of "better journalism," the latter is mostly true. John Hailes, the pioneering editor who introduced convergence at the *Orlando Sentinel*, believes convergence can only succeed if there is a top-down shift of corporate culture. However, very few organizations do this, "choosing instead to focus on the relationships, newsroom layouts, [and] titles" (cited in Quinn 2005: 4). Hence convergence relies on management's willingness to train staff to be able to practice convergence, to prepare them, as Quinn and Filak suggest, for doing journalism and telling stories, "using the most appropriate media" (2005: 7), and more specifically, to train staff to use a combination of relevant media to tell stories. It is this multimedia aspect and skill set that defines the journalistic level of convergence.

Table 4.1 Types of convergence

Types of Convergence	Descriptor	Impact
Ownership convergence	Machinations for creating a more effective use of resources by owning, for example, radio, print and television under one umbrella company.	Aimed at maximizing audience reach, it is driven by lower costs and increased efficiencies. It impacts the structure of newsrooms and cross-platform content aggregation practices.
Tactical convergence	Content sharing between media organizations at ground level, where producers swap tapes, or at the more formal corporate level, where output deals are struck. A common relationship is print with television.	Driven by commercial imperatives and the news cycle it impacts relationships between media organizations and a media's own level of content output.
Structural convergence	Management process associated with changes in news-gathering and distribution and converging areas of the corporations business like employing multimedia journalists (curation team) to repackage print for television.	Frustration amongst journalists, redundancies, loss of DNA, less output in favor of curation. Cheap content for television.
News-gathering convergence	The result of an internal decision to retrain staff to work across platforms, they need to learn multiple skills to in effect become multimedia journalists.	Commercially driven, this multi-skilled approach is not unlike the digital skill sets required by a mojo and, like structural convergence, can cause great frustrations and fears amongst journalists.
Storytelling convergence	Skills-based convergence resulting in a more holistic approach and an amalgam of story styles, technologies and platforms, to create a more dynamic and interactive web-based multimedia style of story called UGS.	This is the creative realm of the mojo where technical and skills convergence work to produce dynamic multimedia stories. Skills that can be taught to non-professionals that enable a more holistic story-teller.

I disagree with Quinn and Filak's contention "that the importance of the news event should dictate the depth and type of coverage, and influence the size of the team involved" (2005: 7). It can, but this is very much an analogue observation. The size of the multimedia storytelling team is not necessarily relative to the depth of the story. Traditionally in-depth stories would have a reporter and a cameraperson working on them. Today mojos can cover these stories on their own. Yet, even a mojo story might involve a graphics person, an archivist or an online editor, depending on the intended use. In my experience, size and input factors are also based on the convergent nature of the business and its use of video. While media convergence may be the result of advanced technologies and restructured practice, in news it is driven primarily by commercial imperatives. Even creative storytelling convergence occurs in news because it is a commercial reality. Until revenues and the advertising dollar shift to online news models,[1] media will be looking for cheap and fast methods of curating (scraping) existing content and repurposing it and their own news, across converging platforms. This shows commercial imperatives still prevail over technological optimism, and that new models will require a balance between the two. What's evident is that as news organizations move into web TV, more thought goes into story convergence and the elasticity of form.

Quinn and Filak (2005) argue their definition of convergence is not about corporate conglomeration, like the AOL–*Huffington Post* merger; nor is it about many technologies converged in one box. Quinn settles on a definition that claims convergence is an activity, and I suspect a thought process, that leads to a cultural shift that "takes place in a news room, as editorial staff work together to produce multiple products for multiple platforms to reach a mass audience, often on a 24/7 timescale" (2005: 4). I agree, but this is also where our definitions begin to diverge. In 2013, the proliferation of powerful handheld pocket creative suites made the converged box definition difficult to discount. This is especially so given that smart mobile technology impacts four out of five of Quinn and Filak's convergence descriptors. Moreover, digital story convergence extends beyond newsrooms through all spheres of communication, including education and community, which plays to Hirst's suggestion that any definition should include the "the social relations of convergence" (Hirst and Harrison 2007: 9).

The dialectic around convergence occurs in the changing relationship between technology and outcome, which results in a dialogue about the way we exist within our media world(s). Hirst likens this to DNA and a process of "interaction, mutation and conflict" (Hirst and Harrison 2007: 19). I would add to this that it is not unlike the underlying metrics described by the social development model (SDM), a theoretical approach to human behavior (Hawkins and Catalano 1992). SDM (see Chapter 7) hypothesizes that development is based on opportunities (interaction with convergent knowledge and technologies), skills (a mutation of existing habitus through social capital) and recognition (conflict as a result of exposure).

Producing UGS requires skills and a political will to make stories that empower change, but in addition it needs an understanding of convergent workflows in order to structure and publish content across multiple platforms. Hence, my definition of *convergence* includes journalistic skills— development, research, filming, interviewing, writing and editing; technical skills—use of smartphone, audio devices and camera, microphone and edit app; and publishing skills—telephony and web. These skills are required to effectively use digital mobile technologies to create convergent stories (video and audio) and participate in convergent practices (filming and publishing). I would add another descriptor: freedom of political thought and speech, which digital convergence enables and requires. The ability to complete converged UGS on a mobile device from start to finish, anywhere anytime, by anyone (citizen or professional), is empowering and distinguishes converging styles of mojo from other video forms.

Further, as UGC fragments are structured into more complete UGS, these converge to form user-generated programs (UGP) that can be scheduled on web TV. More specifically, UGC and UGS are examples of the news gathering and storytelling convergence discussed above. UGP incorporates news gathering and storytelling, but it also plays a role in *ownership, tactical and structural convergence*. At the ownership level UGP enables a better use of existing internal resources. On a tactical level UGP enables program sales to occur between media and UGP to become part of output deals. Structurally, editors who are assigned to create new production strands can commission UGP from internal and external suppliers. But organizational attitudes to convergence and commercial pressures to succeed will impact how traditional media makes the switch to convergent technologies and practices and the connection with external suppliers. There is no denying this shift will involve the citizen content creation sphere. Like UGS, UGP such as *HuffPost Live*, Al Jazeera's *The Stream* and a raft of programs from *Ekstra Bladet*'s EBTV, provide formats around which to curate UGC and UGS into more bankable hybrid forms. Examples of a type of neo-journalism that marries social content and traditional production forms designed to draw the public and advertisers to new online platforms, they are more interactive, but also look much like formats we are used to watching on TV.

Convergence Impacting News Business

> A good newspaper, I suppose, is a nation talking to itself.
> —*Arthur Miller*

Michael Gawenda, former editor of *the Age*, suggests that "no newspaper in a democracy has ever been a nation 'talking to itself'" (2008: 1). Literally, of course not, but Miller's statement might suggest either a good newspaper can get a nation talking or the only real newspaper is one that is influenced by a nation that's talking, or both. Today, Miller's statement could also include the words "and this is happening more via smart devices." Notwithstanding the importance of communicating and the value of all sorts of communication, the question remains, how do we get *the talk* to be more purposeful? How do we get the nation talking to itself in a more reflective way? Indeed, how do we ensure that convergent practices don't aid to diminish net neutrality or editorial independence?

Consider this scenario: the volume of UGC reaches its current massive proportions, and as more citizens turn to the Internet for news and information, the print newspaper faces extinction in as little as five years. The managing editor of the Danish tabloid *Ekstra Bladet* predicted that in three years their print edition wouldn't be making a profit. The Digital Futures Project at the University of Southern California Center for Digital Futures predicts that the only print newspapers that will survive will be at the extremes of the medium—the largest and the smallest (Cole 2011). In *News 2.0* Martin Hirst paints a similar picture of a media sliding into depression, albeit a few years earlier: "In the first few months of 2009, obituaries were being prepared for a number of American newspapers ... the *Seattle Post-Intelligencer* closed after 146 years of continuous publication" (2011: 51). In 2012 Fairfax Media in Australia slashed 1,900 jobs, advising it was going to make the *Age* and the *Sydney Morning Herald* tabloids. According to Hirst, the slide commenced in the early 1960s when, in a sign of early corporate convergence, large media organizations, like U.S. media giant Gannett, began buying smaller newspapers to create cost-effective monopolies and increase profits. At about the same time in the 1960s, print, screen and audio platforms began a process of corporate convergence as a response to falling revenues; they created a more dynamic immediate electronic one-stop shop for advertisers and called it television.

Regarding the rise of Internet connectivity, in U.S. households broadband connections rose from 10 percent in 2000 to 83 percent in 2013. People who use the Internet to buy online rose from 45 percent to 78 percent in the same period (Cole 2013). These shifts have made traditional media, including television, and especially daily newspapers, look slow and unresponsive. The advent of online classifieds like Craigslist negatively impacted advertising in print and created a sense of doom. In simple terms, based on Audit Bureau of Circulation figures, "average newspaper sales have dropped 23 percent since 2002 (O'Donnell et al. 2012: 11). This has resulted in budget cuts, bureau closings and layoffs. In Australia, shrinking revenue led to an announcement in July 2012 that Fairfax Media would cut 1,900 staff and begin charging for content on the websites of its two main metropolitan newspapers. Fairfax chief executive Greg Hywood said that if the cuts did not work, Fairfax still had the option "to move to a digital only model" (Ellis 2012). Managing director of *Ekstra Bladet*, Poul Madsen, sees no options except to go digital, and in 2013 he cut 22 print staff to further digital expansion.

Deciding on a convergence strategy can be a costly exercise. But it is one that Geir Ruud, former editor in chief of digital news at *Ekstra Bladet*, believes needs to be a long-term plan. In 2009, when Murdoch felt pay walls were needed to protect the exclusivity of online news content, *Guardian* editor Alan Rusbridger suggested Murdoch's idea would result in a "sleep-walk to oblivion" (Greenslade 2010). Murdoch's response, "that sounds like BS to me," signaled there were two distinct ways of thinking about the online news business. As an advocate of open journalism, Rusbridger believes accessing the "on the ground," especially mobile communicators is becoming more critical for survival in the news business. It is a view shared by Ruud, who believes "what's changed is that we don't own the news on our own anymore, now we are sharing it with the audience, asking them for it" (2012).

In his Hugh Cudlipp lecture Rusbridger further argued that:

> we've moved from an era in which a reporter writes a story and goes home and that's the story written … the moment you press send on your story, the responses start coming in. And so I think journalists have to work out what to do about those responses … if you go along with open journalism, you're going to be open to other sources.
>
> (Rusbridger 2010)

Rusbridger's philosophies extend to pay walls. He said "we charge for mobile, we charge for iPads. It's not that we're against payment altogether … we don't think that the revenues we would get from a pay wall would justify making that the main focus of our efforts right now" (cited in Greenslade 2010). Rusbridger believes it is philosophically wrong to have a wall that separates content from the readers who want to contribute (2010). It is an open news view of journalism that has former editor of the *Sydney Morning Herald*, Amanda Wilson, asking, "Will we soon see a tech giant like Google or Facebook buy an ailing legacy media outlet and its newsroom so that it can offer the whole package to its connected users?" (O'Donnell et al. 2012: 3). The reality suggests this is already happening. AOL has moved quickly with its $315 million purchase of the independent online news site the *Huffington Post*. In a merger designed to provide AOL with "a sort of democratic alternative to Fox News" (Zaponne 2012), the *Huff* gets to fulfill several strategic objectives; "we know we'll be creating a company that can have an enormous impact, reaching a global audience on every imaginable platform" (Huffington 2011). One main aim was gaining access to AOL's Patch.com sites, which covered 800 towns across the United States. Patch offered "an incredible infrastructure for citizen journalism in time for the 2012 election, and a focus on community and local solutions that have been an integral part of *HuffPost*'s DNA" (2011). The *Huffington Post* offered AOL brand identity and a way for Patch to access their "reader engagement tools" (Peters and Kopytoff 2011). But just months after the *Huffington Post* came on board, 450 Patch sites were closed because 2013 revenue was

40 percent down on projections (Wilhelm 2013). In Australia, Kim Williams, former CEO of News Limited, was cautiously optimistic when he said his figures speak for themselves. In one week, in July 2012, he said his company sold 17 million newspapers and hundreds of thousands of dollars worth of magazines and had 12 million weekly digital users. This, he said, is "hardly the portrait of a failing company" (Williams 2012). However, six months later the revelation that the Australian publishing arm of News Limited was posting a $476.7 million loss, with projected "lower future forecast earnings" (Kwek and Kruger 2012), suggested turbulent times ahead.[2]

Ruud, in an unwavering commitment to convergence, believes it is a matter of trial and error: "I went from paper to online in my old newspaper 14 years ago," but it's not easy" (Ruud 2012). Ruud believes that success will only result from corporate willingness to experiment: "It doesn't happen by clicking fingers or a keyboard for that matter, you need to go out and make [digital] stories try out a few things, make lots of mistakes and then make a few good things from time to time" (2012). It is a formula that has seen *Ekstra Bladet* swim against the digital tide and make some revenue online; "maybe this year 3–4 million euros go to the bank, it's not a lot but it is something" (2012).

Ekstra Bladet's online revenue still comes from advertising, and 70 percent from its ailing newspaper. "Most news organisations will lose money [online] in their first years … we are only able to do this [make money] because we have spent years building our online journalism base [and] we reinvest by hiring a few new reporters [each year]" (2012). The key, according to Ruud, is to understand your market: "We are not the *New York Times* … with 300 million potential customers and a couple of billion people understanding English in the rest of the world, so we need to offer them something more online; more interactive sport, better almost live investigative journalism, than they would get from a public station" (2012).

Williams and Ruud both argue that working in convergent news is about changing the news culture to provide a more dynamic and responsive news. Williams believes this is done best through changing the business culture. Ruud agrees, but says this happens in concert with education. He believes education on all levels is the key to successful convergence:

> I think they [students] should start with social media training on day one of the academy, if you want to be a carpenter you get a hammer and nail on day one, start training as a mojo … it's about getting the thing done and delivered that's what mojo does. And it doesn't help that in academies we train reporters to be like Hemingway. Hemingway has been dead for 50 years.
>
> (Ruud 2012)

Poul Madsen believes you can only succeed if you have multiskilled journalists with traditional skills working with young journalists, learning from each other. It seems this more proactive neo-journalist approach—early adoption, experimentation with style and content, and marrying new and relevant traditional skills, which requires a strong commitment by management—is a fundamental formula for converging business practices, skills and technologies in the news business. Madsen's view that video is key for an audience he describes as "viewers" and that the binary approach (the old way vs. the new way) can only lead to business ruin is a common, if slow, realization. His more neo-journalistic approach, where the best of traditional storytelling skills are maintained and married with relevant new social and multimedia skills, might be what journalists need, especially if AOL CEO Tim Armstrong's prediction about the rise of web TV is correct. Armstrong, who was a vice president at Google, is trying to transform AOL into a content platform. If he succeeds, and the latest change of direction at *HuffPost*, from platform focus to content creator, suggests that taking on Google and Facebook might be difficult, then we are only beginning our convergence to video. Whether producing content for a platform or as a supplier, we need to increase our emphasis on training about video storytelling, using multiple devices and creating content for different screens and platforms.

A Journalist's Perspective on Convergence

Current trends in online news indicate three complementary development models. The first is a type of traditional model where journalists interview people and record video on their smartphone—which they can also use to record an audio interview. The video clips are delivered to the newsroom via systems like Xstream.[3] Here they are topped and tailed, or undergo a basic edit, if B roll vision is used, by journalist editors who assemble content, before.[4] The aggregating journalist, or the field journalist, writes around the pictures. The second trend is an aggregation model that relies on journalists scraping the Internet for stories, especially those with video, and writing around these pictures. The third trend is a more complex web TV model that media houses like *Huffington Post* in the United States, VG in Norway and *Ekstra Bladet* have adopted. In some cases though, a lack of in-house television skill and a shortage of production dollars, to buy TV-trained staff, are resulting in predominantly studio-based formats. These are fronted and produced by journalists, who often work alone on niche programs (money, food, travel, politics, etc.), until the studio recording phase. Built around small live streaming tricaster[5]-type studios, these programs are mostly conversational and rely on technology like Skype, LiveU, Dejero, Bambuser and smartphones to provide live vision and audio streams.

In circumstances where journalists get the opportunity to learn multimedia story creation skills, like mojo, they are able to produce magazine style UGS for motoring, cooking and other UGP. Anders Berner is one journalist who made this shift. He produces and hosts a new motoring format, *Topfart*, for EBTV. In *Topfart* location-based UGS is formatted into a 15- to 20-minute weekly UGP. Berner believes it is a big transition to move from print to UGS and then to a UGP produced by one journalist who records, hosts, writes and edits the program. He sees a willingness to learn as critical. As he says, "It's actually a nice feeling where you can evolve yourself and your skills" (Burum 2014). Jon Pagh, journalist and host of weekly sports format *Football with Attitude*, agrees, but says enthusiasm should be tempered by reality: "If you produce for the paper, you talk to two or three sources on the phone and write your story. To produce a video segment, you need appointments, you have to inform them before you go, organize the camera, shoot, edit, write the article, basically you are doing everything yourself and that's the big difference" (cited in Burum 2014). This of course leads to perceived issues of quality. Former executive producer for ebTV, Massimo Grillo, says it is "an ongoing psychological battle to convert print journalists to making simple video content" (cited in Burum 2014). Grillo believes many print journalists are initially reluctant to cross the digital divide, fearing it will result in shoddy journalism. "It's true we can live with the unfocused shot in a good story, we are web TV," but signaling "your work is not good, but we'll publish it anyway" (2014), is a red rag to journalists. As the media business becomes more networked and managers look for enterprise bargaining to replace unionized labor, the increasing precarity that permeates journalism and its labor force also, ironically, impacts journalists' willingness to embrace digital. They are often afraid of letting go of the sources that finance their everyday lives—the journalist's "job for life"—which creates a kind of ongoing anxiety that Neilson and Rossiter (2005a) contend is another form of precarity. Although new digital skill sets could potentially reduce the risk of unemployment, they are resisted because journalists see digital as increasing workload and downgrading craft.

To assuage journalists' fears that online means shoddy, and to raise extra funds to create quality journalism, *Ekstra Bladet* is following an EU trend and trialing a freemium[6] soft pay wall model that provides more in-depth content for paying customers. Online users have the option to subscribe to the EKSTRA page, where they will find more developed news once these stories have been teased on the free online or mobile sites. According to editor Lisbeth Langwadt, EKSTRA plays to "our quality news traditions, in disclosures, detective journalism, crime investigation, critical consumer journalism, politics and sports" (cited in Burum 2014). A small EKSTRA team works to refine and develop stories from *Ekstra Bladet*'s print version, focusing on quality journalism that people are willing to pay almost 4 euros a month for. "Almost every journalist at *Ekstra Bladet* takes part in the process to produce EKSTRA content," the key focus being "converting existing users into paying customers so we can keep creating journalism that matters and of course, keep our print journalists" (2014).

However, producing short television-like stories for the web, or extended print-plus video versions behind the pay wall, does not immediately create the required revenue to keep investigative journalists and sustain quality online journalism—hence ebTV's mandate to develop commercially driven web TV formats. They are banking on formats being familiar territory to advertisers who look for more on-air advertising real estate to sell to their clients. Thomas Stokholm, CEO of ebTV says, "I was hired to build on the commercial side and take the EB brand to a new level in TV and possibly to a full-blown station by 2015, to give advertisers a strong alternative to current TV providers" (cited in Burum 2014). Notwithstanding his commercial mandate, Stokholm sees one of ebTV's key roles as assisting print journalists to make the jump from articles to programs: "print has its own life," but "TV is a long haul that requires a shift of mindset from the 24-hour cycle to a 365-day operation, where planning is key" (2014).

Rudd believes what is required are long-term strategies. When newspaper sales in Denmark dropped by 15 percent, *Ekstra Bladet* knew they had to get involved fully and not as an excuse. So executives played to their strength–investigative journalism—and converged it "... to the web and we always concentrate first on web, then web TV and newspaper. It needs to be purposeful, you need to be committed no excuses based on dropping circulation" (Ruud 2014). Grillo sees this convergence shift as an ongoing psychological battle. "There is a big difference about making TV first and not thinking we need to make the article first and then stick the pictures around it" (cited in Burum 2014). In a modern newsroom this philosophy can cause dilemmas on a front page driven by print imperatives, where everything is still called an *article*. This shift in mindset from article to program becomes a consideration when a web TV program, which may have taken weeks to produce, is relegated lower down the online site's front page due to its perceived lack of news currency. Imagine, said Grillo, if your TV program was "pulled five minutes before the news cast and you were told you can run it between 9 and 10 p.m. ... try saying that to a broadcaster. That's the hardest thing about making web TV on an Internet news page" (2014). This clash in priorities plays out at the various daily editorial meetings where assigning editors choose and shift stories up and down the front page depending on how they are trending. Because this page can be a meter and a half long, stories can invariably get lost. Berner acknowledges that "EB is an old publishing house with news traditions" (2014). However, from a marketing perspective, he feels a 15- to 20-minute program is a big investment and needs more time to settle. "If we are only on the front page for 2 hours we'll only get 5% of our readers" (2014). Hence web TV programs, like *Topfart*, are segmented, and these interstitials are published following the program. This can double or triple the number of viewer impressions. Finding the right publishing formulas, including alternative community and school-based media, is a key to attracting advertising revenue.

Screen Choice and Revenue

Today *Ekstra Bladet*'s investment in the various forms of convergence has made it the most popular Danish online news site, with more than 15 percent of the population visiting every day. Madsen believes that a successful digital plan must involve mobile. However, one of the major impediments to monetizing the mobile space is the relatively small amount of screen *real estate* for advertising on a mobile. While the team at *Ekstra Bladet* is producing news stories and programs made specifically for the smartphone for people to watch on the mobile on the train, they are hoping the game changer will be their investment in freemium and web TV. This provides their mobile audience with natural segues to a larger screen once they land at home, and advertisers with substantial formats they understand.

While media bosses may disagree on how to save their business, there is no denying that mobile will be at the heart of any converged rescue operation. Eighty percent of the world's population own a mobile, and more than 2.5 billion people own smartphones. In the United States mobile penetration has hit 91 percent and smartphone use is estimated at 56 percent (Smith 2013). In 2015, world smartphone sales increased 1.4 billion (Judge 2016). In Australia more than 50 percent of the population has a smartphone:

- 74 percent of people don't leave home without one;
- 51 percent search on their smartphone every day;
- 83 percent use their smartphone for communication;
- 43 percent use it to read news;
- 65 percent use it to access and watch videos;
- 94 percent use it to research purchases; and
- 39 percent of those users actually make the purchase. (Rosenberg 2011)

The focus for publishers is multiscreen. Given that mobiles are now powerful enough to live stream, people are tuning in on their way to and from work and during breaks. Consumers are demanding more, including live or catch-up programs, on the go (McKendrick 2013). The growing mobile consumer society is looking for tasters, small bite-sized packages that provide a heads up tease to longer, more in-depth formats that might be watched when a user lands, either as free or pay wall content. In this environment the set-top box, once the center of paid-for home entertainment and information, is now relegated to fighting for its use value as OTT[7] providers deliver mobile browser-based shell-covered 24-hour anywhere content streams.

On a global scale, social behemoths like Facebook and Google are moving the pieces of the puzzle into place to become the *platform of platforms*. Google chairman Eric Schmidt believes "the core strategy is to make a bigger pie" (Womack 2012). And, since 2011, Schmidt's vision has been mobile:

> As I think about Google's strategic initiatives ... I realize they're all about mobile. We envision literally a billion people getting inexpensive, browser-based touchscreen phones over the next few years.

Can you imagine how this will change their awareness of local and global information and their notion of education?

(Schmidt 2011)

One year later and of the 1 billion Facebook users who log on daily, 934 million do it via mobile. Facebook's 1.59 billion users have increased its mobile ad revenue to 80 percent of the total revenue (Constine 2016). This is an increase of 27 percent of mobile ad revenue in the few months it took me to complete my final draft of this book.

Summary

After 400 years of print domination, the current shifts in our media landscape, brought about by the convergence of new technologies, practices and institutions, are so profound that analysts like Robert McChesney (McChesney and Pickard 2011: 3) are asking, "Who will have the dubious distinction of publishing America's last genuine newspaper?" The implications of convergence are transformation in the organization, type of media, type of content, use and distribution of content, redefinition and relocation of the audience, professional changes and a shift in values (Schmidt 2011). While traditional media converges its business online, McChesney believes we will need to wait to see the degree to which citizens embrace the possibilities of the above changes, or leave matters to the state and communication giants like Facebook and Google, whose business models are defining convergent practices and technologies. Google's purchase of Motorola's mobile business, Facebook's $1 billion purchase of Instagram, AOL's purchase of the *Huffington Post,* News Limited's purchase of Myspace and Storyful and Alan Kohler's niche online financial advisory business, Australian Independent Business Media, are examples of corporate convergence designed to short-cut a move into specialist sectors of the online media business.

On the one hand, newsroom convergence will need to address all of the above-mentioned descriptors. It will need internal corporate protocols for dealing with convergence at the ownership level—sharing content between platforms. In the case of output deals, the newsroom will need to understand *tactical convergent practices*—content sharing between media organizations. As the new newsroom responds to and creates new news opportunities, understanding the impact on journalists of *structural, information and storytelling convergence* will be especially critical. To compete online with millions of bloggers and citizen content creators, who are already part of the Facebook and Google families, many experienced journalists and photographers will need training in multimedia story production using new practices and technologies.

Ruud believes that to develop a strong online presence, journalists will need to keep in touch with public attitudes and their mobile-created UGC, which is the new face and pace in news.

If you go to a basic traffic accident, that's boring. We publish and as new facts come in we check them and then we continue the story, which could be published 30–50 times in that hour while we continue the reporting ... together with the audience because they always know more than you, because they have seen the accident. That's complicated because we as journalists are used to thinking that we know better than the rest of the world and we don't, at least I don't. (2012)

It is this self-perpetuating aspect of media, as the omnipotent sentinel of people's rights (now acting as a filtration system for public-to-public views) contrasted against their corporate responsibility, that Ruud feels has led to a shift to niche online newslike offerings. More than just being a supplier of news content, he believes that today's fragmented audience needs to be treated as a partner. Hence, there is a need to teach journalists what could become a common user-generated language. As Ruud said at the end of our mojo training, "They [mojo skills] have been useful to change thinking. You taught people how easy it was for traditional journalists to make video [and] how easy it is to edit great stories like in traditional television, told on the website with shorter and more dynamic editing" (Ruud 2012). However, producing niche television-like stories for the web does not immediately create the revenue stream needed to sustain quality online journalism. "We have seen spikes of up to 20 percent on the web site when a story includes video" (Ruud 2012). EB management hoped the trend would continue into their web TV, a shift to more formed video that AOL's CEO, Tim Armstrong, believes is the next convergent frontier (Taylor 2013).

While the audience is extremely capable of delivering large quantities of UGC, it, like print journalists, needs relevant digital storytelling skills—research, interviewing, writing, on-camera presenting, camera work, sound recording, editing and publishing—to produce more professional and politically aware content. The delivery of these skills—transforming UGC into the more professional, informative and political forms called UGS and UGP, which are content forms designed for web TV—sits at the core of the mojo practices described in this research. As digital network societies (Castells 2008), or Rheingold's "virtual villages," where we participate in the "self-design of a new culture" (1994: 2) creating even more networks of connected nodes, a support and filtration mechanism, like Cairo's Mosireen collective, is needed. The Mosireen (2012) gives form to the fragmented energies and citizen witness moments by producing and archiving content, and by providing training, hopefully in the same digital literacies that media are learning, to locals to create more politicized and professional media. In Los Angeles the VozMob network also provides migrant "day laborers, household workers, high school students, and other community correspondents" (Constanza-Chock 2011: 33) with the resources to participate and counter "anti-immigrant voices" (2011: 33), aims similar to those of the Indigenous mojo projects, except for their reliance on cheaper technology. This is a key difference. The mojo described here uses the same technology and skill set that media use, thereby creating the possibility of a digital bridge between media using communities.

In conclusion, I contend that with more than 150 million hours of UGC being uploaded in 2015, we need a filtration mechanism. The media acts as one filter and legislation as another. Self-moderated filtration, a product of training in common digital literacies, is also required. This is the responsibility of the education sphere that needs to take a more proactive approach to training citizens and students to embrace convergent opportunities and links between alternative and legacy media. The level of change that's achieved during this critical juncture in communications which, according to Robert McChesney, will last "no more than one or two decades" (2007: 9), depends on the degree to which scholars embrace the potential for media reform. Because mobile is proving to be the communications glue between platforms and screens, any reform will need to include training community, school, university and professional media in digital mojo storytelling skills. These skills will enable them to function in convergent news and other communications environments. How we develop and implement digital storytelling pedagogy and associated skills is a primary motivation of this research and the driver for the mojo case study workshops discussed in the following chapters.

Notes

1. Seventy percent of *Ekstra Bladet*'s revenues still come from its print edition.
2. Williams resigned from News Corp in August 2013, only 20 months after taking the CEO job.
3. Xstream is a proprietary toolbox for aggregating video content.
4. This is when the beginning and end of a shot is slightly trimmed and it might have generic leader or bumper attached to it.
5. A control room that creates virtual studios and uses robotic cameras.
6. Freemium is where publishers provide aspects of stories for free and users pay for the subscription to get extra, more developed, longer and in-depth information.
7. Over-the-top (OTT) content describes broadband delivery of video and audio (Netflix, Now TV) without a multiple-system operator being involved in the control or distribution of the content itself. OTT content is an advertiser-funded delivery model for smart devices, including mobile and TV.

5 Mojo Working in Communities

> For many such as I, our lifetime experience has been one of racism at
> the individual level, reinforced by the powerful institutions of the law ...
> and without doubt the media ... there has been very little challenge to
> the media about the way in which that institution practices, promotes
> and perpetuates racism ... in our community.
> *Indigenous magistrate Pat O'Shane*

Overview

This chapter discusses the major case study workshop, NT Mojo. It outlines
a process of introducing mobile journalism skills and technologies to remote
Indigenous people. NT Mojo was conducted in remote communities in the
Northern Territory in Australia. It tested a combination of media tools
alongside relevant multimedia storytelling skills aimed at scoping how
mobile journalism practices might be used to help create a local Indigenous voice. It further investigated skills that would enable community-based
mojos to work as local journalists and stringers for media.

Pat O'Shane's comments represent the plight of many marginalized groups
globally. All too often media carries views that are based on ignorance, prej-
udice and editorial and financial gatekeeping practices (Shoemaker 2009).
This was the case when I went to work in Indigenous media in central Australia in the early 1990s, where I witnessed the rollout of the Broadcast for
Remote Aboriginal Communities Scheme (BRACS). I saw a lack of training
turn a potential media and education tool into a delivery mechanism for
Western media. Over the years this researcher has returned to the Northern
Territory many times to visit some of the communities and people he worked
with to try and understand the impact of Western media on remote Indigenous cultures. This research is a direct result of working with marginalized
Indigenous communities over more than 20 years.

This research also includes a number of supplementary workshops run
in the community, schools and with media. The supplementary workshops,
discussed in Chapter 6, were designed to research aspects of mojo implementation. The primary and secondary workshops scoped early adoption;
in Technical and Further Education (TAFE) and in journalism schools where
mojo was trialed to determine its relevance as a professional training tool.

The media workshops scoped the relevance of mojo as a tool to help print journalists and photographers become multimedia practitioners. The overall aim was to investigate whether mojo could create a revolutionary digital and pedagogical bridge between spheres of communication.

Case Study: NT Mojo Workshop

The NT Mojo workshop represents a first step in determining how to transform individual citizens in remote indigenous communities in Australia into producers of more relevant local content. The research is timely because the deployment of Australia's National Broadband Network (NBN) provides a platform (fiber, WiFi and satellite) to address a number of the key recommendations of the Indigenous Broadcast Review (Stevens 2010). The workshop's significance is further enhanced by its focus on key principles identified in the independent review established to examine the policy and regulatory frameworks of converged media and communications in Australia. These principles state that citizens should have opportunities for participation in a diverse mix of information, content and news, produced locally and sourced across platforms, which reflect and contribute to the development of national and cultural identity (DBCDE 2011a). This is especially true for citizens living in remote marginalized communities.

Digital has created possibilities for new cross-cultural online communications. People with similar social and cultural backgrounds, even those in remote areas, can engage in activities concerning local issues (Meadows 2005). Digital potentially enables a more diverse balance between source, content and exposure key factors in determining what Professor Philip Napoli calls the diversity principle. This balance is critical in a "process of developing well informed citizens and enhancing the democratic process" (Napoli 1999: 9). But meaningful change requires more than technology; it requires education to alter the state of consciousness of marginalized people to enable them to seek change (Freire 1970). The NT Mojo training package scoped the degree to which Indigenous Australians, trained to use portable mobile technologies, can become change agents in a new subfield of local alternative multimedia journalism, called mojo.

A Historical Context

Indigenous Australians living in remote communities are world pioneers of community-based participatory broadcasting. The roots of the mobile storytelling described here lie in the workshops Eric Michaels ran in the 1980s in central Australia. All the content the Warlpiri Media Association transmitted in the 1980s was "locally produced ... community announcements, old men telling stories, young men acting cheeky" (Michaels 1989: 7). There was a need for local media skills because of media's gatekeeping approach to volume and news type, compounded by what media scholar

Axel Bruns sees as a journalist's "feel" or desired "news beat" (Bruns 2005: 12). This resulted in news from communities being obtained primarily from non-Indigenous transient community workers, reported by journalists living in larger cities hundreds of kilometers away. Often this was ill informed, lacking in grassroots diversity, and more interested in shock portrayal. The political economy of the mainstream media is such that commercial and political imperatives still shape the social image of Indigenous people through negative portrayal. This commodifies Indigenous people more as news items than valued contributors to the Australian mosaic (Bell 2008). And while "Aboriginal newspapers since the late nineteenth century in Australia, have played a crucial role in the symbolic reclamation of space for an Aboriginal public sphere" (Meadows 2005: 1), the reality suggests these papers have given voice to a select few, heard by a niche group of Australians.

One of the founders of the Central Australian Aboriginal Media Association (CAAMA), Dr. Phillip Batty, says in the film *Satellite Dreaming* (1991) that the camera is one of the most powerful tools used by Indigenous Australians. Marcia Langton, former chair of Australian Indigenous Studies at the University of Melbourne, who was involved with the video experiments at Yuendumu and CAAMA, believes all Indigenous uses of the camera for cultural preservation can be "traced to those early Warlpiri policies of representation" (cited in Michaels 1994: xxxv). Notwithstanding this, those willing to tell their story on camera were often criticized by anthropologists and community members for giving away information. Therefore, in an attempt to safeguard the local culture against appropriation by visiting ethnographers and media, Michaels developed a series of rules—effectively the community's own gatekeeping practices (Michaels 1994).

Concerned about the impact of satellite content delivered into remote communities by AUSSAT,[1] Indigenous people requested resources to enable them to interrupt the signal and insert programs they created. In 1987 the government recommended the establishment of BRACS,[2] which included a cassette recorder, radio tuner, microphone, speakers, switch panel, VCRs, television set, video camera, two UHF television transmitters, FM transmitter, satellite dish and decoders (Willmot 1984). Based on the Yuendumu participatory model, the initiative had enormous potential, but failed to provide enough training to enable people to create their own video content, and some units closed down (Batty 2012). Only those communities, like Yuendumu, that had already developed a response to television coped with the responsibility of creating local content (Bell 2008: 121). Batty believes the key to success often involved finding the funding for an "enthusiastic whitefellah" who would live in community and "work for almost no wages to keep it going" (Batty 2012).

When I arrived in central Australia in 1990, Warlpiri Media, in Yuendumu, was active and the CAAMA was well established with a video unit, music recording business, radio station and new RCTS television station, called Imparja. While Yuendumu and CAAMA employed mainly Indigenous people, at Imparja, the scale and technical intricacies of television meant that a large number of non-Indigenous staff were employed. The CAAMA Imparja model was seen by some as an example of how sophisticated expensive equipment transformed Indigenous-owned television into a Western-looking network (Michaels cited in Bell 2008). Michaels observed that once an Indigenous media organization moves away from traditional cultural and social organization, "they produce mainstream type programs and need Westerners to operate and manage them" (Michaels 1986 in Bell 2008: 82). This was certainly true at Imparja, where Indigenous people owned a TV station that employed large numbers of white people and in the main broadcast aggregated mainstream non-Indigenous content, like soaps, sports, game shows, movies and news. Batty says of Imparja, "It's one of the many tragedies of Aboriginal affairs ... it could potentially offer educational services and health," which he says are "still dysfunctional" (Batty 2012).

Warlpiri Media in Yuendumu and EVTV in Ernabella in the south were creating what Batty hoped Imparja would create—what Meadows refers to as "overlapping public spheres," communication spaces that "articulate their own discursive styles and formulate their own positions, on issues that are then brought to a wider public sphere where they are able to interact across lines of cultural diversity" (Meadows 2005: 38). Batty wanted Imparja to perpetuate a discursive Indigenous media space by acting as the cultural aggregator for community and CAAMA and BRACS content. He also wanted the BRACS communities to take CAAMA/Imparja content (Bell 2008). The aim was to use the Imparja footprint and the BRACS units to create a diverse Indigenous content sphere. Unfortunately, politics and responsibilities to advertisers led to commercial content being broadcast on Imparja. CAAMA also found producing daily, even weekly television, much more difficult than radio, and hence could only deliver a small amount of its own video content. Batty's vision and the reality were at times difficult to reconcile. As to which vision—Batty's, Michael's or the government's—created the more diverse cultural sphere can be determined by applying a test for diversity.

For many scholars source diversity sits at the heart of a healthy public sphere (Jakubowicz 1994; Dahlgren 1995; Napoli 1999; Hartley and McKee 2000; Meadows 2005; Deuze 2006; Bruns and Schmidt 2011). This is primarily because source is often defined through ownership and "can be measured in terms of diversity in ownership of media outlets, the workforce and content" (Napoli 1999: 12). To this end the originators of BRACS believed that a larger number of outlets—80 units were deployed nationally—would lead to more diverse ownership at the source, delivering a diverse content stream that would receive national exposure. According to Napoli (1999), these are the primary components of the diversity equation. However, as discussed earlier, the lack of effective ongoing training about how to create video programs diminished the potential for BRACS to create diverse local content. "The policeman's wife would take it over and be the program director and bring in all that commercial junk like *Dirty Harry* on a Friday night" (Batty

2012). In those central Australian communities where training was lacking, many BRACS were reduced to being a radio rebroadcaster, or no more than a retransmitter for the RCTS (Imparja) broadcasts of sports, soaps and to transmit commercial DVDs. Exposure can be distinguished by content "sent" or content "received," and seen from the perspective of either the broadcaster or what the audience selects. The assumption is that an audience with diverse content options consumes a diversity of content (Napoli 1999: 25), which would provide "exposure to a diversity of views and public issues" (Sustein 1993: 22). However, this did not occur at Imparja, where choice of content was restricted primarily to mainstream aggregation, with the odd Indigenous program. In providing a reason for not broadcasting a one-hour Indigenous documentary coproduced by CAAMA Productions and Channel 4 (UK), the director of Imparja said he was driven by commercial imperatives. He advised that no one would watch the program because it was Indigenous. The network's position was that because of its commercial imperatives, it was caught between a rock and a hard place. The interesting fact is that many Indigenous people liked the Western programming, especially the sports.

Meadows advises that the utopian goals of an Indigenous public sphere "should not be understood in terms of a nondominant variant of the broader public sphere" (2005: 38). CAAMA, Imparja, Warlpiri Media, and also BRACS need to be viewed as unique offerings in confrontation with the mainstream public sphere. They are relevant because they enable Indigenous people to deliberate and develop their own counterdiscourses, identities and experiences that enable interaction with the wider public sphere (Meadows 2005). While huge gains were made, real opportunities to create a unique Indigenous subfield of communications were missed: "to expand the organization you had to take the Aboriginal people with you and the prime example of that not happening is (was) Imparja TV" (Batty 2012). The type of deliberations Meadows refers to are "central to democratic theory and practice," with new technologies becoming society's "central nervous system" (McChesney 2007: 10), in ways previously unimaginable.

After more than 25 years of campaigning by organizations such as Warlpiri Media and CAAMA, in 2005 the Australian government supported the development of National Indigenous Television (NITV), with funding of $48.5 million. Even though NITV eventually delivered more than 350 hours of first-run Indigenous content per annum (Stevens 2010: 92), its first three years were turbulent. Grassroots organizations, including Warlpiri Media and CAAMA, felt the funding could have been better spent on programing at a local community level rather than on urban producers and infrastructure. These were the same criticisms leveled against Imparja 20 years earlier.

In 2010, the Australian government held a review of its investment in the Indigenous broadcasting and media sector (Review of Australian Government Investment in the Indigenous Broadcasting and Media Sector [IBR]). The key terms of reference were a consideration of cultural benefits for Indigenous Australians from investment in Indigenous broadcasting and media, and consideration of the impact of media convergence on the Indigenous broadcasting and media sector. Submissions to the IBR acknowledged the relevance and contribution of NITV but were critical of its centralized aggregation model. The IBR found that a "one size fits all" approach would not work given the significant differences between communities (Stevens 2010: 2). Hence at the heart of the IBR recommendations is a need to empower and resource a more diverse media, especially in remote communities.

One aim of the NT Mojo case study was to investigate whether multimedia storytelling skills and digital technology could enable a more diverse local content sphere. NT Mojo continues traditions of participatory Indigenous content creation, and capitalized on current changes in communication technologies, practices and government policies, by delivering control of all phases of digital story production and publication at a local level. Conducted at a seminal point in our communication history, this research provides one possible road map for introducing mobile journalism practices to remote Indigenous communities. What is hoped is that the program is embraced by the education sector, and local and mainstream media acknowledges the results, screens the mojo stories, and uses the mojos as suppliers of locally produced content.

Parameters for an Evaluation

As explained in the chapter on methodology, studies such as NT Mojo are often seen as prime examples of qualitative research. Like all qualitative research, this investigation adopts an interpretive approach to data, in part defined by the context and the subjectivity of researchers (Clough and Nutbrown 2006; McNiff and Whitehead 2006). The case study investigates a group of participants (mojos) working in a growing community of practice, who are engaged in a process of collective learning (Schramm 1974; Wenger 2007). Based on a concept of generational learning, the NT Mojo participants were a group of people who have had similar life experiences or significant life events. The mojo workshops are designed to augment these experiences with skills and technologies to create trained mojos able to work as community media practitioners, or be employed by more mainstream news agencies and TV networks. In all workshops participants were required to undertake practical journalism work based on a training manual and a set of guidelines. The primary emphasis was to produce and publish complete digital stories. In keeping with usual qualitative research practice, the mixed-method case study approach of this thesis involved a process of action research that situated the researcher as a participant agent of change (McNiff and Whitehead 2006; Wadsworth 2011).

Evaluation occurred across three phases: identification of communities and participants, the training package and the immediate impact of the training. Researcher Yolande Wadsworth observes that we evaluate all the time: "every time we choose, decide, accept or reject we have made an evaluation" (2011: 7). In action research we do this by taking a piece of the world and holding it up against a known value (Wadsworth 2011: 7), in this case the representation by media and the use of media by remote Indigenous communities, contrasted against the possibilities offered by the mojo training package. This type of evaluation by the trainers occurred daily during workshops. Communities and the funding body evaluated the finished videos against previous media output from communities.

The phases of action research as they applied to NT Mojo evaluation are as follows:

- *Noticing:* We bring a set of expectations and values based on previous experience and we notice the discrepancies between what we observe and what we expected. In the case of NT Mojo these were prior observations of Indigenous media and prior experience and understanding of previous attempts to alter the situation. For example, in 1990, it was difficult to get Indigenous people to appear on camera. In 2011, following two decades of commercial television penetration, it was a different story. In 1990, communication with communities was almost impossible; today each community has access to 3G telephone reception. In 1990, finding accommodation and food in communities for an extended research period was difficult; today there are air-conditioned "dongas" for hire, and community supermarkets.
- *Design:* This phase explores the problem in more detail—who is experiencing it, to what extent and what is the fix? Part of the design involves determining who or what is being researched; who is the research for and who is the researcher? Based on this a program of recovery was developed, in this case mojo training. The aim was to explore changes in remote communications possibilities since the 1990s, and the government agency that funded the workshops wanted information on the possibility of being able to deliver locally generated in-community messaging. The researcher was an experienced television producer with a track record of working with nonprofessionals to create and deliver video-type content. These factors impacted the design, the skill level being imparted and the outcomes. The researcher's background in television and self-shot content meant professional skills were being taught and outcomes could include job possibilities.
- *Fieldwork:* This occurred around a formal training workshop followed by a further four weeks of supplementary training. Being on the ground with mojos, the researcher was able to better understand the historical and cultural imperatives (sorry business, family commitments and social structure) that potentially impact this form of storytelling (see below).
- *Analysis and conclusions:* These are based on the researcher's immersion and associated observations of mojo reactions during production and the reception to the stories by mojos, community, public and networks. These observations are contrasted against survey responses, the

final shorter comments from mojos and interviews with experts. An element of quantitative research also occurred and the evaluation of this data is represented in a series of graphs. This data was vetted by a highly experienced quantitative data academic and used to supplement the action research findings (see Chapter 6).

- *Feedback and planning:* This began on the ground during the workshop. In this case it led to a number of other workshops to determine sustainability, transition and implementation of mojo skill sets into media. To facilitate supplementary training in the other spheres the program required a tonal shift.

The NT Mojo Workshop Primer

The mojo concept was based on the researcher's previous experience working with citizens on self-shot television series and from time spent producing content and running training in remote Indigenous communities. During travels around NT communities the mojo concept was discussed with a number of elders to gauge interest. Early scoping was essential to enable the completion of ethics proposals (Ethics). The program lasted eight weeks and comprised formal training, in-community training and production, and follow-up discussions. The various stages of the workshop are outlined below. While many stages overlap, they have been listed in chronological order, primarily to provide a guide for researchers wanting to replicate the process and activity.

Once the project had Ethics approval it developed in the following stages:

- *Funding:* The Department of Families, Housing, Community Services and Indigenous Affairs (FaHCSIA) was approached and agreed to fund the workshop, primarily because it provided an opportunity to train local people with job-ready skills, increase literacy levels and create local messaging to augment their Closing the Gap[3] campaign responsibilities. FaHCSIA suggested an NT training partner would make it easier for them to fund the project. Batchelor Institute for Indigenous Training and Education (BIITE), which provided training to Indigenous people, was chosen as a partner.
- *Partnership:* It was hoped that the association with BIITE would provide the mojo program with an opportunity for long-term sustainability. Mojos came from a number of communities, so BIITE would be viewed as neutral ground for running the one-week formal training workshop. Two BIITE teachers were trained to mojo to help with the in-community training phase. The fact that BIITE is located in Batchelor, 100 kilometers south of Darwin, meant students did not go walkabout while there. However, during training we observed that many community people did not like being away from their communities. But having mojos together

for the training phase made it easier to begin the process of creating a community of practice where mojos could help and inspire each other. In hindsight, while this had a positive impact, there may be a more effective model. In subsequent workshops formal training was run in community or in nearby communities. This familiarity relaxed mojos, introduced their work to community earlier, and enabled them to record local content for their training stories. But it was also fraught with peer group pressure.

- *Community support:* A project overview was sent to 30 NT communities. Local elders were asked to discuss the project and its requirements—to photograph people and homes and create digital stories for publication online. We chose communities where we had previously worked and where elders were receptive to the concept. This decision was made to save time and money during the selection phase. Discussions were held with elders and community representatives about excluding professionals. This decision was based on a desire to scope the relevance of mojo training for ordinary citizens and to determine how willing they were to record their own stories. The elders and community representatives agreed. Choosing to omit semiprofessionals is a form of gatekeeping like any form of limitation, whether essential or not (Wadsworth 2011: 7).
- *Permissions:* Beginning the collaborative process by meeting elders before a camera arrived was important. It enabled a more relaxed setting for discussions about cultural restrictions on photography that included difficulties showing certain material, controlling the mass mediation of photography beyond the face-to-face exchange, class and gender restrictions, the need to account for temporality (what is authorized today is not necessarily authorized tomorrow) and mortuary restrictions (Michaels 1994). Elders thought having mojos film their own story was one way of managing cultural protocols at a community level, where mojos understood local customs. There were no transgressions during filming and elders, like Mavis Ganambarr from Galuwinku, were generally delighted by all the stories: "I'm so happy about the stories and to see them kids working this way ... so proud" (cited in Burum 2012a).

    Candidate mojos received a project description prior to being selected, which also advised they could withdraw at any time. Mojos provided permission for us to film them and for their work to be broadcast. Mojos required permissions from people they filmed. This meant explaining the story, which meant mojos had to think about their story and why they might need to interview a particular person or film a specific event.
- *Project guidelines:* Having developed a number of UGC television series, it was clear that there were benefits to using guidelines. While these may appear restrictive, they establish clear working parameters and legitimize the project as something more than just movie making. Guidelines also assuaged some of the fears the funding body had that mojos would use the cameras to record and publish nonauthorized content.

The guidelines proved to elders that we had thought about possible issues as they outlined the parameters and actions to be taken if a transgression occurred. Candidate mojos were provided with a copy of the guidelines before they decided to become involved.

Also, in traditional communities the notion of ownership can be gray. The guidelines helped establish an ownership pattern for mojos to protect their equipment and their right to participate. The guidelines described the project in detail, including project partners and the roles and responsibilities of mojos. They outlined the selection process so mojo candidates knew on what basis selection occurred and what was expected of candidates selected for the program. In traditional communities, where everyone knows everyone, recording and broadcasting material that is incorrect can prove disastrous. Hence, the guidelines included information on editorial aspects, such as what could and could not be filmed or said, and a reminder of the importance of checking facts and not defaming people. This information was reinforced throughout training.

It is worth noting that there were no transgressions of using iPhones for unauthorized browsing and filming, which was a concern of the funding body, given the government's intervention[4] response to allegations of child abuse. The guidelines were used in one subsequent educational workshop and were replaced by educational guidelines and educational scaffolds for those workshops. This effectively tested educational and mainstream scaffolds around the issues dealt with in the guidelines.

A selection of the guidelines and their outcomes are listed in Table 5.1.

Table 5.1 Guidelines and outcomes

Guideline	Outcome
G 1.3: Each participant will have to produce one short video during the training phase and a series of 4–8 short videos during the production phase of the NTM project.	All mojos produced a video during training and produced 23 videos during the production phase, an average of 2.5 videos per participant. The lower number was due to two factors; a cyclone and mojos' low literacy levels, which made writing voiceovers and structuring stories a longer process than anticipated.
G 1.4: In keeping with the rules of the NTM project, videos will focus on these suggested themes: health, sport, music, employment, family, my community, art and culture. Final themes will be confirmed at the training workshop after considering your suggestions for themes.	We found this broad set of themes covered mojos' theme areas.

Guideline	*Outcome*
G 1.7: The NTMPT reserves the right to change or amend rules at any time. Any such modification will take effect as soon as the participants are advised of the change.	This was included as a request from the funding body, but there were no transgressions and the only modifications were stylistic, at the request of the mojos and as part of training.
G 2.6: Participants can be disqualified if they regularly fail to attend the course and produce material as directed, or if they fail to meet any other requirements of the course, as set by NTMPT.	We had one transgression during training where two mojos were up all night and missed a morning training session. Participants were not disqualified but chastised by their peers for letting the team down. How they took this reaction was not investigated. But they did not miss training after that.
G 3.3: If a participant younger than 18 is considered this will only be with the approval of community elders, the school and the parents of the participant.	We chose a number of participants who were under 18 at the suggestion of the community, but they could not do the training because local floods resulted in crocodiles swimming through the community.
G 5.3: Each participant will be supplied with a Telstra mobile account with predetermined cap and data allowance. Calls to the NTM production office and for other NTM-related matters can be made. Participants must not use their NTM Telstra accounts for personal calls. Each account will be itemised and records kept.	This did not work. Participants used the accounts to talk with each other across communities. They were running up bills and using all their credit, so at times were not contactable via the smartphone (G 6.7). BIITE did not cap the calls and so found it was responsible for large bills. In subsequent workshops I insisted on capped plans and bills were not an issue.
G 6.8: During the production phase NTMPT representatives will visit participants to further assist with video production.	Mojos found this essential and beneficial. In fact this is one of the main elements that made this multi-community project difficult. It was why subsequent projects were community specific.
G 6.9: All participants are encouraged to keep a video journal each day of the production phase.	This could not be policed due to the number of communities and was not a factor in the final analysis. Post workshop interviews were used instead to gauge responses.
G 7.2: Each participant will be responsible for their equipment and keeping it safe and in working order.	We had one breakage, whihc occurred on the plane returning from training to community.
G 7.3: This equipment remains the property of the NTMPT until NTMPT deem the participant has successfully completed the NTM project after which we will enter a discussion about the possibility of mojos being allowed to keep the equipment.	We decided to give the mojos their iPhone kits because we reasoned they would need them to continue mojo. However, a month later many of the kits were lost, damaged or unaccounted for, except in the communities where a local media center existed, and had become responsible for the kit.

(Continued)

Guideline	Outcome
G 8.1: Prior to any recording, participants must make sure that all necessary authorisations and clearances have been obtained concerning the subject or the object of the video. All potential legal problems must be avoided.	Participants made sure everyone depicted on camera agreed at least verbally. There were no complaints and hence no transgressions. Participants understood well the need to be ethical in community settings.
G 11.1: The participant acknowledges the stakeholders will have the exclusive right to use all material recorded by the candidate without limitation in any and all media, including but not limited to television, radio, videotape, disk and multimedia throughout the world without any limitation in time.	These are wordings government required for funding and it was expressly agreed that mojos would hold copyright on their work, with stakeholders having the right to use the work only in line with project imperatives and in a non-disparaging and professional manner.

- *Participant selection*: We received a positive response from eight communities to our call for participants: Daly River, Lajamanu, Bathurst Island, Gunbalanya, Ramingining, Angurugu, Numbulwar and Galiwinku. In each case community leaders like Mavis Ganambarr sanctioned the project: "I think that's a great opportunity for young people to be doing something that they can learn ... and I'm really happy very, very happy," she said (cited in Burum 2012a).

Community leaders discussed and chose an appropriate community mojo support person whom we also trained. This provided a friendly face during out-of-community training and an extra hand during in-community training and filming. Support people were generally senior community people, either teachers or those working in a media-related field.

The selection team, who spoke with 54 candidates, were looking for mojo participants interested in telling digital stories. Following the in-community briefings and interviews, possible participants were discussed with community representatives. A list of candidates was presented to the community for consideration. In the early 1980s, when Eric Michaels ran his video experiments, elders were concerned that any proposed television model should focus on languages (Michaels 1989). In 2011, elders wanted to use mojo to create positive television and web images to get young people "off the mischief and sniffing and all that is happening here" (Mavis Ganambarr cited in Burum 2012a). So elders looked for participants who would be able to convey this.

When I first came to work in the NT in 1990, the choices about which person in a community could be involved in a video production were limited. Michaels (1989) said these would be made according to skin groups and a person's position in the community. By 2011, this requirement was no longer overarching. Agreement from community leaders and representatives was generally based on their knowledge of the candidate, whether they thought he or she could stick it out and if they were a "humbugger"[5] or not. In 2011, television was not seen as ceremonial, but as utilitarian. Once senior community representatives agreed, candidates were approached to discuss commitment and the project guidelines, and collect signed participation forms. All candidates identified and asked to participate agreed to be involved.

- *The mojos:* Thirteen mojos and one support person were selected from six communities. One of the support people wanted to make stories as well, and this took the number to 14. We based our choices on candidates' availability and passion to be involved. "I was praying for this ... and one lady tell me, we got job multimedia job (mojo course), this old lady tell me and I was, thank God!" (participant in Burum 2012a). The mojos' ages ranged between 16 and 32, and there were eight males and six females, a spread we felt necessary to ensure a diversity of stories ideas and content. All mojos had been to secondary school; two were still attending and all but two of the others had completed year 12. All mojos spoke some English, a prerequisite we imposed because of time constraints and the level of job readiness we hoped to achieve.

At the commencement of training the group from Daly River had to return home due to floods and crocodiles floating on their football field. Following training two female mojos, one from Ramingining and one from Numbulwar, withdrew for family reasons. The support person who wanted to make stories found they were too busy, so we were left with nine mojos.

In the pretraining interviews we discussed the following with 14 participants. As indicated in Table 5.2, some mojos had more than one motivation for wanting to learn to mojo.

The digital storytelling aspect of mojo interested participants for traditional storytelling reasons: "The mojo workshop it's a new thing for me, it's all about to tell stories ... it could be a dreamtime story, it could be football ... stories are very important, passed on from generations ... my grandfather always told me stories and I tell my young ones" (participant in Burum 2012a). Others saw mojo as an opportunity to pass on lifestyle messages: "We can teach kids not to do bad things through mojo work" (participant in Burum 2012a).

- *Equipment:* Harrison et al. (2004), addressing the holistic nature of convergent story practices, point out that any story produced will need to form part of a larger publishing model. Their example was a convergent newsroom model in a tertiary environment called Newspace. While receptors like Newspace are essential, students need to have the tools and skills to make strong digital stories. Further, change research

Table 5.2 Pre-training interviews

Question	No of response	Typical response
Why they wanted to be a mojo?	11	They wanted to share positive stories with the rest of Australia and they liked how mojo gave them an opportunity to tell the stories their way
	7	Wanted to work as journalists
	2	Just wanted to use the skills at school
	4	Wanted to make community messaging
Type of stories they wanted to produce?	4	Wanted to produce stories that supported their cultural practices such as art
	5	Wanted to produce stories on how they live in harmony with their surrounds, such as bush medicine
	2	Wanted to produce sports stories
	3	Were very specific about wanting to promote a healthy life for young people
Whether they would be able to attend out-of-community training?	14	All said they could.
	6	Were concerned about the time away from community.
Demonstrated mojo kit	14	All mojos took to the technology immediately.
Explanation of timeframe	14	All were happy and able to commit to the one week of out-of-community training and four weeks in-community filming/training
Explanation of guidelines and project requirements.	14	Understood the requirements, the need for the guidelines and all were happy to sign and commit to the project

informs us that how we define mobile technology at the outset of its use will determine how it is used for generations (Boczkowski 2004). Hence, a neo-journalistic approach and digital storytelling skill set were employed to test the technology. A semiprofessional production kit (discussed in detail in *Mojo: The Mobile Journalism Handbook* published by Focal; see Appendix A) was developed that consisted of an iPhone 4, which was chosen as the camera because (1) it shoots in high definition (HD) and records digital audio, (2) it has great hedonic appeal—no mojo had owned one and everyone wanted one, (3) it has excellent functionality, (4) it offers the required 3G and WiFi connectivity, (5) it enables certain functions to be restricted and (6) it works with the 1st Video edit app (Voddio). The fact that it was first a phone, second a camera and then an edit suite made it less threatening and immediately accessible. *Mojo: The Mobile Journalism Handbook* includes a chapter describing equipment options in detail.

- *Edit app:* VeriCorder in Canada developed a commercial-grade editing App enabling multitrack vision and audio editing and mixing. The current iMovie 2.0 and the Kinemaster 3.1 Android apps are the only other edit apps that offer multitrack vision editing. As the intent was to scope the commercial application of mojo training, it was critical that we use a professional edit app. Two video tracks are essential when teaching students how to make *content at speed*, or how to use a B roll, which can be the difference between dynamic multimedia and static video stories. The apps include a subtitle feature, which is essential for language work, a tool for creating *name supers* and a facility to enable an audio mix. The iMovie 2.0 app released in 2013 has features that make it a viable, easy-to-use alternative. The mCamLite[6] iPhone cradle was used to steady the smartphone, a small shotgun microphone was used to enhance sound and we had a portable light.

- *Telephony:* Having both 3G and WiFi functions enables the user to choose the fastest upload connection. WiFi is not common in private homes in remote communities. At some in-community organizations like government agencies, WiFi is inaccessible because it is wrapped in proxy servers and government security protocols. So we mainly used 3G to upload stories.

Table 5.3 indicates video upload speeds from remote communities in 2011–12.

Table 5.3 3G upload speeds

Upload Test—1 minute file sent using 3G		
Resolution	File size	Upload speed
1080p	170 megs	34 min
720p	80 megs	16 min 30 sec
360p	27 megs	4 min 45 sec
270p	6 megs	1 min 30 sec

Training, the Transfer of Knowledge Elements

NT Mojo training occurred in three stages: a five-day formal workshop, a four-week block of intensive in-community training based around story production, and follow-up discussions. The aim throughout was to find a balance between theory and practical training, to produce what media scholar Lee Duffield refers to as "start-ready recruits for media jobs backed by a study of contexts" (2011: 141). The context in our case was location-based mobile journalism skills, which include writing, recording voice and audio, editing and basic legal and ethical considerations. The formal training workshop, which lasted one week, involved four phases:

- Basic journalism: Simple elemental research and storytelling techniques including a community-relevant primer on defamation and ethics;
- Technical: Use of the iPhone for recording audio and video;

- Editing: Using the 1st Video edit app (Voddio; now iMovie); and
- Publishing: Uploading stories to a website.

To cover these phases, a comprehensive mojo training manual was developed to teach basic mobile journalism and associated technical skills, which each student received with their mojo kit.

Journalism Skills

Participants were introduced to simple story building blocks—actuality, narration, interviews, overlay (B roll), piece to camera (stand-up) and music (see *Mojo: The Mobile Journalism Handbook*). Training involved treating the elements like Legos and learning about their individual shapes, before learning how the elements form story. When learning how to drive a car, we first learn to use the accelerator, then the brake and finally the steering wheel. Combine those elements in various sequences and you have different driving experiences. Learning to tell stories by learning individual story elements first, then structure, is less daunting than learning complete story structure from the outset. This elemental approach places the emphasis on coverage and editing. Finally, the training exercise demonstrated how these elements are used to create a beginning, middle and end of a mojo story. Story rhythm, or what I call the "story bounce," which differs depending on how elements are constructed, was the most difficult aspect to learn. While a third of the mojos were confident enough to tackle this on their own during the training production block, the majority relied on trainer intervention. By the end of the one-week formal training block, mojos had a strong grasp of story elements and a rudimentary understanding of story structure.

Mojo participants were required to outline their in-community stories during the formal training workshop. This was achieved with the support people to establish this way of working. Once participants had developed their own stories I made suggestions about content and structure. This process was chosen to try to avoid the danger of story choice being a reflection of what makes the teacher happy (Worth and Adair 1972).

One of the advantages of having all mojos attend formal training was that when learning occurs through engagement in a group, the group becomes a community of practice, and participants learn from each other (Wenger 2007). According to Duffield, a community of practice is particularly helpful in the transference phase, where skills are mastered to form new knowledge (2011). For transference to occur, Duffield suggests providing guidelines in the form of readings. NT Mojos received a slide show, a comprehensive training manual or workbook, a set of guidelines and an interactive workshop. It was the group dynamic, and working in front of others repetitively, that enabled transference and helped overcome what Indigenous people call shame,[7] which can lead to disengagement.

Hanrahan and Madsen (2006) make the point that any training using digital media sets up a dichotomy between learning styles, in particular writing and storytelling conventions. New, more innovative ways of learning multimedia storytelling lead to participants having higher expectations. Our participants experienced the immediate gratification resulting from actuation. The growing realization was that a balance between the *hedonics* and *tech creep* (which drove the higher expectations) and storytelling and traditional journalistic skills was required for effective mojo. Communal practice was helpful in reducing individual frustration by locating mojos in a group experiencing similar issues. When mojos returned to their communities, we found this changed and some were sidetracked by peer pressure.

Another aspect of journalism skill that was easier to convey was the need for ethical reporting and the care required to avoid defamation. Ethical concepts made sense to the mojos who lived in tight-knit communities and had firsthand experience of unethical treatment by the media. An interesting discussion ensued about how mojos should portray negatives, like alcohol abuse, which they believed needed to be addressed. They reasoned that those types of stories should become an exploration of what is being done about the problem, rather than focus on the problem. Mojos initially agreed to seek elder approval to tell this type of story primarily to ensure, through traditional tribal osmosis, that the community knew they had permission. Two mojos tackled these types of stories.

iPhone Recording

I left the introduction of the iPhone and camera until participants received basic journalism training. This proved a valuable decision for two reasons: (1) it enabled a focus on the importance of journalism techniques before technology, and (2) it contextualized the use of the iPhone as a device for doing journalism. Seven trainees answered the question relating to mobile phone use. All seven had previous experience with mobile phones, but only one had a smartphone. Figure 5.1 shows that all but two used their mobile for recording audio and all but one used their mobile to record video. The video was unedited and kept for family and friends and was distributed between community members using Bluetooth. The high percentage recording video and audio is probably due to the fact that five mojos had previous training in video production at school. At 71 percent, this is a much higher percentage of previous video training than we saw in the secondary and journalism school workshops we ran later.

What was a revelation to the group was the level of coverage (actuality and B roll) required to make stories look professional. This was a difficult concept to convey and was best achieved through demonstration and editing during the production and post phases. It required that all mojos record and edit specific shots, voice-overs, narration and a piece to camera. Having this exercise scripted meant that elemental decision making was taken out of

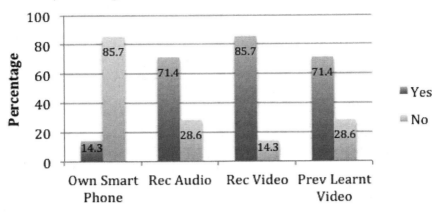

Figure 5.1 Mobile phone multimedia use.

mojos' hands. Mojos could concentrate on essential aspects of training, such as style, technique and how elements come together to create story bounce. Once mojos began editing their shots, they began to learn how sequences are created—how story elements marry to create narrative—and they saw what elements were missing. Half the group learned this during the formal training stage, while the remaining members needed extra time.

From the outset, the aim was not to underestimate the potential for people to learn new skills. For example, the ABC in Australia had underestimated the possibilities for ABC Open[8] by focusing primarily on *still* content. The ABC producer's rationale was that many of their contributors would be elderly and would find it difficult to come to terms with video. In 1993, in *Home Truths*, self-shot video production was introduced to people as old as 82, who loved the experience. On further investigation it was determined that much of the reason the ABC and many teachers of multimedia choose a stills approach, or an ineffective edit app, may have been due to digital trainer skills lag. A lack of digital storytelling experience can hamper trainers' ability to teach students to create dynamic and professional multimedia.

Editing

Multimedia storytelling can involve a variety of media, for example, actuality, archival, pictures, documents, narration, tweets and music. These can be constructed using online placeholders like Storify to provide form for UGC. In our case we were using mobile edit apps that turned iPhones into pocket creative suites capable of producing complete user-generated stories (UGS). Bathurst Island support person Louis Kantilla found the edit technology liberating. "Small mojo portable digital, you know the screen is better than a camera where you take out the cassette and do it in a mixer in a computer. But this little gadget, you do everything by snapping the finger, bang you can do it" (participant in Burum 2012a). All mojos learned the practical aspects of editing on the iPhone. This involved creating a project, choosing content and moving around a timeline. As indicated in Figure 5.2, the 1st Video edit app (and iMovie 2.0) has two video tracks: a feature that enables more professional checkerboard editing and a more visible element integration with B roll on a separate video track.

V2		B Roll		B Roll	
V1	Sync		Sync		Sync
A1		Narration		Narration	
A2	Music	FX	Music	Music	Music

Figure 5.2 Checkerboard edit example.

Participants created a short 35- to 45-second training video that incorporated all the basic story elements—pieces to camera (stand-ups), narration, overlay, actuality and music. Creating a finished video to demonstrate how quick the process is and to provide a sense of achievement early in the training phase is a key component of successful mojo training.

On a mobile device, which enables almost instant story creation, the thought process associated with the edit needs to extend beyond the kinesthetic or mechanical experience of stitching one shot to another. Mobile editing occurs on location, and this impacts the type of content and style of the edit. The edit begins with the shoot where a greater level of handheld actuality will make the edited story feel more dynamic. Dynamic editing in and out of pictures, to create a news-type story bounce, will help create an edited-while-it-is-happening feel. Editing in general is a way of *thinking* influenced by *ways of seeing* various states of immediate possibility. This is particularly relevant in close-quarter storytelling like mojo, where the immediate is an essential story component. It is based on a state that has been described as fluid where "the relationship between what we see and what we know is never settled" (Berger 1972: 7). Yet when training people to mojo we need to impart skills that settle perceptions. In this context mojo praxis, especially the editing skills, work as a filtration system to make sense of the flowing relationship between two separate unsettled realties— traditional Indigenous and Western worlds.

Given the above, two aspects of the edit process need to be discussed. First, because NT mojos came from six different communities, and spoke different languages or dialects, in a sense, mojo was like a common digital language. Worth and Adair note that "although the parallel between film and language is not exact, it may be that the manipulation of images ... and structuring in editing is not a random activity" (1972: 44). This is often true as a screen language follows structural forms like any language. Hence, the premise was that if mojos were shown how to edit (by introducing an understanding of story elements) and how to sequence stories with a journalistic bounce, they would learn that language style, and "develop (those) patterned ways of filming" (1972: 45). It was presumed these patterned filming structures would be based on their already known culture and languages, which influence not only their "semantic and thematic choice of image," but the "very way they put images together in a sequence" (1972: 45), the way they might naturally structure story. For the most part, what actually occurred was that mojos were happy to follow the structural patterns, or bounce, they had learned during the formal training course. In fact, a mojo story produced 18 months after the mojo workshop was made in exactly the same style with the same story bounce mojos had been taught. This indicates participants were happy with the style and required more time to enable them to break away from story structures learned at training.

Secondly, mojos felt that the story bounce we established was just like television, and they liked television. This raised a question as to the relevance of the patterns of journalistic story structure that were introduced, which in one sense seems so different to their traditional storytelling structures. As Worth and Adair observe (1972), there is a universality involved in working with pictures and music that most people understand that transcends cultural boundaries. If this is true, then additional training time is required to enable stories produced during training to be deconstructed and restructured in a number of ways to demonstrate different outcomes and editing possibilities that take into account other possible structures. The question is, when should they be introduced?

The In-Community Training and Production Phase

This involved putting into practice what mojos learned during the formal training workshop. It also involved trainers moving between communities to assist with aspects of story production and ongoing training. Below are listed a number of observations about this phase.

- *Story choice:* The majority of mojos recorded one of the stories they had identified during the formal training block. Mojos chose their own stories generally based on location, family, local issues and availability of interviewees. The mojos produced 20 stories in four weeks: 5 health, 3 sport, 4 art and culture, 3 youth, 3 media and 2 local news stories. The two news stories, a response to the flooding caused by cyclonic rains, were produced after trainers had left the community. Mojos produced six issue-based stories: *A Natural High* (petrol sniffing), *Bush Medicine* (native healing plants), *Chooky Brothers* (youth delinquency), *Youth Pathways* (learning to work as a team), *Aged Care* (looking after the elderly) and *Numbulwar Night Patrol* (fighting and alcohol abuse). Issue-based stories were difficult to develop in small communities where everyone knew each other. However, one of the mojos spoke with elders about wanting to produce a story about petrol sniffing, which elders thought was important. The mojo constructed a method, without help from trainers, for telling this aspect of the story without offending locals. The mojo used drama reconstruction laced with interview grabs from elders. It was a smart and effective way of dealing with a sensitive issue and an indication that the workshop was having a positive effect on ways of seeing stories. It also showed that mojos could think outside the patterned story bounce style described during training.

- *Production and edit:* Mojos were concerned with some aspects of production, especially recording interviews. Because they had never recorded interviews, they often felt shame. This sensitivity was weighed against the importance of their possible new role in the community— as *modern-day storyteller.* All nine mojos who made stories said their biggest difficulty was constructing the story—choosing which bits to shoot and which bits to include or edit out. This was expected. However, when they were shown how narration works and explained why it might be required, they settled into the task to develop their own draft form of words. Trainers worked with mojos to massage these before the mojos recorded their voice-over on location, often at night, directly onto the iPhone.

  All mojos had friends attempting to borrow their production equipment. Mojos agreed that signing the project guidelines enabled them to tell friends they weren't allowed to lend equipment. In a communal existence, where people share almost everything, this proved essential.

- *Publication:* We established a discreet website at ntmojos.Indigenous. gov.au, where edited and moderated stories were uploaded using 3G or WiFi connections. Publishing stories was critical for a number of reasons. First, it was the icing on the cake that made mojos feel they had achieved something special. Publishing on the web is seen as professional and like television; it legitimized the extra effort required to "get it right." Second, publishing is a way of getting a less marginalized message out to other communities and to the non-Indigenous population. Finally, publishing provides an opportunity to sell content and for mojos to be compensated for their story, as occurred with sales of mojo stories to NITV.

  The irony was that even though communities had terrific 3G connectivity, the digital divide meant that not many households had computers. Hence, many families often could only view stories on the mojo's iPhone, or when they went to the school or the local media and community center, or when mojo stories were broadcast on television. As one of the mojo's mums said, seeing those stories was just the incentive families needed to ask their communities for computers and computer training.

  All NT Mojo stories were shot in high-definition 2 (HD2) 1280 × 720 and most were uploaded in that resolution. Current technology has advanced to high-definition 1 (HD1) 1920 × 1080 resolution. If the 3G signals were slowed, stories were rendered and uploaded in 640 × 360, which is a typical YouTube resolution.

Outcomes

The NT Mojo project was developed because access to technology with relevant journalism skills meant that citizens living in remote communities could become producers of their own politicized content. This ideal, first envisioned in remote Australia in the late 1970s, is another way of attempting to overcome Indigenous marginalization brought about by geography and the gatekeeping practices of the media.

The success of the NT Mojo's first-stage mojo training program can be gauged against a number of criteria:

• *The transference of skills and the level of learning:* One major question arising out of the mojo workshop is the degree to which participants might become self-sufficient after trainers leave and be able to work on their own, or with other community members, to develop, produce and publish stories. Table 5.4 shows a summary of what participants did and what skills they had learned following the mojo workshop.

Table 5.4 Mojo skill audit

Skill	Details	Level achieved
Story choice	All mojos determined their own stories and provided an initial list of interviewees.	Intermediate
Story structure	Mojos decided on the type of material they wanted to cover in discussion with support people and in some cases trainers. In other instances mojos began filming even before trainers arrived in community. One example is found in the petrol-sniffing story from Galiwinku described earlier. In Ramingining the mojo continued to work with community support people after trainers left. They choose, developed, filmed, edited and published two stories (Ramo News and NT Bula Bula Arts) without assistance from the trainers.	Intermediate
Coverage	Mojos mainly did their own filming. Occasionally trainers would intercede to provide advice or describe technique. Where there were two mojos in a community each would be encouraged to help the other with filming pieces-to-camera or other difficult on-camera material.	Intermediate—more practice required covering and editing sequences
Sound	Mojos recorded their own actuality sound and they recorded their own narration.	High
Writing	Where possible, mojos tried to write their own narration after discussing with trainers what was required. Mojos often got the thought of the narration piece right, but sometimes needed help with words. In some instances trainers helped augment and write narration with mojos. A great deal of training time was spent on this key element during the training/production phase.	Low—needs more specific and longer training beyond the scope of this workshop.

Skill	Details	Level achieved
Editing operation	All mojos did the mechanical aspect of their editing. They learned to operate the edit system very quickly. Some were very proficient.	Intermediate to high
Story editing	On those stories completed without trainers in community, mojos did all aspects of editing. Where trainers were present and as required, they helped with editing and offered advice on structure. The degree to which mojos edited without trainer input was determined by their understanding of story structure and not the mechanical aspect of editing on the device, which all mojos could do relatively well. More training is required in story editing. This might be achieved using the training exercise and re-editing it using different structures to see the difference.	Low—this was the most difficult of training elements and requires more time and more specific work.
Supers	Mojos entered their own name supers and subtitles on their stories.	High
Render and upload	Mojos learned to render stories at various resolutions and to upload their stories.	High
Ethics and defamation	Mojos received basic information on ethics, defamation and copyright. There were no issues. As expected mojos were aware of local cultural protocols and the proclivities of living in small communities. However, given the interest by media in their stories and skills, I believe a greater emphasis is required in this area.	Intermediate— more specific modules required, especially given story reach is global.

- *Recognition of achievements:* When two of the mojos beat professional filmmakers (at the Fist Full of Films Festival in Darwin) and won major awards, media and the education sector began to take interest. The Northern Territory Department of Education and Training wanted to know how to implant mojo in schools and media began to make inquiries. All nine mojos were offered fee-for-services community stringer work on a story-by-story basis by ABC TV news in Darwin and NITV news. Mojos secured video commissions from the government, and two secured ongoing media work in their communities. Winning awards indicates to mojos that mojo is a professional toolkit. Being offered stringer work is critical to creating a less marginalized voice and local jobs. This is a first and empowering step to creating a grassroots alternative Indigenous voice that overlaps with the mainstream media sphere.
- *Youth sport and recreation:* Following from the success of the project, an NT government department has purchased 36 mojo kits for use in communities across East Arnhem Shire.
- *Improving the model:* Table 5.5 identifies aspects of mojo training that will need to be incorporated in future programs.

Table 5.5 Improvements

Element	Change
Training location	Workshops need to occur in community to enable mojos to feel more at home and to slowly introduce their communities to mojos" responsibilities.
Training partners	Could include community media centers, schools and local media interested in the region. Partnering mojo with existing in-community media and schools provides it with its best chance of sustainability.
Equipment ownership	One of the major issues during the community phase of the workshop was equipment control. Mojos found it a constant battle to keep the mojo kits away from interested community members. This poses a conundrum, as one of the aims of mojo is to create a greater awareness of the possibilities of mojo. In our case we determined that the mojo kits should be left with mojos after the workshop in recognition of (a) their empowerment as mojos, (b) to enable mojos to react to stories without having to ask permission to use the mojo kit, and (c) to enable mojos to earn income from mojo activities. Some of those mojo kits are now unaccounted for.
In-community supervision	A more substantial training/production phase is needed which includes a facility to have trainers oversee the program on an ongoing part-time basis over an extended period of time.
Ethics and defamation	As discussed above, a more in-depth component is required during formal training. This will be required when mojo is taken to a next, more investigative stage and when developing UGP for web TV.
Story construction	More time and more exercises are required to enable the re-edit of the training story. The creation of a second and third more comprehensive story during formal training will enable exploration of interview styles and recognition of associated issues, including varied styles of editing.
Coverage	More specific coverage exercises are required during formal training. These exercises need to be structured around sequencing so that the focus is on story coverage and not shot-gathering.
Community contact	Government instrumentalities, agencies and interested media will need a community contact point for mojo content. Following NT Mojo I received calls from media wanting mojos to cover stringer-type activities like car accidents and floods. On these occasions I was not able to get hold of the mojos, who were out bush. Subsequently I provided ABC TV News in Darwin and NITV with the names of mojos and a number of community contact points. Formalizing this process by early association with in-community media and schools will help. I also had an approach from ABC Darwin to advise mojos to provide free content for ABC Open. I advised mojos of the offer. Their response was that they would rather get paid for content, and if not they would prefer to upload to a community website.

Element	Change
Guidelines and consents	These are helpful to any mojo project and need to be comprehensive; they also need to provide a no-penalty mechanism for withdrawal.
Safeguards	A series of safeguard protocols were available. The degree to which these need to be employed depends on the nature and location of the project. I have supplied an example of these as Appendix B.

In summary, projects like NT Mojo potentially deliver tools to enable the creation of dialogue with Indigenous people at a local level. This potentially overcomes the sensitivity, identified by Professor Marcia Langton (1993), that requires an indirect approach to news interviews and extensive negotiation with communities. With Indigenous communities able to publish their own local stories, bypassing even the more mainstream Indigenous media, this negotiation becomes an ongoing internal cultural process that media will need to buy into, if they don't want to miss the real news.

Because of the low cost of mobile technology, the real potential of mojo is to create in-community employment opportunities. Achieving this for all mojos was one of the key outcomes that was not fully realized. Even though there was overwhelming interest in the mojo concept and the mojos, offers of work beyond those discussed above were not forthcoming. The study showed that mojos received ongoing community employment only through in-community media organizations, not as a result of external offers, which came from ABC news, in the form of stringer requests. Mojos, however, were not in community when the stringer call came through. Notwithstanding this, and with media showcasing mojos' work (ABC TV and NITV news), the opportunity has never been greater to create a more sustainable early-adoption model in remote, regional and urban schools, and that is the focus of the workshops discussed in Chapter 6.

Notes

1. The Australian communications satellite launched in 1985.
2. Remote communities' broadcast facility.
3. Closing the Gap is a government initiative to address the disadvantage faced by indigenous Australians in life expectancy, child mortality, education and employment.
4. A package of government initiated changes to welfare provision, law enforcement and other measures, introduced in 2007 to address allegations of child sexual abuse and neglect in Northern Territory Indigenous communities.
5. Someone who is persistent in creating problems and might not want to stick at something.
6. Cradle for the iPhone.
7. Indigenous people from isolated communities often get embarrassed about having to stand out in public or in certain other situations (Freire 1970: 16), which is due to attention rather than action (McChesney 2007: 221).
8. ABC Open is a receptacle for people from all over Australia to create great videos, photos and written stories to share on the ABC.

6 Supplementary Workshops in Education and Media

> I don't know if you realize but before I did the mojo course I couldn't
> hold a complete conversation.
> —*Robert French in* Cherbourg Mojo Out Loud *(Burum 2013)*

Overview

This chapter investigates the introduction of mojo across two other important spheres of communication: education and media. This was done to test the workshop training methodologies and training manuals across multiple spheres and to

- Validate mojo and user-generated stories (UGS) as more than an alternative community-based toolkit and form;
- Investigate the accessibility (level and pitch) and sustainability of mojo within the education system; and
- Assess the relevance of mojo skills to helping print journalists across the digital divide. A positive outcome would further validate the training package as being an effective tool for creating alternative journalism.

One overarching aim was to determine whether mojo skills and literacies could form the basis of a common digital language (CDL) across multiple spheres of communication. I contend that mojo's digital language could form a digital bridge that links community, education and media communications praxis.

After conducting the NT Mojo workshop, it became apparent that if mojo was to succeed, especially in remote environments, it needed to be tied to sustainable in-community programs in order to provide ongoing support. The success of the NT Mojo project resulted in numerous inquiries from education departments, schools, universities and the media. Inquiries from schools indicated educators were looking for a way to modify and transform literacy programs to make them more dynamic and relevant. As Robert's comment shows, students were inspired to achieve beyond expectations (theirs and others) and schools were interested in using mojo to provide challenge-based literacy training. Hence, series of short supplementary workshops were conducted in Australia and internationally.

Two primary schools were identified in far north Queensland that had a mix of Indigenous and non-Indigenous year 6 students. The secondary schools were in the Northern Territory, Victoria and Western Australia. The mojo program was run in tertiary journalism schools in Australia and China to determine its effectiveness as a multimedia tool set to prepare journalism graduates with the skills they need to work in digital newsrooms. Table 6.1 lists the skills learned in basic mojo training 101. The level at which these are taught depends on whether the students are primary, secondary, tertiary or professional journalists.

Table 6.1 Skills learned

Skill	Benefit
Research	Enables the mojo to undertake investigation and to use social media to develop the story while analysing their intended structure and thinking about the editorial implications.
Camera	Enables mojos to cover sequences on a mobile that can be edited, are dynamic and relate to the story being covered.
Audio	Enables mojos to record clear audio in a number of environments using a number of digital methods.
Interviews	Enables the mojo to learn how to conduct and record interviews on location using a variety of styles.
On camera	Mojos learn to work in front of a camera creating stand ups.
Writing	Enables the mojo to write narration in and out of pictures to make dynamic use of media, including an ability to create sharp headlines and editorial segues.
Editing	Enables the mojo to combine pictures and audio in a dynamic structure to gain the most impact and to edit these on mobile non-linear edit equipment.
Publication	Enables the mojo to use YouTube and WordPress, or to upload via FTP, to create their own voice or supply UGC or UGS to professional agencies.
Web and blog	Training on Word Press and YouTube (to which students uploaded their stories).
Budget and schedule	Scheduling a multimedia story is different from a print story. Knowing how to do this provides the mojo with skills that enable them to cost stories and teaches them producing.

Publication, web and budgeting skills were not taught at the primary level. My aim was to scope

- Skills translated into schools and whether teachers and lecturers would find the skills accessible and transferable across the curriculum;
- Student engagement;

- Impact of short class times on mojo training; and
- Optimum group size.

In working with media in Australia, Timor-Leste and Denmark, the aim was to determine the effectiveness of the mojo workshops as a tool for providing print journalists with digital skills training. If effective, this would validate mojo as a relevant university unit to prepare tertiary students for journalism and web TV work.

Primary and Secondary Mojo Workshops

In the education sphere the mojo program was first introduced to two Queensland primary schools, one in remote Queensland and one in Cairns, who came together for a workshop. As one aim was to scope its effectiveness in large class sizes, two teachers from each school were trained to provide support during the workshop and to continue with the program in their schools. Most students used iPods to create their stories. The workshop was difficult to run and 43 students proved to be the limit of control. The class included five deaf students who used iPads and required specialist attention from one of the teachers. This left three teachers and I running a workshop with 38 students. Once the formal training was completed, students formed small practice groups to develop stories and storyboards. The smaller, more manageable groups made it possible for students to take on production roles—as writer, camerapeople and journalist or editor. All participants in the team had a role that suited them. Once teams developed a story structure each group recorded their stories over a two-hour block.

Most of the students, who were around 11 years old, found the mechanical aspects of filming and editing accessible. Developing story and structuring the story edit proved a little more difficult. A number of the students commented that they felt they were too young to understand this aspect of the training. However, Dan White, one of the teachers involved in the workshop, said he was already seeing mojos' potential to build storytelling and communication skills. Robyn Thompson, the specialist teacher working with deaf students in the workshop, felt deaf students responded well because the more visual aspect of mojo helped overcome their general reluctance to write. All mojo participants produced their own in-class mojo story exercise, and all mojo collectives produced one group story. The cohort viewed all stories with the Cairns principal, who wanted to integrate mojo into the curriculum.

While I have listed some findings at the conclusion of this chapter, the clearest observation in the primary setting was that students loved making digital stories and teachers welcomed the integration. The students found the edit app confusing, but I believe they would find the new iMovie 2.0 app accessible because it functions very much like their other iOS devices. Story editing was also slow, but it was remarkably successful. Students created their own rhythms but managed the concept of stand-ups, narration and cover shots, or B roll. They also felt comfortable devising questions and recording interviews. Students at this level relied heavily on teacher input.

Workshops were run in a number of secondary schools across Australia, using the same mojo package employed with NT Mojo and with primary schools. It proved effective across all levels from years 7 to 12, primarily because a large number of students were mobile phone users with experience using iOS devices. The modular way of teaching multimedia storytelling was also effective, enabling students to grasp individual elements, before having to build their cache of elements into a story.

Two mojo workshops were run in the Northern Territory for secondary students. Both workshops included a train-the-trainer component. One of the schools set up a WordPress site, http://gunbalanyamojo.wordpres.com, to publish their mojo stories. Prior to the workshops, I ran a train-the-trainer course for two teachers. During the students' workshops I slowly relinquished more of the training to the teachers as they became more comfortable. There were difficulties getting more teachers to the train-the-trainer workshop because schools were reluctant to release teachers and teachers were unwilling to undertake training on their own time.

The train-the-trainer workshop is designed to create a mojo knowledge base within the school and begin the buy-in process with staff. The train-the-trainer workshop was incorporated as an integral component of future school-based training. In Western Australia a series of workshops was run for teachers from six schools. These schools decided to scope a hyperlocal network to share UGS and views about their education programs and communities. In doing so they hoped to empower students with a unique journalistic voice and promote community-based civic ideals as described by Clark and Monserrate (2011).

Despite initial success, the process has not progressed as quickly as expected in participating schools because of competing scholastic imperatives. Carly Follington, a teacher from Kolbe College in Western Australia, who attended a mojo workshop, feels that pressures of everyday teaching get in the way of initiatives like mojo. The head of IT at Corpus Christ College in Perth, Trevor Galbraith, believes teachers still don't understand the potential of mojo and the power of a child's voice. Galbraith believes this attitude leads to scheduling issues, which has led him to write his own mojo program and run it as part of the IT curriculum at his school.

The network set up by the Queensland government to broadcast mojo stories from the primary school workshops restricted access to only schools. This defeated one of the major aims of mojo—to disseminate content to the broader community. It's uncertain how to overcome these reservations, which are based in part on school's *loco parentis* and pastoral care responsibilities. The workshops show that editorial skills that come with mojo training deliver student-driven moderation at the source and before exposure.

One way to change attitudes is by promoting mojo's success stories. When one student we trained during the Gunbalanya mojo workshop won the

ATOM Award for middle school video production, it created an unprecedented interest among the student body and the teaching staff. As identified by Funk (1998), this sense of community responsibility, that's tied to creative ability, leads to a growing social identity and interest. Clark and Monserrate (2011: 419) found that students with a "commitment to benefit the collective, were more likely to engage in behaviors that would benefit the societal interest than those who did not express such interests." Mojo praxis promotes a eudemonic philosophy, where students begin thinking about more than immediate hedonistic gratification. They begin to interact with the wider community and think as citizens. Mojos' effectiveness as a cross-curricular cross-disciplinary pedagogy potentially enables eudemonic attitudes to develop across school and community. This concept is expanded in Chapter 7.

Primary and Secondary Effectiveness

The mojo kit proved accessible, with students and teachers who took to the smart devices intuitively. Even though 73 percent of the primary students who attended the workshop did not have a mobile, the training package could be adapted for primary students because they regularly use the iOS platform in class. Multimedia storytelling skills were more difficult to impart at the primary level. Hence for the primary program, the modular storytelling elements and the explanation about the use of mobile technology was simplified. Partitioning story elements as modular items, with their own story function, makes them manageable, moveable and accessible. However, the workshops showed that editing these into a structural form—wrapping them in a journalistic story bounce—requires more time at the primary level. Most teachers, even media teachers at the secondary level, suffer from digital trainer skills lag. Teachers who have some digital experience generally have an IT background and a technologically determinist view. Teachers who have never produced multimedia stories will require professional digital skills development. This training should focus more on digital storytelling than on the use of technology, which teachers picked up very quickly. While teachers saw mojo as an excellent tool for creating innovative literacy programs, the major problem they foresaw was scheduling it. To overcome scheduling difficulties at his school, Dan White formed a mojo club that meets two lunchtimes each week, and even more often before school events. At the club students plan and produce mojo stories. To overcome scheduling issues in high school, some teachers are scheduling mojo across junior years, where they have more flexibility with the curriculum. To overcome timetabling issues, mojo can be taught in 13 distinct phases run in 70-minute to 2-hour classes. The phases are as follows:

- Students receive an overview of the basic storytelling elements of mojo. The story elements, including SCRAP,[1] are reinforced and developed over the following weeks as per the mojo training manual.

- Students receive instruction in shooting strong video and recording clean audio. They record the mojo story exercise.
- Students are introduced to the edit app by editing the mojo story exercise. They learn about two-track vision checkerboard editing.
- Students complete the edit and learn the onboard titling tool and the mix features of the edit app. Students learn how to use up to four tracks of audio.
- Students create a YouTube channel and a WordPress site before uploading their story, writing a post and embedding the link into the blog.

Secondary students also learn the following:

- Students develop a final outline for their second story, a 1- to 1.5-minute local issue–based in-community story they have been researching at home. Teachers check sources and the story plan for structure and safety.
- Students shoot their second story. They set up and record a greater number of interviews, work with multiple sources and shoot more specific actuality[2] and B roll. Particular attention is paid to lighting, sequencing coverage and clan audio.
- Students edit their second story where they learn to plan, structure the edit and use B roll and narration. Specific attention is paid to writing in and out of pictures.
- Students insert name supers, mix and upload their second story.
- Students plan their third story, which will be 2.5 to 3 minutes long and include at least four sources, with at least two sources being used more than once.
- Students shoot the third story. They learn to interview more effectively. They learn to cover sequences that are specific to the story, and particular focus is paid to interview-specific B roll.
- Students prepare the edit by choosing grabs, grading footage and writing a paper edit map and an edit script.
- Students edit their third story, with the focus being on creating a journalistic story bounce with a strong story structure. Writing in and out of pictures to create story bounce is a key skill.
- Students insert supers, mix and upload their third story. The focus here is key frame or more advanced audio ducking and mixing.

In subsequent classes secondary students learn how to use UGS to form longer user-generated programs (UGP).

All the teachers involved saw mojo as a relevant tool for increasing literacy skills across the curriculum. The editorial aspects (choice making) that occur in mojo are helpful when teaching students to make structural choices in writing. Galbraith believes mojo will help improve kid's literacy, storytelling and self-confidence once they see their work published. White believes it is too early to tell how successful mojo will be across the primary curriculum, but he is already seeing improvements in some students' writing ability. White puts this down to the choices that need to be made during the editing and scripting stages of mojo. Galbraith (2013) believes the engagement, or interactive aspect of mojo, helps develop communication skills between students and the community: "Mojo is the one single factor in my time in teaching that's exploded the connection between school and community." Researchers have identified this connection as leading to an increased level of *citizenry ideals* among students (Clark and Monserrate 2011). Mojo potentially modifies previous literacy practices, turning them into new undefined methods through a series of challenge-based learning tasks—research, planning, interaction, filming and editing. Mojo works to redefine ways of structuring interaction, conversation and story elements. This will be discussed at length in Chapter 7 on pedagogy. The development of mojo UGS involves a shift in thinking from the personal to the collective or the eudemonic. At a story level this involves developing UGS into UGP, which can be the basis of web TV formats. At an interschool level this can involve forming hyperlocal networks to create collective UGP constructed from school-based UGS. This will be discussed in Chapter 7 and in this chapter's conclusion.

Tertiary Journalism School Workshop

I trialed the package in a tertiary environment to determine the degree to which journalism students were exposed to multimedia storytelling and the effectiveness of the mojo training package for journalism students, and to further scope a mojo training pedagogy for training skilled multimedia journalists. Given the critical nature of the transition phase between study and work, particular emphasis was placed on eliciting student responses around the above criteria.

On investigation, the websites of a number of leading journalism schools did not include UGS training of the caliber advocated here. At the 2012 Journalism Education Association of Australia (JEAA) conference, in Melbourne, not one of the journalism lecturers I spoke with was working with mobile, let alone to make user-generated stories. This was also evident among journalism lecturers at the International Symposium of Online Journalism in Texas in 2013. Keynote speaker Andy Garvin summed up the trend when he advocated that we need to "use these incredibly powerful tools to talk with them, listen to them, and help us all understand the world a little better" (Garvin 2013). I agree with Garvin, but believe the audience is capable of providing more relevant and complete content offerings than is available in a 140-character tweet.

During this research, the work was discussed at more than a dozen conferences. It appeared the idea of creating UGS was something of a side step from the main game, which was to keep it traditional, or to promote engagement through *social media*. Journalism schools were still thinking of mobile as a medium for connecting UGC, tweets and other social media content. Many journalism schools were stuck in the analogue and print-to-digital transition phases. At best, they were delivering curriculum based around an exploration of social media, when what is needed is a neo-journalistic approach where elements of traditional storytelling are wrapped around new multimedia tools and literacies. Only then will we, as Garvin suggests, "slow down the news cycle" (Garvin 2013). What's required is time to be reflective and question the public, ask them for more and collate this information into multimedia stories, rather than a never-ending stream of curated witness moments we call headlines. But how is this possible in a 24/7 always-on news environment?

Deakin University Workshop

I ran the *mojo* workshop with a number of cohorts of third-year journalism and communications students at Deakin University over two 6-week blocks. Following the Deakin experience, I thought that the workshop is best run in 4-, 8-, 16- or 24-hour blocks (see Chapter 7) and not 2-hour sessions. A two-hour session can end at a crucial point and the student leaves without having been taught the complete skill set, making homework frustrating. On further investigation, and after further developing training, I found that the first and possibly the second class would benefit from being three or four hours long. The following classes could be run in two-hour blocks.

The style of workshop was similar to that run in secondary schools, predominantly because the students were only available for six 2-hour classes (half a semester). We established a WordPress site called Go2News. The group consisting mainly of third-year students, with a number of second-year students, was asked to load the 1st Video edit app (Voddio) onto their iOS device.

At completion of training, 53 students were given a survey including structured and open-ended questions asking about previous digital experience, the usefulness of the course, how they would change it, and so forth. Forty-three (81 percent) completed the survey, and a summary of the key findings follows.

Questions about whether students had previous digital training and whether they found this helpful are presented in Figure 6.1. A third-year elective, "Broadcast Journalism," is available to students, but only six students (14 percent) had any video journalism training during their course. Thirty-seven students (86 percent) didn't receive video journalism training while enrolled in their course. Forty students (93 percent) felt they either benefited or would have benefited from previous digital video training.

Those students who thought that mobile journalism training was important gave a number of reasons:

- Knowledge about multimedia story structure (creating stories using pictures and words) is essential.

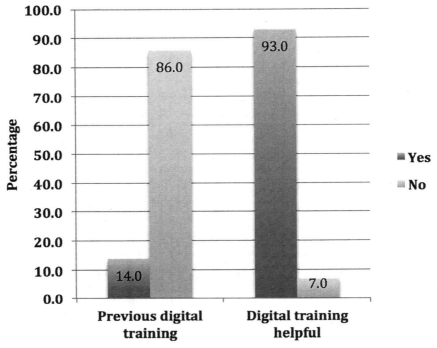

Figure 6.1 Relevance of digital video training.

- More time to develop the skills to be better prepared by third year and deal with the realities of the current journalism industry.
- Could help strengthen their practical portfolio by placement time.
- Would help with their placement where they could "try it out for real."

Students received basic training on identifying and recording story elements, recording strong vision and clean audio and editing on the smart phone. They were required to produce one training exercise and one video of their choice, which was assessed and uploaded to the Go2News blog (Burum 2011). A more complex introduction section was run that included definitions of journalism and a discussion about styles of storytelling and, more specifically, journalistic multimedia storytelling. Students were also asked to write an assessable report on the mojo experience.

- *Length of classes and the course*: As mentioned above, the short two-hour classes impacted on the practical aspect of mojo training.
  Thirty-six students answered the survey question: Should the mojo training course be changed? Of those who answered, eight students (22 percent) felt the course should not be changed. The majority, 16 students (44 percent), felt the sessions and the course duration needed to be longer, possibly a 12-week course.

- *iOS device*: As described earlier, the choice to use iOS devices was based on hedonic appeal and accessibility to the preferred edit app, which is only available for the iOS platform. We found that 34 of the students (79 percent) who enrolled in the mojo unit, and completed the survey, owned their own smartphone. Of those, 23 students (70 percent) owned an iPhone. It was anticipated that students who owned an iPhone would use the edit app beyond class requirements.

Students who owned a smartphone gave the reasons shown in Figure 6.2 for buying their device.

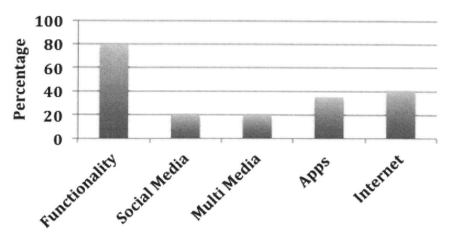

Figure 6.2 Reasons for buying a smartphone.

Figure 6.3 shows what percentage of students used the various functions on their smartphones. Phone (73.5 percent) and text (64.7 percent) were lower than social media (accessing the Internet) which was at 76.5 percent. I concluded that some students did not mention phone because all students used their phone for calling. What was initially surprising was that fewer mentioned they used their phone for music, but this is probably due to these students owning an MP3 or iPod for listening to music.

- *Technical*: Many students who owned a smartphone had never shot video on their smartphone, and almost none had edited video into a story using their smartphone. Hence, during the workshop they experienced issues in the following technical areas:
  - *Coverage*: Students had problems with shot steadiness, exposure and the level of coverage. More practice and a 12-week training block would allow time to run exercises to fix this. Knowing how to cover a scene requires some practice and is closely linked to understanding screen structure and language. The most common mistake was a lack of coverage or not enough close-up or usable overlay

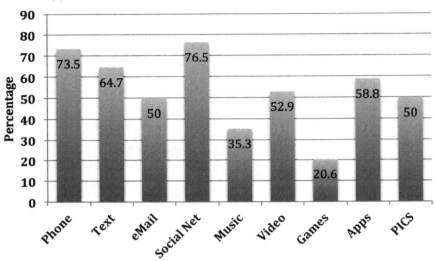

Figure 6.3 Functions used on smartphone.

(B roll), to help tell, compress and expand the story. Thinking in terms of sequences, and not shots, is a first step to thinking *video and not stills*. Exposure was also an issue. Mostly the problem was backlit, or dimly lit, subjects. This can be rectified through more hands-on exercises in how best to use natural lighting to advantage. A video grading app is available that can be used to enable poorly exposed shots to be partially fixed.

- *Focal length:* Students often complained that they could not get close enough to the action. It is not the camera's fault that a mojo is not close to the action. It is best not to use a long lens,[3] which may mean moving closer to the subject and the action. A wide lens up close provides a sense of being there and is more stable when using the camera handheld. In some cases, the mobile journalist is not able to get close to action. In this case, a zoom may be needed, or a doubler lens[4] for the mCamLite[5], or an adaptor[6] to use DSLR lenses. Current iPhone cameras have a zoom and the FiLMiC Pro app enables greater control over focus. It's best not to zoom (see above).
- *Sound:* This is a critical element and is often disregarded, especially when using smart devices. The golden rule is to get in close to try to eliminate background sound. This is another reason why using a zoom during training is a not a good idea. Many of the students did not have a microphone plugged into their iOS device, because they didn't own one.
- *Edit:* All participants thought the edit app and the ability to make mobile multimedia stories on the run was the key to this mojo

workshop. At the commencement of editing, a number of participants said they were having difficulties with the small screen. This
changed as they became more proficient. The issue could also be
resolved by transferring data to an iPad for the edit, or to a laptop,
which could negate the advantages of using mojo on location. The
complexities of editing pictures and words are not resolved in a
12-hour course. One way to begin this process is to have specialist
story edit training modules, which occur in phase 2 and 3 of mojo,
or to run a 12-week course.

- Detailed information on recording vision and sound and editing on
  an iPhone is included in *Mojo: The Mobile Journalism Handbook* (see
  Appendix A).
  - *Experience blogging:* The survey results presented in Figure 6.4
    indicate that only 23.8 percent of students had a website, while
    48.8 percent had a blog site.

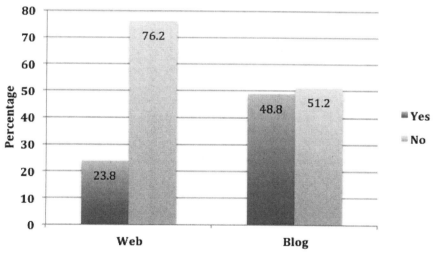

Figure 6.4 Students' use of web and blog sites.

Of those students who had a blog site, 10 (47.6 percent) used it for
accessing news, while 5 (23.8 percent) said they used it for gossip. No one
who used it to access news said they also used it for gossip. The vast majority, 18 students (85.7 percent), said they used it for other reasons, which
were identified as music and travel type info. No student who had a blog
site said they used it for uploading video. This is not surprising given that
before the mojo workshops, most students said they had not done any video
multimedia training or made videos.

This correlates with the findings of Hirst and Treadwell in *Blogs Bother
Me* (2011) They found that many of the journalism students they surveyed

were not digital natives. "The point is we cannot assume every student participates in the Twitterverse, understands Photoshop or Dreamweaver, or can write PHP code and manipulate audio or video files in editing software without some frustration and learning through failure" (2011). I think many digital natives couldn't operate Photoshop or Dreamweaver. The point is, even if they could do all those things, they may still not think like a digital native or multimedia journalist, and may not have the skills to produce multimedia stories. In fact, understanding Photoshop or Dreamweaver still has little to do with being a multimedia journalist.

- *Go2News blog:* Due to a lack of funding, we could only set up a free blog, which we linked to a YouTube site. We chose WordPress and named our site Go2News (deakinnews.WordPress.com). We set up a YouTube site also called Go2News (www.youtube.com/user/go2news). Students from the two cohorts produced 76 UGS. In my experience in researching and training mojo participants over the past three and a half years, the Go2News experience, in 2012, was the most advanced use of mojo skills at an educational institution.

Students' Reports

Following the unit, students were given a series of questions and asked to write a report to evaluate the workshop. The report was completed by 86 percent of students and the responses to five specific questions relating to different aspects of the workshop are shown in Figure 6.5.

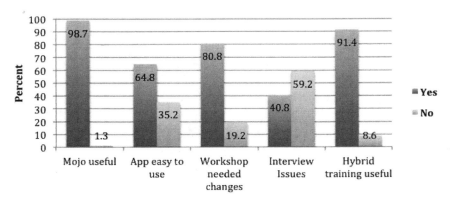

Figure 6.5 Mojo evaluation questions.

All but one participant felt the workshop was useful for their future work prospects. Students mostly found the edit app intuitive, but felt learning a hybrid workflow—mojo to laptop and desktop systems like Final Cut Pro—would also be beneficial. Many students had issues sourcing interviewees (see Figure 6.9 for further details).

Students had the opportunity to provide more information for the first four specific questions presented in Figure 6.5. They responded to why they found mojo useful or not, what was or was not easy to use, if and how they would change the workshop and what issues they had with interviewees. Using a qualitative theme analysis process, where evidence is extracted from data values to provide new knowledge (McNiff and Whitehead 2006), the responses were grouped according to the main reason or issue given. The pie charts in Figure 6.6 show the proportion of students who mentioned each reason or issue in the further inquiry into each of the questions.

Mojo Usefulness

The reasons students gave for why the mojo training was useful are presented in Figure 6.6.

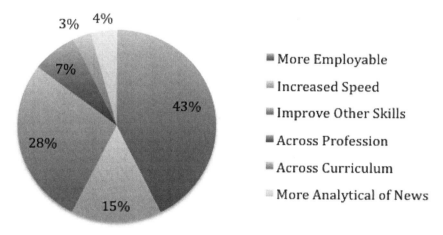

Figure 6.6 Main benefits of mojo training as identified by journalism school students.

ANALYSIS

Many students (43 percent) felt a key factor was that mojo provided multimedia skills that made them more employable. Discussion with online news editors suggests that mojo skills will make journalism graduates more employable and useful. Twenty-eight percent of students believed mojo practices sharpened their writing, camera, editing and interview skills. Fifteen percent felt that breaking stories was a critical aspect of being a successful journalist, and being able to produce every phase of the story on a mobile and publish quickly, without leaving location, was an important benefit. Some students (7 percent) felt mojo skills would be valuable across professions and different tertiary disciplines. Students are already using the skills in other areas to pitch ideas, and 4 percent believe it has led them to be more analytical about news stories on TV.

Device and Edit App Accessible

Even for practitioners experienced in working with pictures and words, their first experience of producing a complete UGS was daunting. Figure 6.7 shows the main reason students found the iOS device and edit app accessible or easy to use or not.

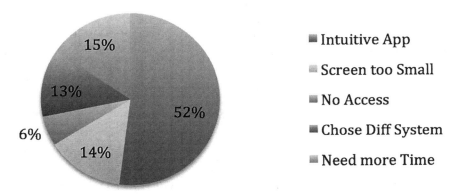

Figure 6.7 App usefulness.

ANALYSIS

The majority of students (52 percent) felt the edit app was intuitive, easy and empowering once they learned the basics. The students thought they would have benefited from at least the first class being four hours long, as this would have enabled more time to understand the basics of the app.

A number of students (14 percent) found the screen too small and had problems making the wipe and tap movements. They would have preferred to edit on an iPad. Because of internal WiFi protocols in the classroom, students were not always able to transfer from the iPod or iPhone to the iPad or PC. A number of students (13 percent) chose a different edit app on their device (iMovie) because they wanted to edit on a laptop that used the same edit program, or because they had problems with their iDevice and there were no replacements. A small group (6 percent) did not have access to an iDevice either because they were off campus or because the university could not provide one. Almost one in six students (15 percent) felt that they needed more time during training. In fact, many students felt the skill sets being taught were so useful that the course should have been run for the full semester.

Workshop Improvements

As this workshop had not previously been tried with students over a six-week two-hour structure, it was important to gauge their response in order to adjust the workshop for future cohorts, and to develop it into a more substantial program across the curriculum. Figure 6.8 indicates student responses to the main thing they would change in future workshops.

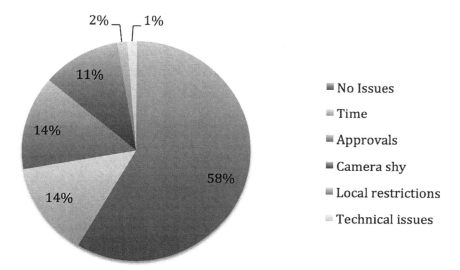

Figure 6.8 How the workshop could be improved.

ANALYSIS

Fifteen percent of students felt the mojo workshop did not need to be changed. Of those who felt change would help, the majority (41 percent) thought the workshops should have been run for the full semester. I was allowed to run the mojo workshop for 6 weeks (six 2-hour university classes) of a 12-week block. I articulated the view that a substantial mojo workshop required 24 hours of face-to-face, or 12 two-hour university classes. I was advised students would do extra work at home. By all accounts, this homework was not done until the last minute, as students had many other competing projects to complete.

Almost one-quarter (24 percent) of the students felt they did not allow enough time to prep stories. The majority felt their focus on print made them blind to the extra work required to produce multimedia stories: face-to-face interviews, shooting B roll, selecting the best footage and interview grabs, writing a narration script and doing the edit and mix.

Approximately 1 in 10 (8 percent) of the students believed they should have collected more footage or that they got the wrong type of coverage.

One of the most common mistakes when starting to make multimedia, and especially UGS, is the lack of what I call story coverage. This overlay, or B roll, relates to story specifics like elements discussed in an interview. B roll helps color the interview to make it more dynamic, enables the use of choice interview grabs in the edit and enables compression or expansion of story points. It also works as cover footage when introducing on-camera talent like an interviewee. Students also wanted more training on sequences, more specifically, how to cover a moving event quickly.

Some students (4 percent) felt their stories needed more interviewees (sources). When broadcasting raw footage, seeing one extended interview grab seems to work. However, when we construct story, we need a number of points of view. For inexperienced multimedia journalists, the need for a variety of opinions often does not become apparent until they begin their first edit. During the edit students realize they need to choose sections of interview and write powerful narration to bounce story between sync grabs and from one structural point to the next. This important realization transforms their next mojo piece dramatically.

A small number of students (8 percent) felt their gear was restrictive. They either wanted a zoom on their iOS device's video camera (current apps can but picture quality is compromised), or they wanted to edit on a PC to enable more control. A number of students thought that it would help if they were all taught on the same gear so that they could help each other when required.

Interview Issues

When moving from a photo-plus voice environment (stills and comment) to a moving pictures format there are many factors that change. Apart from the creative considerations, there are logistical and psychological issues that require attention. One of the main comments we often hear is "There was nothing or no one to shoot; everything was boring." This is a comment first heard in 1993 from participants on *Home Truths*, an ABC self-shot series that was a precursor to the current mojo format. We also determined that when students said a location was boring, they meant that they were embarrassed to dig below the surface to find information, or ask people to be interviewees on camera. Figure 6.9 outlines the main issues the journalism school mojos had with interviewees.

ANALYSIS

Fifty-six percent of students had no issues doing interviews. Further research is required to determine whether these were journalism students who had previous experience with face-to-face interviews. Students were all experienced in doing print interviews, but not necessarily face-to-face video interviews, and the realization that the formal interview could not

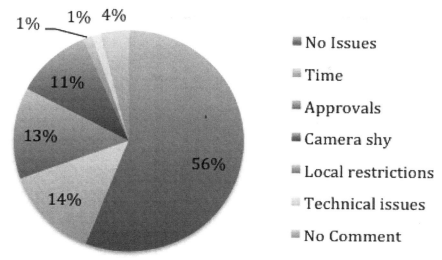

Figure 6.9 Issues with interviewees.

be done over the phone caused a number of scheduling conflicts. This is a common finding when moving from print to more interactive video formats like UGS.

Many interviewees, 14 percent, said *no* due to time issues; 13 percent could not agree to an interview because they weren't able to get approval from their superiors; 11 percent didn't want to appear because they were embarrassed. They would have agreed to a print interview but not on camera. Local and technical reasons caused some issues (1 percent).

Introduction of Digital Video Training

The survey results suggest that modern journalism courses should include a multimedia component, similar to mojo. Students were asked for their views on when mojo studies should be introduced in a journalism course, and their responses are shown in Figure 6.10.

ANALYSIS

Of the students who responded, 27 percent believed mojo should be part of the foundation skills in a communications and journalism course.

Approximately one in five (19 percent) felt that it should be introduced in the second year, after students received grounding in writing and interview skills. A similar proportion (17 percent) believed it should be developed over three years of the course, creating new and more advanced mojo skills each year. A quarter of the students (25 percent) felt that its current placement in

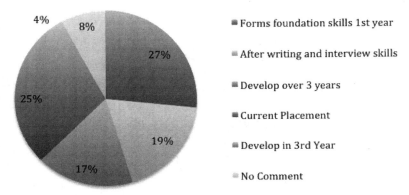

4%
8%
27%
25%
19%
17%

■ Forms foundation skills 1st year

■ After writing and interview skills

■ Develop over 3 years

■ Current Placement

■ Develop in 3rd Year

■ No Comment

Figure 6.10 Stages students think mojo should be introduced.

second semester in the third year was right. Industry employers want graduates who can make multimedia stories, write headlines and have experience running interviews. Beginning this training early would assist in developing UGS skills to a high level, including the production of user-generated programs (UGP) required for web TV.

Ningbo University Workshop

To assess the impact of short class times and course duration, I ran mojo over three consecutive eight-hour blocks for a cohort of communications students at Nottingham University in Ningbo, China. The program was successful and all students found the eight-hour sessions enabled substantial immersion in the various phases of the program. Moreover, it was apparent that at critical points of mojo training it was important that the program was continued over the next hour or so to answer a new batch of key questions. I found that during this phase students who had grasped the technology and, in particular, the edit app, were able to support slower students. This student-to-student teaching approach is more difficult to achieve in short one- or two-hour workshops, after which students leave class and become busy with other school commitments.

The Ningbo stories all had a political edge: safety, lack of amenities and dangerous traffic, were some of the topics. This is possibly because of the repressive regime, and the recent bans on Internet search providers in China. The fact that YouTube was unavailable caused issues when publishing. A number of the students indicated they would continue mojo to become citizen journalists even if they couldn't get work with the media in China. According to journalism professor Stephen Quinn, as a result of their involvement in mojo, Ningbo students formed a China chapter of NUTS, the Nottingham University Television Station. NUTS produces student-generated news and entertainment programs.

Media Workshop

The contention is that because mojo skills form part of the journalist's tool-kit, it is important they are taught at journalism school. Hence, it is important to determine if the mojo program is relevant to professional media. This is particularly important given that traditional print media is losing its revenue source and its audience, and print journalists are facing the prospect of being underskilled and unemployable, as print journalism moves online. To test mojo in the media, I ran three workshops at Fairfax in Australia; at the *Dili Weekly*, a bilingual print and online publication in Timor-Leste; and at *Ekstra Bladet*, a large Danish tabloid.

Except for the *Dili Weekly*, where a three-day version of the phase 1 workshop was run, we ran eight-hour mojo programs with groups of 10 journalists. The reason only one-day workshops were run was because management could not release journalists for any longer. This was despite mojo training being determined as an essential skill required to keep journalists functioning in the digital age. The aims of the workshop were to provide journalists with an overview of the technology, basic multimedia skills to enable them to record video and audio, and to complete a short story. In Australia and Denmark, the modified workshop involved creating an in-class exercise in the morning and an in-community or workplace exercise in the afternoon. In Timor-Leste, because of the language barrier, we needed three days to complete the same level of training.

Participants in the Fairfax workshops (journalists and photographers) gained useful knowledge and advised management they believed all their journalist and photographer colleagues should attend. As a result, they petitioned management and a number of workshops were scheduled. The outcome was positive, but convincing management of the benefit of teaching journalists and photographers to edit was another matter. Fairfax management was of a view that all they wanted their journalists to learn was how to upload raw unedited footage from location, in low resolution, as quickly as possible. I argued that teaching staff to edit was crucial on two levels. Initially I described how my experience working internationally for *Foreign Correspondent* demonstrated clearly that the most useful camera-people were those who worked in bureaus, primarily because they edited their own footage. Knowing how to edit helps journalists decide what to record. Second, I proposed this scenario: The chief of staff sends a journalist to a missing person suspected drowning five hours away from the office. The journalist covers the retrieval of a backpack at 7:00 a.m. and, using his iPhone, uploads this and a short on-camera grab from attending police. The journalist knows the body will appear sooner or later. While waiting, he interviews some witnesses and begins to write and edit a complete news package. Around lunchtime a body appears and is recovered. The journalist covers the retrieval and records a few sync grabs from the attending officers who advise the parents are on their way to identify the body. The journalist uploads the retrieval footage. While waiting for the parents to arrive, he keeps editing the package, which now includes the retrieval. When the mum arrives, he records a very emotional and highly sensitive interview with her and uploads this before completing the edit, which he uploads via 3G just before leaving location to begin his long drive home. The journalist has been on the scene all day working with police and locals to create a series of breaking news reports that correctly tell the evolving story. Because he hasn't had to leave location and is unobtrusive (small camera and no other gear), his relationship with police and other services develops and he receives unfettered access to family and other story moments. The journalist is mobile, more responsive, more involved and hence more sensitive to the events, the police, family and friends. He has used his mobility and the advantage of small equipment to provide a very in-depth view of a breaking story. Hence, the office receives three updates and an exclusive edited package for the evening bulletin, which no other media has.

The primary aim of running mojo workshops for six journalists working at the *Dili Weekly* in Timor-Leste, was to determine if mojo training translates to non-English-speaking environments, and smaller news operations. Some mojos couldn't speak English, while others spoke only a few words. Even though workshops were run using a translator, the skill level achieved was high. Participants began using mojo immediately to create stories around the 2012 national elections. Stories were uploaded to a new video page on their website, http://www.thediliweekly.com/en. Post training, *Dili Weekly* mojos are producing UGS each week, and have been doing this for more than three years.

My hypothesis is that *Dili Weekly* management was more receptive to the holistic nature of mojo and UGS because they lacked options. Mojo enabled journalists to produce the type of multimedia coverage that would otherwise have been cost prohibitive. *Dili Weekly* journalists are now able to earn income working as stringers for large news organizations, and are creating their own saleable content archive. Because of the low bandwidth of the Internet system, uploading stories was a major issue for mojos working in Timor-Leste. With the Internet monopoly now broken, new, more powerful Internet services will enable *Dili Weekly* journalists, who are trained and ready, to supply their mojo skills to a global market, and train others.

Further along in their conversion to online (15 percent of the population visit their site daily) *Ekstra Bladet* (*EB*) management, like Fairfax Media, initially wanted their reporters to deliver raw UGC. However, because of their convergence, to what I call phase 3 of online multimedia conversion, user-generated programs (UGP) and web TV, management realized the importance of journalists being able to deliver complete UGS.

Three or four years ago we decided there was no way back—we needed to be delivering in the channel people wanted, on the web, and not newspapers as a free service. It's been working well, but now it looks like without paid content and other ways of capitalizing on our web traffic we won't be able to keep all our staff.

(Ruud 2012)

At *EB* management decided that advertising alone was not enough to keep journalists employed. Also needed was paid content offered on the *EB* website. This more developed paid-for content also demonstrates to the company's journalists that *EB* is still interested and able to deliver powerful journalism. Available 24/7, this content begins its journey to the public via their smart device.

EB research indicates that 50% of Danes 14 and up look at the site daily. Research also shows that as much as mobile is the conduit in the home–work–play–home continuum, journalists need to be trained to be prolific using their mobiles to create the stories, so as Ruud says, they will "consider the smartphone just like they think of the pen" (Ruud 2012).

Media Workshop Outcomes

Even though for many of the experienced print journalists mojo was the first time they had broken story down into its components, overall, working journalists and photographers found the mojo skill set valuable and accessible. The modular way story elements were dissected and taught made sense to journalists.

Analysis

The editing component is an integral aspect of mojo. In my view the reasons why Fairfax training managers did not consider editing important before our workshops is that they:

- Already had editors on staff;
- Did not believe journalists would welcome being asked to edit;
- Believed any edit process would slow the upload process; and
- Believed raw UGC is more usable.

At *EB* journalists have already used their new mojo skills to deliver complete stories. One of the journalists who embraced the mojo training developed his skills to a point where he could run mojo workshops for other journalists. Understanding the edit process is now recognized as an important skill for *EB* journalists working online. There are two reasons for this: (1) editing teaches journalists how to shoot the right type of coverage to create stories that will be required across their platforms, and (2) there is not enough editing support to edit the extra video content resulting from mojo activities.

The reality is that news agencies[7] want raw footage and have always wanted complete stories as well. You can have both. Sonja Pastuovic, a fixer and producer during the Bosnian war, describes the relevance of being able to edit and supply complete news packages from the field.

> I worked for APTV, a pocket bureau based in Zagreb. My role was to quickly decide what to cover and who to send. Many times there were actions that required a pool cameraperson, so it was critical we sent someone who could put a story together. In the field, in action, you don't have the time to think. Without the right logical pictures you wouldn't have the battle on tape even though you were caught right in the middle of it. The cameraman had to be able to edit—the great ones shot with an editor's eye—because we needed to piece a three-minute story together very quickly. Agencies preferred the longer stories with a script, which I wrote, as these could be delivered long and short for our list of more than 150 clients. Therefore knowing how to edit is an essential skill for camerapeople, journalists and producers.
>
> (Pastuovic 2013)

EB journalists are not wading through rivers of blood every day, but as management develops formats for its web TV platform, mojo UGS creation skills become a jumping-off point for print journalists wishing to work online. The current danger is that because many online editors are ex-print journalists, without multimedia training, web TV becomes radio with pictures. For example, one of the first *EB* formats was an extended studio interview profile concept run as a radio with pictures style—talking studio heads. Yet creating videotape (VT) package inserts—short UGS—around at least three stages of that interview would provide another editorial level and a format that could more readily be sold to other networks, or wrapped into their paid content area.

Subsequent mojo workshops at about 30 newspapers and web TV operations in Scandinavia have established mojo as a useful form for gathering video content to support or drive news and feature stories. With hundreds of journalists now trained to mojo, the form is becoming an indispensable cost-effective content creation tool, which plays to the elasticity of the web. There is now a growing desire from online editors for more long-form UGS, in the five- to seven-minute range, especially in news services that have transitioned to web TV, like VG in Norway.

In summary, it's clear from supplementary workshops conducted as part of this research that mojo is a useful toolkit for developing cross-curricular literacy skills. In all cases, teachers were receptive to new ways of teaching literacy and welcomed the shift in emphasis from classroom to community challenge-based learning activity, which mojo encourages. Many teachers believed the emphasis mojo puts on interactivity (school and community projects) is an essential step in creating citizen-minded students. Mojo's holistic approach combines literacy and investigation skills into a communications package where storytelling becomes an integral part of community life. Many teachers felt that scheduling mojo would be difficult, but that its strength as a cross-disciplinary tool could help create more dynamic curriculum.

Secondary and primary students welcomed the opportunity to learn digital literacies in an interactive way. They enjoyed the teamwork aspect of mojo and found the technical skills easy to learn. Younger primary students found the story aspect of mojo challenging, but understood the story bounce when they saw it edited. In a composite workshop with year 7, 10 and 12 students, younger students helped the older ones with the technology, while the older students helped with story elements. The modular way of teaching mojo storytelling helped overcome some issues with teaching narrative structure to younger students.

Publication is key to literacy training and to the outcomes that mojo espouses, such as generating higher self-esteem and greater confidence, through more command of language, and hence a willingness to interact with community. Showcasing students' UGS on a website that is accessible to the community is a crucial part of this process. However, schools will need to resolve internal proxy server and other security protocol issues that can inhibit viewing of school websites.

The media workshops seed mojo praxis and philosophies into the professional newsroom. In a market searching for revenue streams, and affordable content, alternative student and citizen journalism has economic value. The degree to which the potential of a citizen content sphere is realized will in part depend on the extent to which citizens create the type of content that mainstream organizations like the BBC need. One way this can become sustainable is by developing alternative citizen UGC to more formed and professional UGS, that is, in opposition to media offerings. This maintains its alternative weight within neo-journalistic and professional story structures.

I believe that the BBC's desire to embrace citizen content (Entwistle 2012) is driven by more than economic rationalism. Just as film theory is more about a wider inquiry into cultural studies, the citizen form of journalism, like film and television, can form part of the wider argument about representation (Turner 1988: 38). This concept of citizen journalism drives the democratic ideals that underpin this research in the same way that television and other broadcast or publication media have depicted culture as a social practice (Turner 1988). Today new forms of expression, such as mobile journalism practices and publication on the web, are capable of taking on that role. The great advantage the digital age has over analogue is that the ubiquitous nature of communication devices means today's conversation does not need to be representative. Because the technology is accessible, the representative becomes local and, as McChesney (2007) observes, inclusive. Findings from the mojo workshops suggest it can be.

Harcup (2011) suggests that the production of alternative citizen-generated media can be seen as an example of active citizenship. He cites Hartley as suggesting that alternative media can provide "a rich vein of journalism which is simply invisible in journalism studies" (Harcup 2011: 15). This rich form is what Atton and Hamilton (2008: 1) identify as activity that "proceeds from dissatisfaction not only with the mainstream coverage of certain issues and topics, but also with the epistemology of news." I agree that citizen journalism *can* be this, if and when citizens shift from their predisposition to recording and uploading anything they *accidentally witness*, to more purposeful citizen journalism, including more complete and politicized UGS.

As discussed in Chapter 3, and identified by Wadsworth (2011), a number of methodological factors, including my own background as a practitioner, need to be considered when evaluating the mojo case study workshops. I am not experienced in running this type of academic study. My television and journalism background brought a depth of self-shot multimedia experience, which I had been testing with citizens for more than two decades. This is one of the reasons the case study workshops were successful in delivering a practical model that:

- That will potentially form the basis of a hyperlocal network being discussed among secondary schools in Western Australia;
- Sits at the core of a new ongoing mojo workshop developed with TAFE in Queensland;
- Is being used by Danish, Norwegian and Swedish print media to help develop their online news and web TV platforms; and
- Is inspiring government agencies to use it as a form of delivering community messaging.

The study followed the three principles of data collection identified by Yin (2003):

- Use multiple sources of evidence;
- Create a case study database—this was done using the survey questions and forms a data set on which the graphs are based; and
- Maintain a chain of evidence—I have kept surveys, the documentary provides evidence of the major NT Mojo workshop, stories published online provide evidence of outcomes, interviews have been transcribed, and a peer-reviewed paper has been published, as have a number of articles in high-profile industry publications (*Channel* and *Walkley* magazines). The research collates these various sources of information into a usable and referenced document, as does *Mojo: The Mobile Journalism Handbook* and the documentaries (see appendices).

There are a number of pros and cons when using particular evidence. *Documentation* was important and the texts and documentaries that are referenced provide important background information. But there is very little or no documentation on the creation of UGS, which is a relatively new subfield of journalism. *Interviews*, especially with Indigenous participants, were important not only to solicit baseline comments, but to relax participants and begin their relationship with the lead trainer. Interviews with professionals were important to provide the media perspective and to begin a record during a moment of change in our media landscape. The interview with Dr. Phillip Batty, 30 years after he, Freda Glynn and John Macumba began Central Australian Aboriginal Media Association (CAAMA), provides a rare insight into their vision. As interviews can be fraught with response bias, or a reflectivity based on what the interviewee thinks the interviewer wants to hear (2012), surveys were included where warranted. These were also fraught with possible bias and, as with all interviews, are a form of their own gatekeeping based on the researcher's own preconceived views and aims.

Hence *direct observation* was critical to this investigation, as it enabled me to witness the unfolding of actuality. Bringing to bear my past experience with Indigenous communities proved to be both a positive and a negative. On the positive side, more than 20 years of experience in remote communities enabled a familiarity with how communities function. On the negative side, reflectivity was, at times, difficult. My experience in communities and also in mainstream television occasionally had participants agreeing with my view. I found I had to work hard to illicit the participant view, and I can't be certain I always got that. The direct observation method of research is time-consuming, and because the observer is not always able to be in one location, he or she needs, at times, to rely on others to provide an overview.

In addition to the findings already provided in Chapter 5, and here, the following is an overview of the major conclusions reached from the case study workshops:

- *Mojo Training Package:* Functions across three spheres of communication, with level and intensity being determined by the age of participants, their language ability, experiences, the context and desired outcomes. Because the package is modular and focuses on story elements, it can be modified to suit different training environments and skill levels. This is explained in more detail in Chapter 7.
- *Technology*
  - The iOS technology is accessible and its hedonic appeal leads to participants being willing to experiment. Many of the participants felt that all participants should learn using the same iOS device. There are training and consistency advantages to teaching students on the same device, however, these don't outweigh the benefits of students learning on *their own devices*. This is especially true now that the Android has an edit app with two video tracks.
  - The Voddio edit app was an effective training tool enabling professional training, multitrack video and audio editing and online publishing from a mobile device. Some journalism lecturers think the app is difficult to use, but not school teachers. This could be because

many of the university lecturers may not have much experience making multimedia stories, whereas school teachers have generally been immersed in technology and multimedia for longer. This form of digital skills lag impacts trainers and online editors in media who have no, or limited, experience with multimedia or video forms. The new iMovie app, which provides almost all of the functions required for mojo work, is more user-friendly for both trainers and participants. We are seeing better skills retention using the iMovie app (see *Mojo: The Mobile Journalism Handbook* published by Focal in 2016).[8]

- *Sustainability*
  - In Indigenous communities a sustainable model is needed to realize the long-term benefits of mojo training and production. Any such model should include funding for online publishing and, if possible, a mechanism for story payment for UGS sales or UGC stringer-type work. Revenue may also result from government contracts for health and other local messaging campaigns or from local business or media. An important consideration is a reliable in-community contact to help mojos coordinate work and negotiate rates and licenses.
  - In primary and secondary education, sustainability relies on being able to train enough teachers to introduce mojo practices and schedule it across the curriculum. The rigid school timetable is one major concern. In one school this is being overcome by forming out-of-class mojo collectives. Sustainability will be enhanced when schools begin to form hyperlocal networks with other schools to share UGS, knowledge, and the benefits of mojo praxis.
  - At the tertiary level, sustainability is being achieved as multimedia storytelling is recognized more as a professional skill set. Students learning mojo felt multimedia storytelling was relevant to their careers and that it should be introduced earlier. Many of the students left their mojo exercises until the last minute and were caught trying to rush them to completion. The Ningbo workshops showed that running mojo classes in eight-hour blocks is extremely effective. I believe the first or second class in a workshop being taught in two-hour blocks needs to be extended to four hours, to get students over the tech crunch phase that occurs at the two-hour mark of the first class on using edit equipment.
  - Media sustainability is based on being able to integrate mojo into the bigger shift occurring in the news business. The media workshops indicated that journalists of all ages are interested in learning mojo skills. Their print training is a benefit, but it can also restrict lateral thinking. School principals, like some media managers, found it difficult to schedule time for journalists to be away from their core business of aggregating stories. Management initially felt

journalists did not need to learn to edit, yet journalists understood that being able to edit helped them understand how elements came together in multimedia storytelling. The relevance of mojo practices will be enhanced as media move away from seeing multimedia as merely a way of enhancing online print stories, and more about creating UGS and UGP for their suite of online platforms.

In concluding this chapter, the mojo training package investigated in this research is designed to provide skills to train citizens, students and journalists to participate in a new subfield of journalism called mojo, which uses handheld smart devices to create stories. Mojo practices transform UGC into more complete UGS. The thought process and effort required to shift from creating UGC to UGS is a first stage in transforming *citizen witness* moments into *citizen journalism*. As Benson observes, the production of cultural discourse is "marked by the struggle for distinction," and to survive, any new subfield "must mark one's difference" (Benson 2003: 122). The final important ingredient is a politicized will that generates a need for a voice and shapes story. But how do we attain this state?

In 1989, I went to Mindanao in the Philippines to make a series of documentaries. On the way back I made a short film at Lake Laguna about a group of kids who spent all their spare time protecting their lake from pollution. On arrival back in Australia I showed this film to a group of 12-year-old students and asked how they spend their time. One remarked, "You know what I do after school? I play video games." Two weeks after he watched the film, that student who was learning digital video production was working for an hour every night after school in the school's vegetable garden. Four weeks later he was documenting that experience and sharing it with others. He was a student videographer, or mojo, demonstrating a eudemonic more civic-minded philosophy.

Digital storytelling enables practical skills based on theoretical underpinning that leads to the communications and action necessary to overcome obstacles and even oppression. As Paolo Freire (1970: 164) so eloquently writes, "Only in the encounter of the people with the revolutionary leaders—in their communion, in their praxis—can this theory be built." Chapter 7, on training, establishes a theory on how to create this revolutionary praxis and a common digital bridge that will enable communion between the three spheres of communication discussed above.

Notes

1. SCRAP is an acronym for story, character, resolution, actuality and production describing the verification stages of UGS.
2. Footage and audio recorded of unfolding events.
3. A long lens is a telephoto lens that makes objects look closer. On a 70–200 mm zoom lens the long end is toward the 200 mm focal length.

4. A doubler increases the focal length of the lens, but it can result in lower-quality image.
5. A stabilizing iPhone cradle with fixed points for lights, microphones and tripod (see *Mojo: The Mobile Journalism Handbook*, Chapter 4).
6. Fits on the front of the mCamLite lens.
7. Reuters, APTV and EBU are three news agencies that provide news services to broadcasters.
8. The Kinemaster app recently released for certain Android devices also has two track video editing features. It includes key frame audio and a grading function.

7 Training

A Common Cross-Sphere Pedagogical Bridge

> True simplicity is derived from so much more than the absence of clutter and ornamentation; it's about bringing order to complexity.
> —*Jon Ive, chief designer, Apple, 2013*

Overview

The aim of this chapter is to discuss pedagogy for creating form around user-generated content (UGC), to provide a road map to a more autonomous subfield of journalism called mojo. This neo-journalistic style of multimedia storytelling shifts the focus away from a technological determinist view to one that posits the importance of digital storytelling skills and reflectivity. A detailed explanation of how I teach mojo is provided in *Mojo: The Mobile Journalism Handbook* (see Appendix A). This chapter discusses issues related to mojo training and pedagogy and will

- Introduce a behavioral perspective that underpins my mojo praxis;
- Investigate multimedia storytelling, specifically at secondary school;
- Discuss how mojo might be introduced into the tertiary journalism curriculum; and
- Introduce various ethical issues that need further consideration.

McLuhan's (1964) well-known trope about communications in the 20th century, "the medium is the message," has been tossed around for almost 50 years. User-generated content that today results from the use of ubiquitous mobile technology has embedded itself in the message. Because of this, the potential exists to develop common digital literacies that enable a common language or digital bridge across spheres of communication. One of our tasks as educators is to find training models to enable this shift in schools, community and the workplace.

McLuhan suggests that the "personal and social consequences of any medium ... of any extension of our selves—result from the new scale that is introduced into our affairs by each extension of ourselves, or by any new technology" (1964: 23). Smart mobile technologies are changing the scale and nature of communication and the power balance between what

Bourdieu (2005) called the various subfields of communication. But how we harness the possibilities of these shifts will depend on the willingness and ability of educators to develop *new relevant media* curricula.

This is a philosophy espoused by cultural critic Raymond Williams more than half a century ago when he said that we need "a common education, that will give our society its cohesion and prevent it disintegrating into a series of specialist departments" (Williams 2000: 34). A lack of standards and a techno determinist view about digital content creation has resulted in a fragmented digital space. What is required is relational digital literacies relevant to all three spheres of communication. Hence, one of the key roles for educators, as Mark Deuze (2006) observes, is to decide the values and expectations of the digital culture. Will values be aligned to technology, skill sets, culture or a combination of all three, and how will educators best help trainees to express these?

There are three components to multimedia digital literacy (Meyrowitz 1998):

1 Content literacy: An ability to understand and analyze a mediated text or other kinds of messages.
2 Media language or grammar: An ability to *read* visual languages.
3 Medium literacy: Understanding the (technological) functions of a medium both on a micro and a macro level.

Mojo training resulting in user-generated stories (UGS) enables these three stages by providing:

- Skills to dissect and comprehend media content messages;
- An understanding of the key elements of a new common digital language; and
- Skills (technology and social media) to enable users to apply the medium to create a local voice or participate in news workflows.

From a cultural perspective, these skills can help build what Barbara Gentikow (2007: 79) refers to as a "nation's cultural canon." Increased levels of cultural capital that can lead to a heightened cultural awareness, this mindfulness is a key to enabling citizens to participate in what Mark Deuze calls "life politics" (Deuze 2003: 4). This identity-forming shift begins once we move from the early sublime stage of artifact evolution, where we are awestruck by hedonic functionality and form, to the banal, when artifacts "lose their role as sources of utopian visions" and "become important forces for social and economic change" (Mosco 2004: 3). Henry Jenkins (2008) believes this shift first occurs in the brain of the individual through what he coins convergence talk, which he says is the time taken to discover, agree and settle on change. This is an attitudinal transition from "passive receivers to proactive consumers, who decide what they want, when they want it, and how they want it"

(Kovack 2005 cited in Hirst 2011: 109). However, as Boczkowski (2004) points out, much of what becomes unique or revolutionary about new technology usually develops at the outset of its use—in the sublime stage. Hence it is imperative we begin the shift to the posthedonic stage as early as possible after adoption. One way to create this shift is through UGS skill sets. It can also occur using UGC, which has its own use value that creates "self-talk" possibilities (Archer 2007). But for sustainable change to occur, the form will need to be auspiced by educational institutions, journalism and associated subfields of communication. As it becomes relational, the form continues to develop, opening up new opportunities for media research and pedagogy. Citizen mojos, students and digitally trained print journalists become interlocutors or "force-fields," "acting and reacting to one another" (Benson and Neveu 2005: 11). Mojo is the binding agent across the spheres.

Bourdieu distinguishes between *heteronomous* forces "external to the field" and *autonomous* forces represented by the "specific capital unique to that field" (cited in Benson and Neveu 2005: 4). The journalism field is predominantly heteronomous, due to its reliance on advertising and, with respect to state-owned media, its reliance on the shifting priorities of the political field (Phelan 2011: 133). The mojo subfield can be more autonomous, relying on a mojo's social capital. Potentially, it can become heteronomous as it becomes increasingly reliant on government, education and media funding to provide its legitimacy and sustain its development as a form of participatory journalism. Increased funding and implementation across curriculum will enable long-term planning and more comprehensive research, but this will require mechanisms to preserve the form's alternative relevance.

Understanding the relevance of the participating voice is as critical to creating a more diverse society as is publication of that voice. John Berger writes that the very act of writing was "nothing except the act of approaching the experience written about" (cited in Goodrich 2010). Understanding the story of relational participant narratives, whether in the workplace, community or school, is a first step to educational reform. Relational properties and the forces that act on them define life narratives; for example, one narrative that impacts marginalized community education is "deficit theorizing" (Bishop et al. 2009: 3). This occurs where teachers believe problems are solely due to students, rather than education programs. Conversely, with the narrative, or *self-talk*, around UGC exalting it to the lofty heights of citizen journalism, the two become self-supporting and the story becomes nonproductive folklore. This, like any "unresolved narrative," can fail "to fulfill its subsequently understood function" (Goodrich 2010)—in this case, a sustained voice that has all the resonance of citizen journalism. Goodrich provides the clever analogy of spinning thread, which can also be used to describe mojo praxis. He suggests that while a single fiber is weak, combining fibers (in the case of mojo, technology, skills and publication) results in a strong thread. Literally, narratives have traditionally been the result of an act by a writer (producer) designed to affect the reader (consumer). But this relationship is changing in the digital world as more audience members become publishers of UGC raw fibers. These can float aimlessly online in fragmented, unwoven, unfulfilled forms until a mojo's storytelling structures and elements glue these fibers into a receptacle called UGS.

Another example of a failing digital narrative is the technologically determinist view—that *technology* alone will fix societies woes—that is often used to describe the Arab Spring revolutions (Hirst 2012). While effective as a short-term change agent, the mobile narrative (rioters with grievances use smartphones to galvanize society into life-changing revolution) loses long-term potency unless it has form that it gets through a marriage of technology and journalistic skills. This is supported by training structures that result in skills and *tasks*, which creates change that results in outputs and outcomes. Figure 7.1 is a mojo techne flow map that works as a self-perpetuating training helix. It swings back on itself, enabling a more advanced use of technology by participants whose skill set is expanding as a result of applying skills to technology. Eventually this results in more advanced tasking, which creates further opportunities and new levels of training, in a subfield of journalism, called mojo.

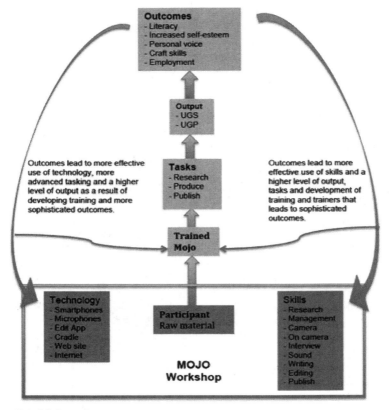

Figure 7.1 Mojo techne map.

Training—the successful marriage between technology and skills—enables a mojo to perform *tasks*—research, produce and publish—that result in *output*. Each *task*, like each individual fiber, becomes more complex and involved as we weave the mojo narrative from research through production (filming, editing) to publication. This *transformative* phase results in *output*, which generates a more digitally aware user with greater literacy and increased self-confidence being able to communicate with people who probably don't know each other. As users begin to recognize each other's content signals (their online UGS), they begin uniting (weaving) in concert as niche online virtual communities of practice, or network societies (Rheingold 2002; Wenger 2007; Castells 2008). They form a collective digital narrative to "gain new forms of social power, new ways to organise their interaction" (Rheingold 1994:12), which results in diverse content and hence the possibility for a greater level of democracy (Napoli 1999). Weaving UGC into "narrative fibers," to create UGS; or turning anonymous network societies into democratic communities of practice, requires an understanding of how fibers weave to form digital *narratives*. Mojo is a very tactile form of storytelling, with an emphasis on hedonic technology coveted by youth, hence my contention that teaching citizens to weave narratives to create a more engaged eudemonic voice should begin as early as possible. That is what is discuss in the next section.

Mojo: Transforming Behavioral Aspects within Communication Pedagogy

The research presented here demonstrates that schools, which practice mojo, can potentially become participants in defining current communications and journalism *subfields* by creating job-ready mojo students. This is a mechanism for exploring the community and for engaging youth with literacy and communication learning. The mojo discussed here was first developed from *self-shot*[1] local journalism workshops that I ran in 1982 with students in an inner-city school in Melbourne. I used storytelling as a *behavioral intervention*[2] to help students engage with each other, the curriculum and their community.

Students are drawn to local journalism because it provides an opportunity to speak out to protect what they view as their collective interest. As identified by Clark and Monserrate (2011), the idea that storytelling can redress alienation tendencies is consistent with emergent concepts of self-actualized and engaged citizenship among students who practice journalism. Clark and Monserrate posit "participation in the culture of high school journalism can provide young people with opportunities to develop the skills and experiences necessary for *civic engagement*, including the experience of collective decision-making" (2011: 417). Pedagogies employed to deliver mojo, for example, in high school journalism studies, promote a state of self-actualization or fulfillment, which fosters collective citizenship ideals and engagement among young people. The pedagogies are grounded in behavioral psychology and educational developmental theories. One such behavioral theory is the social development model (SDM), which hypothesizes that we adopt the beliefs and practices of social units, including family, schools, peers and communities, to affect change (Hawkins and Catalano 1992). SDM is based on broad risk and protective factors within these key domains of a young person's life. Drawing its foundation from processes embedded in the life course, SDM suggests that individuals and groups exist within the social contexts, values and structures—cultural norms and economic factors—of their society (1992). This aligns with Bourdieu's (1986) previously discussed theory that early development is determined through an introduction of *cultural capital*, which stems from social interaction or *habitus*. The SDM posits that the following key identifiable *assets* are required for young people to learn, effect change and enhance well-being within their social domains. Table 7.1 shows how these assets align with mojo practices.

Table 7.1 SDM assets and mojo intersect

Asset	Effect	Impact of mojo
Opportunities	Encourage interaction with family, community and workplace	Mojos learn new technologies and new skills, and become part of a subfield of communications, a coalition that encourages the interaction necessary to tell local stories, publish globally or work as a mojo.
Skills	Prepare the student for social, emotional and practical interaction and application of skills with peers, family and community	Mojo provides technical, journalistic, publishing, organizational and motivational skills to fulfill *tasks*, which create *outputs* and deliver *outcomes*. In the process mojos develop increasing skill levels, self-esteem, which potentially leads to engagement, and further learning.
Recognition	Reward from the social unit, peers and the wider community and/or workplace based on application and result	Mojo enables *outcomes* such as local reaffirmation from peers, school and community, real job prospects and publication online in a growing subfield of journalism.

While the SDM model is generally used to explain behaviors with marginalized youth, its significance is enhanced because its input assets can work to enhance the diversity principle, as described by Napoli (1999). In mojo praxis:

• Source diversity occurs as a result of the individual opportunity the mojo content creation package provides.

- Content diversity occurs as a result of input of skills—journalism, editing and publishing—which lead to a more thoughtful politicized voice and hence more healthy and diverse public sphere.
- Exposure occurs at communal (family, school and industry) and global levels when mojo stories are published and recognized locally and online.

The aim of any intervention, such as mojo, is to encourage bonds between the individual and a socializing unit (family, school, peers, community media center, media) to impact behaviors by increasing an individual's stake in the values of the unit. Even if they do not participate in ongoing creation of mojo stories, journalism training makes the student more discerning of professional journalistic services (1986). This is what happened to Shayha Watson, one of the participants in the *Cherbourg Mojo Out Loud* film.[3] "I'm starting to see things differently. I can't really explain it, but ... when I watch TV and stuff I see it in a different way now, the voiceovers, the music and the pictures and you know how they do it, it's mad" (cited in Burum 2013).

The SDM model is often institutionalized in schools and large community-based programs that require long-term funding to provide an overarching social construct for dealing with young people's issues (Duffield and Cockley 2006). And even though SDM includes provision for individual strands (Leffert et al. 1998), the positive development model (PDM) offers a more personalized approach to traditional problem-solving paradigms for increasing the well-being of adolescents. The PDM typically includes a broad set of individual attributes that impact all youth and emphasize the assumptions (Small and Memmo 2004) noted in Table 7.2.

Table 7.2 PDM assets and mojo intersect

Asset	Impact of mojo
Helping youth achieve their full potential is the best way to prevent them from experiencing problems.	Mojo builds literacy and holistic multimedia skills, which develop confidence that increases potential.
Youth need support and opportunities to succeed.	Mojo is based on core teamwork skills that enable mojos to recognize and work with support networks to achieve immediate and sustainable goals while also having the holistic skills to enable individual success.
Communities need to mobilize and build capacity to support the positive development of youth.	Mojo promotes community journalism practices and principles that politicize engagement and increase local capacity for civic-minded action.
Youth should not be viewed as problems to be fixed but as partners who are cultivated and developed.	Mojo advocates local and hyper-local working models, where mojos, community and local media integrate through respect based on mutual skills and goals.

Built around specific developmental assets, or building blocks, essential for promoting healthy youth development, PDM assets reflect internal and external qualities that can be categorized into eight types:

- *Support development*—Mojo praxis encourages development of the individual and their role as a team member. This leads to a greater appreciation of their role in the family support unit and increased community relationships. This initiates the family–school conversation, which more actively involves family in scholastic ideals.
- *Empowerment shifts*—As mojos begin to appreciate their individual worth and communal values, new opportunities emerge for engagement with local service sectors.
- *Boundaries and expectations shift*—Production, organizational and editorial mojo skills help establish an understanding of the need for structures in society, at home and at school. This leads to a growing ability to work with authority figures such as teachers, parents and positive peer models, which develops social capital that supports and encourages expectations.
- *Constructive use of time*—Mojo praxis requires and encourages time management skills.
- *Commitment to learning*—Published mojo stories lead to positive reinforcement and generate energy, motivation, engagement and a thirst for further research and learning.
- *Positive values*—As a result of immersion in community (home, school, workplace), mojos become more aware of the value of a eudemonic consciousness and share skills with others. Training focuses on integrity in reporting style, and mojos agree to take responsibility for their new politicized actions.
- *Social competencies*—Successful mojo praxis requires planning interviews, filming, editing and publishing. It also involves weaving school and family relationships to form a basis for mojo interaction and narratives. During workshops this enabled a resistance to peer group pressure and an ability to work in a team and show a willingness to resolve conflict.
- *Positive identity*—Overall mojo praxis leads to greater self-esteem as mojos connect with family and community and begin to make statements about their lives, receive recognition and plan for the future.

Another young Indigenous participant in the *Cherbourg Mojo Out Loud* film, Irene Sandow, believes mojo "gives a person a voice [and] if that person is smart enough, they can use that voice to speak for their community, they can take it to the news stations and what not, they can put it up on the Internet" (cited in Burum 2013).

During the research for this book, I found that mojo praxis can provide a framework for evaluating and intervening in youth behavior by providing skills that provide opportunities to

- Communicate with peers, teachers, family and community to create a unique narrative;
- Express personal views to create a less marginalized and more healthy grassroots politicized school and community voice;
- Generate new online communication environments for sharing knowledge, which inspire a greater level of confidence;
- Create job-ready skills in communication that can be used in environments where infrastructure is marginalized; and
- Create new and more interactive ways of fulfilling and redefining core requirements across curriculum.

The use of mojo within curriculum offers exciting possibilities for encouraging youth to become part of a larger collective consciousness. Robert French, also from *Cherbourg Mojo Out Loud*, says, "We were all friends and acquaintances when we started the program. Now we are more like a family; we can sit there and talk to each other in trust and confidence. It's great how the power of mojo changes people" (cited in Burum 2013).

How we initiate this transformative process within schools is what will be discussed next.

Mojo as a Transformative Tool for 21st-Century School Learning

Professor Ruben Puentedura also believes we need to rewrite our definitions of communications, especially the relationship between technology and learning. He identifies three tiers of consideration relevant to the use of technology in education. Puentedura suggests that because we live in a mobile world we should not be thinking about "a computer in fixed location 'A' at school and a computer in fixed location 'B' at home" (2013). We should be thinking about "what can a student do at all locations between school and home [and] how do we go from traditional learning places to a continuum of learning spaces so that the entire world becomes a place of learning for the students" (2013:1). Indeed, this philosophy translates to journalists on the beat and travelling between work and home.

The second consideration is past research on technological approaches to education. Bloom's taxonomy (Figure 7.2), developed in 1956, expanded concepts of learning from behaviorist models to those that are more "multidimensional and more constructivist in nature" (Marzano 2007). However, the model has a number of identified shortcomings, including that evaluation is listed as occurring at the top of the scaffold. Evaluation, as defined by Bloom, is a judgment based on criteria either "determined by the student or those which are given to him" (Bloom and Krathwohl 1984). Hence it follows that evaluation should occur at every stage of the learning process and should include exercises in reflectivity, which is also critical to the student's understanding and participation in evaluating each move, from one stage to the next.

Evaluation	Use knowledge and learning to make judgment about the value of thing or product
Synthesis	Structure information in new way to propose alternative solutions
Analysis	Break information into segments to better understand possibilities and support thesis
Application	Apply used knowledge in a learned or new context
Comprehension	Grasp the meaning of information, materials and or facts
Knowledge	Recall facts or remember previously learned information

Figure 7.2 Bloom's taxonomy.

The final tier of consideration is a delivery model, which helps teachers transition from the promise—of the *digital classroom sublime*—to the reality of having to teach students with differing levels of uptake. One of these transitional models, substitution, augmentation, modification and redefinition (SAMR) analyzes technology use by placing a scaffold under the cycle of technology adoption in the classroom. The SAMR adoption cycle (Figure 7.3) is divided into the four SAMR stages and two subsections, enhancement and transformation. The model explains how technology and practices such as mojo can be integrated into classrooms. Unlike Bloom's taxonomy, the education level in SAMR is the same at any stage, but the use level of technology at each given stage changes, either *enhancing* or *transforming* the task.

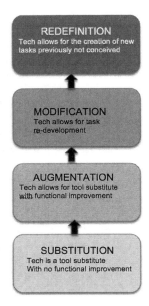

Figure 7.3 SAMR app map.

Figure 7.3 describes the various developmental stages of the SAMR model. Following is an example of how SAMR pedagogy applies to the creation of mojo stories:

> *Substitution:* Technology acts as a *substitute* without functional change, for example, using a word processor to write a script instead of a pen. *Mojo provides a story construct around which to discover the impact of the technology.*
>
> *Augmentation:* Technology acts to augment the task, resulting in functional improvement, for example, searchable word tool, spell checker, font enhancement or format to write and pretty up the script. *Mojo provides research parameters with technology enabling searchable characters in a script commenced at the substitution stage.*
>
> In the next and first stage of the transformation phase, mojo acts as an educational tool for enhancing classroom experience and literacy levels and building student confidence.
>
> *Modification:* Technology modifies and transforms the task, for example, creating a visualization of the script with a storyboard in a form that can be rearranged on the page, with associated audio grabs of readings and a data mind map of links to themes, plot settings and character, which can be presented via Word document, spreadsheet or PowerPoint. The task is modified to a level not possible without technology, from a flat individual task to one that can be viewed online and modified by others. *Mojo requires visualization and an understanding about coverage, editing and publication.*
>
> *Redefinition:* Technology enables the creation of previously inconceivable tasks. Mojo skills transform a written story or script into a digital UGS and enable immediate global exposure. This leads to online communication between schools and other communities to provide a level of feedback and perspective previously thought inconceivable. Previously, if a student made a movie using stand-alone video, generally it would be seen locally by the teacher or peers—arguably there's not a lot of incentive or motivation. Suddenly, using digital online publication as a catalyst for challenge-based learning activity, the student thinks, "The world will *see my product*, hear my voice," and it becomes a visceral lived and authentic experience even while still at primary school. In my experience, publication is a strong incentive to work harder to improve outcomes.

Clark and Monserrate have found that school-based journalism models can transform an individual student's perspective "beyond peer groups to some form of collective identity" (2011: 429). Constanza-Chock (2011) also identify this with the VozMob[4] program. They contend that the eudemonic conscience, which lies beyond hedonics, can only be achieved through a search for identity and a desire to belong to a broader world that encompasses school, home and community. This holistic approach becomes a first step to promoting citizenship ideals (2011: 429). Mojo focuses on student life experiences and their relational narratives. These inform teacher practice beyond deficit theorizing, which often leads to a use of remedial and behavior modification programs (Bishop et al. 2009).

The one-to-one form of mojo training enables instant feedback on personalized learning outcomes. Participants are encouraged to be reflective about the hands-on approach and the developing pedagogy. Authorizing this type of immediate student feedback informs teacher practice in a meaningful way to make "what they teach more accessible to students" (Bishop et al. 2009: 735). With an instant overview of the level of classroom understanding, teachers can alter their approach and level of collaboration accordingly. This leads to a fresh focus by teachers on problem areas and motivates students to participate more constructively in their education and their lives. This type of expansive classroom approach, that authorizes the student voice and encourages a discursive reflectivity about family or community, empowers students "as knowledgeable participants in learning conversations" (Bishop et al. 2009: 735).

Authorizing student views in this way accords with findings that young people express citizenship through self-actualization that's informed by issues that enable them to express their own values (Bennett 2008). Using mojo or journalism at school supports the above hypothesis. It helps young people find their own identity, which Bennett (2008) argues is important to civic action. Clark and Monserrate identified that when young people engage in citizen actions, the process "enhances their own goals of self-actualization, personal expression, and identity" (2011: 429). Mojo helps young people become more expressive, a process that is centered on identity and civic-mindedness. Enabling this process potentially begins a new dialectic in education: around the relationship between curriculum and the community, theory and praxis and alternative and mainstream perceptions of the role of the media, and the relationship between the three spheres of communication discussed above.

Moreover, it's anticipated that students will carry their civic-minded attitude from the school community into home, work and adult life. In some cases, this may involve transitioning through tertiary journalism studies, where students will modify their evolving attitudes, about *participatory citizen journalism*, in line with professional multimedia praxis. Hence, if primary and secondary education are embracing mobile journalism training, tertiary institutions will need to provide something complementary to entice students into journalism school. This is discussed next.

How Mojo Might Be Introduced into Journalism Curriculum

Working to develop my training pedagogy with the Norwegian Institute of Journalism and the Schibsted Journalism Academy, to help large-media transition journalists across the digital divide, it's apparent to me that the old silo model of teaching journalism units in print, radio, television and online may no longer be viable. However, knowing what is required and being able to make the relevant curricular shift, in a large university, is often very difficult. Recent experience running mojo workshops at Deakin University revealed journalism students were only receiving one unit of multimedia training in their three-year course. At the Journalism Education Association of Australia (JEAA) conference in 2012 it was evident from comments like "You do that on an iPhone?" "You actually edit on the phone?" and "Really, broadcast quality?" that journalism academics are still finding it difficult to make the shift from the traditional journalism curriculum to more relevant multimedia skill sets.

The appointment of a traditional journalist as the dean of the Columbia School of Journalism was labeled a "disgrace" (Rosensteil 2013). It was viewed as an unwillingness to acknowledge current trends in a profession that needs to augment the skills that graduates require. Indiana University has done away with traditional stand-alone journalism training, fearing the trade school model of teaching journalism is not working. The thinking is that because of the pace of change, a range of options is safer than a single one. The Reynolds Institute for Journalism at the University of Missouri has prioritized more scientific economic research into the news industry. In 2013, Columbia University was about to graduate its first double-degree majors in computer science and journalism. At Munk, in Toronto, they are recruiting subject experts to become journalists in their own disciplines. Poynters is researching distance learning, and Rosental Alves at the University of Texas is training across international borders (Rosensteil 2013). However, when I introduced UGS creation at the 2013 International Symposium of Online Journalism (ISOJ) in Texas, it was still strangely underconsidered in the new journalism landscape. Is it because storytelling is seen as old hat and irrelevant in a fragmented space? If it is, then what should journalism schools teach their students?

Raju Narisetti, managing editor of the *Wall Street Journal* Digital Network, believes a first step to deciding this conundrum lies in redefining the news business: how organizations develop the experience around content. News has been trying to integrate print and online, but it might need to "integrate technology and content" (cited in Bürén 2012: 15). Narisetti believes video is one key to this shift and that mobile is the key to delivering video (2012). Ole Molgaard, who heads the Media Executive Program, a cooperative research effort between WAN-IFRA and CBS, believes companies "have to redefine themselves and rediscover their core reasons for existing and their goals" (cited in Jolkovski 2013). Hence relevant journalism education will also need to redefine itself, in order to address innovative models for creating and delivering news.

Geir Ruud of *Ekstra Bladet* agrees and says education will continue to play a "pivotal role in transforming journalists' perceptions and business practices from analogue to digital" (2012). He adds, "There's a role for the

traditional journalist if the traditional journalist is not *too* traditional. ...
I had some students who weren't used to writing their own headlines ...
it seems they [professors] are not interested in what we [online news] are
doing because it was better in the old days" (2012). Ruud believes "journalists should start with social media training on day 1 of the academy. If you
want to be a carpenter you get a hammer and nail on day 1, start training"
(2012). And that's a perfect fit for mojo, says Ruud, "getting the thing done
and delivered that's what mojo does ... most days you can make 3 stories a
day or 13 if you work for our website. Give them a computer and an iPhone
and see if they can float" (2012). However, with academic institutions experimenting around forms of journalism studies that go way beyond the hammer and nail approach, the formula for the new curriculum may be more
complex than merely supplying technology or relying on traditional skills.

One aspect of journalism training that needs to be considered is whether
it is taught as a discreet course or as an interdisciplinary unit across, for
example, communications, law, science or teaching degrees. Moreover, tag-
ging journalism within varied disciplines provides students with a broad
range of skills that potentially make them employable across industries.
Ruud believes teaching mojo will give graduates the skills to make them
employable in a frenetic online news environment. My research indicates
both are right. It is clear that journalists will benefit from an understanding
of citizenship and a reminder of their Fourth Estate ideals. As identified by
Clark and Monseratte (2011), teaching student journalists to mojo might be
a way of attaining citizenship and eventual employment as journalists. At
its core mojo employs holistic journalist skills and supports public sphere
ideals.

While journalism schools continue to decide whether their curriculum
should include science and computer majors (Rosensteil 2013), trends suggest they need to include online video content. With organizations like *Time
Magazine*[5] and *Ekstra Bladet* developing traditional formats like documentary or magazine across digital platforms, we can assume that web TV will
be one of journalism's new receptors. It is hoped that advertisers will understand and support these longer, more traditional formats. The skills required
to produce these formats also make journalism graduates employable across
television and web TV nonnews areas.

Current trends in news and communications indicate that 33 percent of
people are getting their news on at least two mobile digital devices, and
average weekly news read on mobiles has jumped to 46 percent (Newman
2015). Mojo's emphasis on mobile supports its inclusion into tertiary journalism training. Like Narisetti, I believe that mobile will drive video and,
in particular, the transformation of UGC into UGS, which I contend will
morph into user-generated programs (UGP), published on web TV. Online
operators are also banking on megastars like Katie Couric, who has moved
to Yahoo, bringing their audiences and advertising dollars. Research indicates that the key to succeeding in today's *punishing media markets* is the

right form of content (Haughney 2013) and, if Yahoo is right, with the right face in front of it.

With social media like Facebook finally able to make large profits from mobile (Husson 2013), it is apparent that mobile is becoming the delivery mode of choice, and organizations like Facebook have become better at monetizing it. Facebook generated almost 0 percent revenue from mobile at the close of 2011, when it had 432 million monthly users. Three years later, revenue figures from mobile account for 76 percent ($2.9 billion) of it's 3.8 billion Q2 advertising revenue in 2015 (Husson 2013). This climbing trend indicates that more people are using mobile to access social media (Husson 2013; Kern 2013). Given its reliance on mobile-generated revenue, Facebook's purchase of WhatsApp, a brand built on no advertising, is a strategy to watch carefully.

Notwithstanding the above, journalism education needs to teach students to search for answers and seek to develop and promote pathways to citizenship. In that sense, journalism training is highly relevant across many disciplines, as evidenced by the directions many of the world's eminent journalism schools have taken. However, it is argued in this exegesis that if journalism is to survive as a relevant tertiary discipline, journalism teachers need to teach the skills current employers are looking for. Journalism lecturer Lee Duffield suggests this shift necessitates offering students "an introductory experience of creating media, using common 'new media' tools with exercises that will model the training of communication principles through practice" (2011: 1). This research suggests that mojo might be such an experience.

Mojo at Journalism School

Mojo training takes a neo-journalistic approach. Elements of *traditional* and *multimedia journalism* are used to form a skill set that includes the intellectual processes and the turnaround skills required in the 24-hour news cycle. At the risk of oversimplifying, there are four essential components to the new journalism and communication curriculum:

- *Digital skills*—Mojo provides skills that enable journalists to shoot video, record audio, write, edit and publish. These skills enable journalists to work across platforms and devices from either an office or mobile. Once journalists possess these skills, they need to refine them to develop their preferred ways of making and delivering news.
- *Journalistic integrity*—Fourth Estate ideals, including a citizenship and community involvement, is what the public expect. Notwithstanding various proposed models of policing media standards and journalistic integrity (Finkelstein 2011) and commissions (Leveson 2012), journalism needs publishing models that will rebuild public trust (Patching and Hirst 2013). Training community and student mojos to publish early in

their training can instill the need to get it right and to publish balanced news.

- *Knowing the business of journalism*—Journalists need to know their market. The more journalists begin to work independently, the greater their need to understand their business, and their audience. Digital journalism, whether alternative or mainstream, requires an ability to quickly identify news that will interest an audience. Knowing the audience helps sharpen news sense, which is a first step to understanding news value. The lower cost of publishing mojo stories (compared to traditional video production) enables more stories to be made for a wider variety of audiences. Understanding audience as both consumer and producer (Napoli 2011) is an area that requires further study.

- *The ability to research, verify and write*—These are key journalistic skills that will always be relevant. Strong research necessitates inquiry, verification requires skepticism, knowledge of ethics and legal implications, and of course writing requires literacy skills and a logical way of thinking. "Journalists need to learn that online writing can be sharper and more dynamic, that lists and subheadings work and that stories with video can get up to 20 percent more hits. And, not surprisingly, they spend much longer time in the story. That has a really high value for the website" (Ruud 2012).

A Mojo Curriculum Model

Mojo uses all the above skills on every story, and as mojos make more stories, these skills are sharpened and an expertise is developed. Hence mojo is ideally suited to journalism school training. The equipment is high-definition broadcast quality, yet relatively cheap, which enables every student to participate. Mojo's neo-journalistic approach includes traditional skills. This means existing lecturers can upskill their current print skills with relevant multimedia skills, so they can participate online.

The manifestations of mojo are from simple UGC to more complete UGS and longer formatted, more complex UGP. These levels can be taught as three-semester-long units across three years. A fourth unit built around specialist UGP is a further option. Table 7.3 describes a typical 12-week curriculum for the Mojo 101 first-year unit:

Twelve weeks is illustrative depending on the length of the term. The above draft course is flexible enough to function anywhere from 10 to13 weeks.

The second stage of mojo introduces more advanced training, with a number of aims to prepare the mojo student for the professional workflows and standards required to complete this unit. The students specialize in an area of news and become more acquainted with story, character, resolution, actuality and production (SCRAP) (see *Mojo: The Mobile Journalism Handbook*), the five-point plan and writing intros and headlines. Finally, a written story will accompany one of the UGS and focus on the theme. The students

Table 7.3 Mojo 101

	Description	Emphasis	Skills audit	Home	Dur
C1	Introduction: overview, slide show, basic mojo information and style, basic copyright, mojo elements and SCRAP	Identify multimedia story construction possibilities.	Teach multimedia journalism skills and identify five main story elements and structure.	Consider two stories and the elements.	2hrs
C2	Mojo exercise: shoot in class 30 second multimedia story that combines the elements	Practice using the iOS device to record shots and audio and speak to camera.	Learn to manage coverage and sequencing, quick lighting, camera presentation and audio recording tips.	Practice doing stand-ups, panning shots and record audio.	2hrs
C3	Editing exercise: learn the edit App and edit the exercise and record narration [Note C2 & C3 best as one class]	Edit pictures and words.	Edit on multi-track smartphone-based system, write and record narration.	Complete the picture and sound edit.	2hrs
C4	Name supers, mix and audio duck tools, grading App.	Complete a professional looking and sounding video, augment narration and grading pictures if required.	Learn to create professional name supers and mix and duck audio, learn about grading Apps.	Smooth out picture and audio edits, plan UGS 1.	2hrs
C5	Create social media site(s) and upload a story.	Create their own WordPress, YouTube, Storify.	Blogging, editing, legal checking, uploading stories, aggregation and curation tools, headline writing and dynamic copy	Plan UGS 1.	2hrs
C6	Plan UGS 1 Advanced research, story and charter analysis	In-depth discussion of story structure, interviewees, shooting, elements	Create a left and right column outline. Write to pictures. Introduce style.	Plan shoot, interviewee availability, and do the shoot	2hrs

(Continued)

	Description	Emphasis	Skills audit	Home	Dur
C7	Shoot UGS 1 Getting everything scheduled and shot on time is the key	Location recording and organization and time management (Dur: 1–1.5 min)	Planning, vision and audio recording, interviews, scheduling	Practice shooting, audio and interview questions.	2hrs
C8	UGS 1 Edit Emphasis is content management, two track editing, story structure and finishing.	Advanced structure and writing in and out of pictures (emphasis on not over writing)	Advanced edit, and narration writing and super skills	Complete edit, narration record and mix, publish, final plan UGS 2.	2hrs
C9	UGS 2 Shoot –Investigative Emphasis is on better coverage, cleaner audio and more succinct line of questioning.	More sources, more advanced edit with pictures and words. 2–2½ minute length, better coverage (vision and audio)	Advanced interviews, more specific shots, clear audio, interview specific overlay	Plan and start UGS 2 edit	2hrs
C10	UGS 2 Edit Emphasis is on doing a base edit and strong investigative structure.	Structure, script and narration to create a professional story	Advanced story structure and edit techniques such as the "Boston layoff"	Complete edit.	2hrs
C11	UGS 2 Post	Finalise mix, publication, screening and class discussion.	Audio ducking, music use, grading, mix, evaluation	Complete 800 word review.	2hrs
C12	UGS to UGP	Overview of relationship between UGS and UGP Phase 2	Analytical and format development	Hand in review.	2hrs

will also need to have one of their UGS published on a mainstream news website. The unit is summarized here:

- Practical: Development and production of three set length UGS around a theme, which will be assessed; understanding of workflows;
- Segue: Advanced writing for the web in and out of pictures;
- Camera: Advanced coverage, simple lighting and lenses;
- Audio: The more complex options, including radio microphones and situational audio;
- Editing: Including advanced nonlinear transfer and application;
- Finishing: Mobile grading and audio mixing;
- Legal and ethics: What can be said and shown; and
- Critical analysis of the form and its place in news production

As indicated above, the further focus in second year is to produce three stories around a specific theme. Emphasis is placed on choice of story, with students required to conduct more in-depth research to establish story plausibility and choose the correct interviewees. The student further develops skills for writing in and out of pictures, using more specific B roll and editing various elements in a different order and structure to gauge impact on the story.

The third stage of mojo is where the unit uses the three stories completed in the second stage, or three new stories, to create a user-generated program (UGP). One format is that the student chooses expert interviewees to speak about aspects raised in the UGS. These interviewees segue stories. The aim of this format is to use the expert interviewee to broaden the focus of stories and link them into a complete UGP. The student can integrate the mobile UGS into a UGP using a video camera and a desktop nonlinear edit system (optional). The student can work with a number of other students in a team. The aim is to achieve a high degree of editorial and presentation skill. A written paper on the theme and the process is also required.

Multimedia literacy, including an understanding of social media, is not optional for communications and journalism students. Alfred Hermida notes social media should be an introduction to "the notion of journalism as a conversation" that reaches out to the audience to "seek out ideas for stories" (2010b: 2). This is exactly what I was taught in journalism school more than 30 years ago—to chase down leads by talking with people.

Finally, creating UGS and UGP will develop program-producing skills that will potentially create more job prospects for students by enlarging the job market. The aim is to equip students with relevant skills to enable them to create a show reel of both journalistic and production work. Mojo provides the required holistic approach that teaches students not only to use the *camera to write*, but also to *write in and out of the camera (pictures)*. In my experience, students cannot learn to use a camera properly without learning about story-specific coverage.

Roger Patching (1996) identified the journalism studies dilemma when he posed the journalism training conundrum: "900 into 300 won't go." Patching saw that there were three times as many journalism students graduating as there were jobs in journalism. His research, based on traditional journalism studies and conducted at the cusp of the current changes sweeping the industry, also has relevance today.

Patching identifies the explosion of desktop publishing as "giving many graduates the opportunity to produce boutique publications" (1996: 60). These opportunities are only small when compared to the possibilities available to graduates today. Mobile digital devices have created a never before envisioned content creation sphere. At fast turnaround rates, the amount of content uploaded to YouTube in 2011 could be worth $1.95 trillion, if only it was accessible and of a high technical and editorial quality. With the right training this content creation energy could supplement new online media, web TV and over-the-top (OTT)[6] digital broadcast models. These new communication environments could potentially alter Patching's 900-to-300 equation, by broadening the definition of journalism, and increasing job prospects for graduates in nascent communication and content production fields.[7] Together with social media training, mojo skills complement the type of training print journalists are currently receiving in digital storytelling.

Pressing and Tapping and Challenges to Implementation in Media

Is it mandatory these days to know how to tap and swipe to be a journalist? Mark Deuze observes that we constantly search for a consensus about this. As journalists working in mainstream and alternative media begin to embrace social media, the definition of journalism, says Deuze, is "constantly reinventing itself" (2005: 447). Social media, described as being in apposition to ideals and values of "real journalism" (Bruns and Highfield 2012), are setting their own agendas and building platforms, where traditional journalism is being questioned. This further blurs the line between consumers and producers of media content (Rosen 2006; Bruns 2008). This becomes even more conflictual when citizens begin learning the craft and creating newslike content. The blurring is a two-way process called normalization. While normalizing their microblogs, journalists appear also to be adjusting these for evolving social media practices (Dopfner 2013). The result is traditional online news content that includes a greater amount of UGC (2013) and occasionally a degree of citizen journalism, for which social media and blogs are important platforms (Bruns and Highfield 2012). This growth led to fast-tracking multimedia training for journalists, and it is in this climate of uncertainty that I embarked on three mojo research studies with media:

- *Dili Weekly*, a small newspaper in Timor-Leste with a new video presence;
- Fairfax Media, an Australian media institution where 1,900 staff were sacked in 2012

- Denmark's *Ekstra Bladet,* a world leader in online reporting and an innovator evolving from print to online over the past 10 years that wanted to train its journalists to deliver digital content for their online and new web TV platform.

The training program used with the media, discussed in Chapter 6, is the same as the one I used for the tertiary, secondary and community case study workshops. While each of the organizations had slightly different requirements, they all wanted their journalists to record video and audio. Simon Morris, video news editor at Fairfax Media, wanted his staff to know how to record and upload raw footage: "We want it low res, we want it when it happens and we want to be the first with it online" (Morris 2012). The managers at *Ekstra Bladet* also thought that teaching journalists to record raw footage would be enough. But four weeks into the workshops they sent an email advising that their pool of curating journalists with video editing skills didn't have the capacity to edit the extra level of content mojo might deliver. They reasoned all journalists needed to learn to edit their own stories. *Ekstra Bladet* editors also eventually realized that being able to publish breaking UGC and also edit it into more developed UGS gave them two bites at the story pie.

For the *Dili Weekly* in Timor-Leste, teaching journalists to edit stories was an economic decision. They were never going to be able to afford to create and edit videos traditionally. So management welcomed the opportunity to produce complete mojo stories, which they have now been producing for the past three years.

My experience working for *Foreign Correspondent,* an international current affairs program on the ABC, in Australia, is that the best camerapeople, those who covered stories more effectively, were those who worked in news bureaus. This is because they edited their own work and editing teaches visual storytelling, which in turn informs coverage, which is what news editors need.

What became apparent is that news needs both raw footage, for breaking news, and stories for behind the pay wall and longer bulletins. At *Ekstra Bladet,* trained mojos went to Spain to cover a sporting event the day after training and delivered raw footage plus two stories each daily. The question was not whether news editors would take the edited story, but what length it should be. A three-minute story produced by an eminent investigative journalist from *Ekstra Bladet* was deemed brilliant, but too long, even though it received a high number of clicks. The general saying, by print journalists working online, is if it's more than 30 seconds, it's too long. So what is the right length? The BBC believes 75 seconds is the maximum length (see later). At the *Dili Weekly* length was kept to about a minute because weak Internet made uploads difficult. Connection speed is a reality mobile journalists will face that impacts story length.

Fairfax Media was not sure about length, as editors were only just realizing their journalists might produce *edited* multimedia stories. *Ekstra Bladet* was willing to experiment with mojo and story length because it believed the future of content delivery will be on mobile and across platforms. Video stories on the *Wall Street Journal* and *New York Times* sites are anywhere from 1 to 10 minutes long. At about a dozen large Scandinavian media companies, where I am currently teaching mojo to journalists, we have begun teaching a longer feature like form of UGS, among short news like UGS. While online audiences surf, research indicates they will also watch what they like. The aim is to create quality story that will hold viewers in the current elastic content environment and to teach journalists to create these on smartphones. Vizibee's Neha Manaktala believes "mobile is where our starting point is and where the audience is as well" (cited in Reid 2013). As Professor Puentedura (2013) has observed, mobile is the conduit in the home–work–play–home continuum.

Summary

In summary, it is clear that media is facing a multitude of issues as it continues on its convergence from print to digital publishing. These issues are manifold and are summarized in the following headings.

Bridging the Divides

As described by Deuze, journalists should be living a "media life extreme" because, like the rest of us, their personal and work life "takes place in media" (2012: 3). Today media is more than an "external agent," and "we can only imagine a life outside of media" (2012: 3). That may be true, but there is a digital divide between imagination and willing immersion in digital. At *Ekstra Bladet* a senior investigative journalist said, "I'm not afraid of the technology, I'm just worried about not having enough time to do it [my job] right."

The 24-hour news cycle requires journalists to do more, much more quickly. Hence finding enough time for training is always difficult. However, multimedia skills are key for journalists, and the lack of these skills might create new professional divisions, between professional users and nonusers (Reid 2013). Mojo's neo-journalistic approach, with its focus on a blend of storytelling (old) and technology (new), is not as frightening. This research identifies the following important considerations when journalists are moving from print to online:

- How do we help journalists transition online?
- How do we introduce digital video (mojo) skills without frightening journalists?
- What skills are required to be a successful online journalist?
- How do print journalists practice mojo in the field while still having to create print?
- What role do photographers play, and does this need to be refined in light of online requirements? What is the relationship between print and

online, web TV and paid content, and will there be an overlap between the aims and mandates of web TV and subscription, or is the relationship complementary?

- What roles will the audience play and what role will journalists play in the intersect between UGC, UGS and UGP? This role is crucial to the dialectic that exists within alternative journalism and skills, which posits that alternative journalism can be produced in community, to a professional standard, and still be alternative.

Once Were Producers

Journalists kept a little black book and refused to reveal sources. Working with social media exposes journalism processes and sources. Corrections are highlighted in real time so that sources like Twitter become part of the evolving story. News organizations need social media, but journalists also need time to learn social media skills, in order to process and verify social media to keep up with the 24-hour news cycle. This creates a shifting state of media work (Hedman and Djerf-Pierre 2013) and a blurring of the lines between producer and consumer (Rosen 2006). Further, growth in citizen journalism creates a real possibility that journalists can be trumped, not only by UGC, but by more complete representations of news events produced by citizens (Deuze 2007).

Social Branding with Hot Tech Tools

Traditionally, many print journalists remained faceless: "a journalist's (often secret) network of sources has always been one of his/her most important professional assets" (Deuze 2007). Some say it was an important part of their strategy for remaining impartial. Social media has tipped that on its head. Journalists now use it to build a brand for their organization and for themselves. They are now more transparent and create their own personal relations and audience loyalty by interacting and being visible. Being retweeted by the *right* followers is seen as enhancing a journalist's social capital in the professional online arena. Conversely, branding may be problematic by inviting criticism from other traditional journalists, guided by anonymity and neutrality. Hence creating UGS that make journalists more visible may pose a problem for some who are slow to change.

Fairfax Media in Australia, like most media, rely on social media to help make the shift from analogue to digital. Social media functions as a branding tool and also as a story idea incubator. The *Dili Weekly*, which exists in a very small market, encumbered by slow Internet, found it difficult to access social media. Mojo gave its journalists an opportunity to have an online presence by working offline until stories were ready to publish. In particular, mojo enabled them to create local commercial content, allowing them to compete with better-funded organizations.

Because of their long-term proactive view about the shift to digital, *Ekstra Bladet* was in a more advanced state of transition. Ekstra Bladet journalists were trained to create UGS and UGP for a variety of platforms, including web TV.

The *Ekstra Bladet* model is a glimpse of one ambitious future from an organization that has invested heavily in transitioning online. Their freemium soft pay wall model, where free online content drives users to a premium layer that is behind the firewall, will require content that citizens will want to pay for and that advertisers will want or need to invest in. This will require journalists who are skilled in producing multimedia and, more specifically, UGS and UGP content. Chapter 8 outlines a few basic principles for mojo praxis.

Notes

1. *Self-shot* is a term I use to define early experiments in UGC.
2. A set of tools designed to address behavioral issues by creating a desire and opportunity for engagement.
3. The making of a documentary about the Cherbourg mojo project.
4. VozMob is a platform for immigrant and low-wage workers in Los Angeles to create stories about their lives.
5. *Time* has established Red Borders to produce long-form documentary for the web.
6. Over-the-top (OTT) content describes broadband delivery of video and audio (Netflix, Now TV) without a multiple-system operator being involved in the control or distribution of the content itself. OTT content is an advertiser-funded delivery model for smart devices, including mobile and TV.
7. My current job as the head of mobile content development at Ekstra Bladet in Denmark is a newly defined position, within traditional print media, to facilitate content development for web TV.

8   Recording Video and Audio and Editing on a Smartphone

Overview

In the 21st century the nature of storytelling and the language and modes of story delivery are constantly being redefined. We've moved from an oral culture of telling stories around the kitchen table, to an era of mass communication where the book, newspaper and text dominated, to a world of convergent medias that capture daily life and play it back to a global audience in real time. Access to powerful and affordable mobile technology means just about anyone can own the tools to tell stories and publish on the Internet anytime from almost anywhere. Moreover, this ability is creating a paradigm shift in the way media does business.

This chapter introduces some basic concepts and techniques for recording media and audio, and introduces basic editing on the smartphone. More comprehensive detail can be found in *Mojo: The Mobile Journalism Handbook* (see Appendix A). Smartphones have become powerful mobile pocket creative suites able to capture, edit and publish user-generated stories (UGS) from location. The technology has spawned a new group of citizen content producers who find it addictive, and the lure of ready-made publishing platforms, like YouTube, irresistible. Mixed with an already rampant voyeuristic culture, born from an immersion in years of reality and self-shot TV, Internet accessibility led to an exponential increase in user-generated content (UGC). In 2015, citizens uploaded a staggering 180 million hours of video, enough to fill more than 20,000 channels 24/7 for a year.

However, being an effective mojo requires more than access to a smart device. It is a holistic form of multimedia storytelling that combines journalism, videography, photography, writing, editing and publishing, all done on a handheld smart device. Story is key in mojo production, and it defines the level and type of mojo that's required. For example, shooting sports or wildlife may require long lenses and a DSLR, or a video camera, in addition to your smartphone. The point is that technology is not the answer to everything, and a focus on story can help determine a level of technology.

Working as a Mojo

The most important thing to understand when working as a mojo is that it's possible to be as professional as the network guys if you are prepared. You may be thinking: How can a single person cover all bases on a breaking news story? It's possible by thinking in advance about the story (theme and characters), knowing the limitations of your gear and the location. If it's a rush job, then preparation occurs en route in the car, train or plane.

Here are some questions that need to be considered before every story:

- Do you have a five-point plan?
- Do you have experts in mind to interview? Will they all be at one location?
- Have you thought of a lead?
- Have you checked the Internet for the latest on the topic or event?
- Do you have archive in mind, and how much will it cost and where is it?
- Is it an overnighter, and can other interviewees be recorded en route?

Five-Point Plan

Stories have a beginning, middle and end—even news stories! Once we begin to understand story, we realize there are a number of additional arc points between the beginning and the middle, and the middle and the end. A five- to seven-point plan is made before the shoot, adjusted as elements develop during the shoot and used as a guide during edit. A plan is not prescriptive or restrictive and is used to maintain focus.

SCRAP

Mojo stories benefit from using a basic modular story development tool like SCRAP, which stands for story, character, resolution, actuality, and production. Mojo praxis also requires an understanding of how to use basic multimedia story elements: actuality, interviews, B roll, Piece T0 Camera (PTC), narration and graphics. Understanding SCRAP helps the mojo recognize the basic building blocks of the story and answer key questions: What's the story? Who are the characters? How will the story resolve? What actuality will I film? What are the production logistics? SCRAP helps put some shape around the story and helps the mojo make sense of the search for reality. SCRAP is discussed at length in *Mojo: The Mobile Journalism Handbook*.

Multiplanar Stories

The big difference is that multimedia or UGS are multiplanar and can be laced with many elements, such as audio, B roll video, interviews, actuality, narration and graphics. Multiplanar stories are discussed at length in *Mojo: The Mobile Journalism Handbook*.

Table 8.1 Multimedia storytelling is multi planar

Graphics		Stills
	Video	
	Sync Audio	
	Narration (VO)	
	Music	

B Roll

Apart from the elements described in Table 8.1, one of the key elements in any video story is B roll, or cover shots. B roll is used to compress and expand story points, and you can never have too much B roll. It's often said that B roll doesn't include footage of interviewees, or on-camera talent, but that's not always true. If the interviewee is talking about a football game and the score, or a fight on the field, your B roll might include these aspects of the game, and it might also include the interviewee. If the on-camera talent is in among the action, then he or she might end up on B roll. Sometimes the audience likes to see the on-camera talent, especially a trusted news reporter, in the fray. At *Foreign Correspondent* (ABC TV) we always shot B roll in our coverage that included the reporter because we got a spike in points.

B roll is crucial for covering edits that we call jump cuts, which often occur in an interview that has been shortened. B roll shots that relate to aspects mentioned in the interview enable the journalist to highlight those points at various crucial stages of the edit. B roll is also used to cover content for legal reasons or to create specific story bounce. Edits in an interview can also be covered with a shot of the reporter listening, often referred to as a "noddy," but effectively this is also a form of B roll.

Once you understand your story at the development stage, here is a pre-record checklist:

- Is the smartphone charged and did you bring the car adapter, solar charger or battery pack so that it can be recharged?
- Have you switched to airport mode (in settings) to stop calls and WiFi interference?
- Will shooting in a dense location such as a jungle require a portable light?
- Do you have the right microphones and batteries?
- Do you have a camera cradle, and can you carry a tripod or monopod?
- Will the onboard camera app be sufficient, or will the location and the job require a more advanced app, like FiLMiC Pro?
- Does the job require a hybrid mojo approach and use of a DSLR and various lenses, or a laptop? If so,
  - Do you have an AirStash or another device to transfer media for the edit?

- Will the edit be done on location? If so,
    - Do you have the right edit app, or a laptop, and is there enough power to complete the edit?
    - Will there be 3G/4G or WiFi connectivity to enable story upload?
- Does someone know where you are going to do the job and have you developed an exit strategy?

Basic Smartphone Handling

Good journalism is partly synonymous with good access, and the better the access—at the scene of an accident, in the fray with water police as they dredge a river, or with fire officers outside a burning building—the more unique the material. If you have access you may find the tripod redundant and your standard iPhone lens will be sufficient to cover the event. The wider lens that ships with some smartphone cradles may be steadier and more useful. Your choice as to whether you shoot handheld or on a tripod can determine how dynamic your footage looks. Using a tripod and shooting from a distance on long lenses gives footage a spy look, and that's not really what journalism and multimedia storytelling is about. It also puts the camera and the microphone a long way from the audio source and the action. Bad access will result in weak location actuality and muddy audio.

Where possible, operate your smartphone without a tripod and only use one when it's absolutely essential; for that super-wide establishing shot of the Rift Valley or that essential long-lens shot of a person drowning in the middle of a river. Shooting without a tripod puts you in a flowing state of body and mind, where you feel the unfolding story and are able to move with it to cover developing events.

Here are a few tips for working handheld:

- Rest your body on a wall or your elbows on a table or on the bonnet of your car to create stability.
- If the smartphone is in a cradle, it will probably be able to support itself on a table. But is that what you want—to leave the camera stationary? Probably *yes* for an interview and *no* when you cover unfolding actuality.
- If you pull your elbows close to your body, you will create a strong triangle with the camera to support the shot. But remember that it's hard walking like that. Try it and you'll see that you look and feel like a Dalek. But pan in triangle form and your shot will be steady.
- Bend your elbows and knees to feel the center of your weight, and when panning the camera left and right, pivot your body, not your hands.

Mojo is really about being mobile, and this means being among unfolding actuality; so move in close to get a variety of shots rather than sit back on a tripod relying on the zoom. Most smartphone zooms are digital, and while they can be used if required, you will do better to track in and shoot close on the wide end of your lens, because the

- Shot is steadier;
- Subject is audible; and
- You're close to evolving actuality and will feel and capture the emotion.

Now that we know how to dance with the smartphone, we need to understand the detail of what we are filming and how to cover a sequence.

Coverage

How the camera is used and what shots are chosen will partly determine the style of a story. An action-packed news story might require a lot of usable short shots with driving narration and choice sync grabs. A slower-paced short feature might require more in-depth interviews with supporting B roll that captures more emotive and reflective moments. The degree to which a style is set in the field will determine the level of creative and editorial complexity during the edit.

Shots or Sequences

A sequence is a number of shots recorded without stopping between them. Follow the action and move from one shot to the next, varying the frame size so that shots are different enough and can be edited easily. For example, if you are filming football training, the sequence might include a wide shot (WS), some tighter midshots and some close-up (CU) shots. A sequence follows the action of the story. You might name a sequence "Training B roll." This will remind you that this sequence contains a number of different clips or shots to cover training.

When covering unfolding actuality such as a car accident, things happen so fast that you'd miss the actuality if you buttoned off and waited to set up each shot. So it's nearly always best to think of those shots as part of a sequence—one following the other.

Framing

Choose the frame that best demonstrates what you are trying to show. Here are some basic frame sizes and an indication of their use:

- Extreme wide shot (EWS): The subject can just be seen.
- Wide shot (WS): The subject is seen full frame and we see the surrounding and background.
- Midshot (MS): Shows the subject in detail while also showing the background. This is often used in a PTC shot on location, with the subject off center to show the unfolding actuality in the background.

- Medium close-up (MCU): The most used shot in news because it is emotive and also wide enough to see some of the actuality in the background. This is often used in an interview and is intercut with an MS and a CU.
- Close-up (CU): Used to convey extreme detail and emotion. Use the wide-angle lens and move the camera closer to the subject. A zoomed shot will highlight any movement by the subject and make the shot appear shaky.

Duration of Shot

One of the most common mistakes people who have just picked up a camera make is they don't hold their shots for long enough. While as little as 18 frames of a shot might be used, it's important to hold shots for at least 10 seconds (if possible). When working fast, concentrate on getting usable information and not shots. While every picture is worth a thousand words, it's pointless having even 10 words if they aren't usable. Always ask, "What's happening in my frame?" Of course shoot special shots, but make sure you cover your story structure with usable story-specific shots.

So what's a usable shot? Well, the more time one spends in the edit suite, the more you'll know about what works and what not to shoot. A more experienced mojo will learn how to use as little as three-quarters of a second of a shot, or even three frames. One advantage of holding a shot for an extended time, perhaps for 45 seconds or longer, is that the camera is rolling if something unexpected happens and you are recording continuous audio. We call these long shots, *tea ceremony shots*, where even the most basic movement can be a work of art. This type of shot (which can include a pensive close-up or a sequence of a Japanese tea ceremony) is very useful for using with poignant narration.

Lighting

Getting the subject to look right (exposure and framing) while working quickly is all about sensing the light. Former multi-award-winning *Foreign Correspondent* and *Four Corners* cinematographer Wayne Harley says it's about understanding and playing with planes of light, which he says we don't notice usually, but which the cameraperson needs to see and use quickly. Working in news and current affairs journalism is about reacting to the moment, and understanding and using natural light is often the key to getting a usable shot. Sensing your light or knowing where it's coming from (behind, in front or from the side) and what it's doing (flat, appearing or disappearing) is a first step to successful lighting.

Outdoor light is difficult to work with because it's not timeless and hence is rarely controlled—one minute it's bright and warm and the next it's cloudy and cool. The best outdoor light occurs in the early morning or at dusk and is often referred to as the "golden" or "magic hour," a favorite time for cinematographers. But when shooting news you are not always going to have the luxury of choosing your lighting moment.

When recording day interiors, use natural light like the sun through a window or available light sources such as desk lamps, ceiling lights or your portable light.

Here are some tips for shooting with light:

- Try to film the subject so that the light is in front of him or her (behind your shoulders) and not behind the subject (Figure 8.1).
- Each light source has its own power, and at dusk and dawn the light is warmer (more golden) and shadows are softer than during the middle of the day.
- At night try to use natural light sources like the moon, fires, flashlights, candles, car headlights or your portable light.
- Low light means muddy or grainy pictures. So add light—lamps, street lamp, a full moon or on-camera portable lights (but stay clear of those with large batteries, as they will unbalance the camera).
- If extra exposure or more control over the shot is required, use a DSLR with a bigger chip and changeable lenses; a wider aperture (low number) on a DSLR means you will have a shallow depth of field, which is great for moody scenes and static interviews, but makes it difficult when shooting moving news or documentary-type footage.

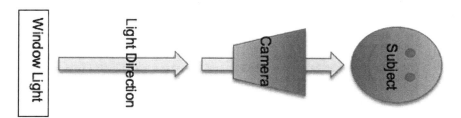

Figure 8.1 Direction of light.

Location Audio

Recording clean usable sound on location is an art requiring practice and the right equipment. While basic sound recording principles remain constant, mojos need to know how to shoot video and record sound at the same time. We begin hearing sounds at about 16 weeks while we are still in the womb and even before we can see. Mum's voice, intonation and rhythms, can all be heard above the sounds of the natural world. In modern times we are bombarded with noise and our senses are detuned to filter out sounds that we hear but don't want to listen to. So listening and filtering out the noise is the key to recording clean audio. If video clips have taught us anything, it's that while we are happy to watch flashing overlit shots, whip pans or blurry close-ups, we like our audio clean. The key to recording usable clean audio is the right equipment, placement and monitoring.

Walter Murch, the famous Hollywood feature film and sound editor and mixer, reminds us that "the most important thing students must learn is 90 percent of film is sound. The picture is far less important" (cited in McDonald 2014). While it's important never to come home without the video, Murch is absolutely right—especially when it comes to factual, location-based recording. Unlike feature films and some large documentaries, which use postsynced sound and dialogue, a mojo needs to know how to record clean audio in the field, especially in noisy locations. A decade ago it was much simpler because, ironically, everything was more complex. You either knew what you were doing or you hired a professional sound recordist. In the late 1980s and early 1990s, when powerful DV cameras became available, the way we made video stories changed. Like video journalists, mojos have to record audio without a sound recordist and edit sound without an editor. The smart mojo needs to know the basic principles of sound recording—which microphone is best and where to place it. He or she will also need to understand to what extent being a one-man band will compromise his or her ability to record and edit clean sound.

For a mojo, as with any journalist working in radio or television, recording location dialogue correctly is vital because in most cases it's the only dialogue the project will have. The key to recording clean dialogue on a smartphone is technique. The second most important aspect of sound recording is the microphone. The other is access. The following information is based on what has been learned over many years working on the road on current affairs programs and large documentary series, and also as a video journalist and mojo trainer.

The word *location* has a number of connotations when used to describe sound recording. In the first instance, it has a topographical meaning that suggests you are not in a studio. But it also describes the proximity of the subject to the reporter, suggesting they are both in the same location. This presupposes an ability to communicate directly and to feel the full spectrum and emotional weight of the auditory experience in a way that watching silent pictures never does. So an important rule of recording location sound is to get in close. If you are among the action, you'll record more dynamic location sound, because you will feel the scene developing before you and see the activity that causes sound to happen.

It's important not to make the mistake of zooming in for audio. Being on the long end of the lens gives grainy, shaky pictures, and if a shotgun microphone is used, the result will generally also be poor audio. Don't forget that on a long lens your subject might look close, but without a sound operator holding a boom, the shotgun microphone is still located on top of the smartphone, exactly where the camera operator is standing, possibly a long distance from the sound source.

Being close to the source is not always enough to record clean audio, especially if your subject is moving about in a developing scene. You'll need to ensure that you can move with the subject and that he or she is facing the microphone when speaking, and this may entail using a radio microphone. Hence, it's important to make a quick assessment of the location and the sound requirements. In short, the key to recording great audio is to know the answers to the following questions:

- Are you a one-person operator or will you have a sound recordist? As a one-person band, your audio recording options are limited and you will be very busy.
- Will your camera microphone be OK, or do you need extra microphones to record clean sound?
- What's the location? Noisy road, quiet but remote jungle, rock band, maybe a football match or an isolated desert lacking backup facilities?

Interview Audio

Recording an interview is the stock and trade of any journalist. A sit-down or walking interview is always a challenge, especially when working solo. The key to getting good interview audio is summarized below:

- *Knowing your subject:* Helps put them and you at ease and will help you get relevant information.
- *Correct microphones:* Ensure that your audio will be on mic and free of background noise (see later in this chapter).
- *Recording in a quite place:* Helps with audio quality, relaxes your subject and helps the journalist concentrate on the interview.
- *Recording lots of B roll:* Will help you edit out unwanted audio glitches or noises, extend or shorten the interview and create dynamic sound-ups.
- *Access:* Being in close to the subject creates less room for unwanted audio and also enables the journalist *to feel the interview.*
- *Atmostrack:* Sometimes called a buzz track, it helps create smooth audio edits. Try to record between 30 and 60 seconds of ambient or natural sound at every location. This track is used to create a seamless audio base between dialogue edits and transitions between different types of audio. This atmos or buzz track will help smooth audio transitions.

Recording clean location audio involves treating sound as a key element, not an afterthought. This attitude and praxis begins long before arriving at location. On location it's all about listening, having the right equipment and being close to the sound source, so you can hear and relate to the story. See *Mojo: The Mobile Journalist Handbook* (see Appendix A) for a detailed explanation of sound recording using a smart device.

Editing

There's a saying that "when the filming stops the story begins." This adage is so true in the mojo era because the edit happens almost immediately after the story is shot, and often on location as the story is being shot. In the era of reality TV and YouTube, two things are apparent: *story* has made way for the *event*—"hey, look at this video of me eating eggs"—and the high level of user-generated content (UGC) that's uploaded each minute (300 hours) represents an example of the decadence that Aristotle said would occur when storytelling dies. But is storytelling dead? Of course not, it's just in a user-generated coma.

Editing footage into structure and story is like magic, except that it often involves very laborious preparation, creative imagination and high-level editorial and publishing skill sets. It's hard work. The more skillful you become as an editor, the quicker you will be at deciding what works and what doesn't.

One great benefit of mojo work is that the story can be completed and published from location. This means mojos can remain on location where they are ready to update the story. The various stages of the edit process are

- *Shoot:* Being able to *edit in camera* is an important skill and the attitude that "I'll fix it in post" isn't realistic in fast turnaround mojo-type storytelling. Successful mojos, like all one-man band journalists, shoot the shots they know they will use in their edit. This is an acquired skill that camerapeople working in news bureaus, who edit their own stories, learn quickly.
- *Viewing footage:* Based on the amount of time you have, scheduling time to view footage before editing is always important. A working mojo will know what shots are good even before he or she begins the edit and will have marked these in a small notepad or on his or her smart device. It always helps to isolate good sound bites, strong actuality and relevant overlay. It's also important to be on the lookout for an obvious structure that supports your intended story line, or an even better one that you hadn't planned.
- *Making a rough edit plan or script:* Your five-point plan is the beginning of an edit script, which is developed before your shoot and adjusted accordingly as elements develop during the shoot. This plan, or *story arc*, is tweaked to comprise the major structural points of the edit. Your edit plan will include reference to sound bites, specific actuality, archive or other material that the editor might need to draw on to build the story and specific narration.
- *Draft narration:* This is a first attempt at gluing story elements into story structure. Narration is the key tool a journalist will use to compress, expand and segue between story elements and structure. Narration does this by relating to the outgoing pictures and introducing the next piece of sync or actuality—writing in and out of pictures. A rough narration is essential if you want to work quickly and effectively.

Use the narration to lay up your vision without worrying about the B roll. The focus at this stage is writing in and out of the sound bites to create a story structure and bounce or rhythm.

When writing narration you can work on three words a second, which is the speed that we generally read at. So if you are writing to pictures and your piece of edited video is seven seconds long, you only need a maximum of 20 or 21 words. This means when working to a deadline you can create your script on the fly.

- *Creating story bounce:* It's best to edit quickly so as to lay a rough narration bed as fast as possible to help understand the story and find the story bounce, which is the rhythm of the story as it bounces between narration, sync, actuality and its five to seven structural points. In news-type, feature and magazine stories, the audience expects a certain story bounce that the journalist or editor sets up very early in the piece. It's best to fine-tune narration after laying down a series of narration and sync sequences to enable you to listen to the statement you are creating with the narration, sync, narration rhythm or bounce. This is called *writing in and out of pictures* and, once learned, will be a very useful editorial and compression skill.

One of the dangers in nonlinear editing, like we do on a smartphone, is that because everything can happen very quickly, the journalist will keep trying stuff and therefore will not get much editing done. Today a journalist needs to be much more prepared for the edit, even when it's being done in the field. The way to work is to prepare well and get the story bed down as quickly as possible. Once the story is structured on the timeline, the parameters are set and the structure becomes much more apparent and manageable. This is most important for mojos who work alone and may not have another pair of eyes to view their work.

In summary, your initial idea is all important, so never lose sight of what interested you in the first place, but be open to new influences. The story will come to life on the road, so don't forget all the best planning and research may change on location. This is the main reason for a plan: It's difficult to know where the story is going, if you don't know where you are. You won't know where you are if you don't understand where the story has come from.

Mojos are inquisitive people who are able to capture their curiosity on a smartphone and then edit and publish the images in a UGS while still at location. A good mojo is well prepared and knows the limits of his or her equipment. If required, he or she is willing to choose hybrid options to make sure that the visuals are exiting. But unless we hear what's being said, we will only get half the story and will lose our audience. If MTV taught us anything, it's that we can tolerate a wobbly shot, but audio needs to be clear. The more thought you give to sound, the better your pictures will look. The audience will forgive bad pictures if the subject is compelling; what they will never accept is poor sound. And the subject is always more compelling when it can be heard clearly. Two decades ago we needed a lot of expensive gear and a sound recordist to get good sound. Today recording sound is much cheaper, but it should never be seen as less important than pictures.

If you record bad sound, you can't really fix it. Aim to record the best possible location sound. Try to avoid extraneous ambient sound and fix any sound issues on location, not in postproduction. Use the right microphone placed as close as possible to the sound source, and be mindful about how you will combine audio and pictures in the edit.

Irrespective of the level of mojo equipment used, the following checklist will assist in recording strong story, visuals and audio with a smartphone:

- To tell the story, we need to shoot the story.
- Plan and schedule the story to allow for all eventualities.
- Switch the smartphone to airport mode or turn off WiFi.
- Shoot in the landscape or horizontal frame.
- Avoid high contrast in lighting situations and shoot with the sun to your back.
- Avoid shots of areas that have high contrast, such as dark versus light settings, or bright sunlight and shadows.
- Always wait for the numbers to start scrolling after pressing record and before you move the camera to lock the gyro into the desired frame.
- Start your story with dynamic CUs or a beautiful WS establisher.
- A change of angle is as good as a second unit.
- To ensure that you have enough usable coverage, hold your shots for at least 10 seconds and even longer for *tea party* shots.
- Use B roll to shorten long sequences.
- Always be on the lookout for scene opening and closing interview grabs and shots.
- Don't use a tripod unless necessary, as it impedes mobility and interaction.
- Don't be afraid to cross the line, but learn how to do it seamlessly using neutral shots.
- Make sure you leave the right amount of headroom or chin room. Don't use a shot where there's excessive empty space above a person's head or too little space under his or her chin, because the name super might cover his or her mouth.
- Depth of field is a concept that describes focus points in a frame and is often controlled by altering f-stops on a lens. On a smartphone use your focus lock to create a sense of depth in the frame, or set the subject to one side of frame to create depth in the frame beyond the subject, or make sure the frame is well lit to create sharper images through the depth of the frame. Also remember that a wide-angle shot will provide a much better depth of field than a telephoto shot zoomed in on your subject.
- Keep quiet while shooting.

Editing in general is a way of *thinking* influenced by *ways of seeing* various states of immediate connectivity and possibility. This is particularly relevant in close-quarter storytelling like mojo, where the immediate is an essential story component. It is based on a state that has been described as fluid. Writer and art critic John Berger described it thus: "The relationship between what we see and what we know is never settled" (1972). Yet in doing journalism we work to create content that settles perceptions. In this context mojo praxis, and especially editing skills and the literacies discussed in this book, works as a filtration system to help make sense of the flowing relationship between separate unsettled realties.

9   Conclusive Ways Forward

> Skilled professionals who can turn isolated units of social content into compelling stories, who can shape the narrative emerging out of the cacophony of conversation flowing through the social web ...
> —*Mark Little, Storyful CEO (2013)*

Overview

This book and the associated artifacts arose from an investigation of the pedagogy and the tools required to enable marginalized citizen groups to create their own local voice. In essence, this book documents an investigation into what's required for citizens to shape their own narratives, in a democratic cyber corridor, to ensure their voice is heard from source through to exposure. Citizens' ability to engage in that activity is seen as fundamental to principles of democracy. In essence, everyone who picks up a smart device possesses the skills to become a potential journalist. However, for this to occur in any meaningful way, citizens will need a skill set to enable them to use current digital technologies to create a more developed, thought-out and even politicized form of citizen content called user-generated stories (UGS).

To test this hypothesis, a series of mobile journalism case studies were run in remote Indigenous communities. In order to further explore aspects of sustainability. the study included supplementary workshops in the education sphere. To understand the possibilities for more formal publishing relationships, the research included an investigation of the impact of mojo training within professional media.

The research outcomes, as discussed in Chapters 5 through 7, validate the following:

- With minor adjustment to tone and language, the mojo pedagogy is flexible enough to work across community, education (primary, secondary and tertiary) and professional communication spheres.
- Mojo praxis can result in grassroots UGS that has a local perspective.
- Mojo provides job-ready skills and advanced levels of digital literacy to enable communication across multimedia platforms.

The accessibility of mobile technology in community, a move in schools to multimodal cross-curricular challenged-based learning using mobile devices, a shift in professional media from print to mobile digital multimedia and web TV—a multimodal version of content creation—all require, as Mark Little of Storyful observes, a profession with a new, more relevant skill set. This skill set will help citizens transform their millions of hours of social online kludge into more meaningful narratives. The mojo skill set brings a narrative structure to social web conversation. This more developed transformation of user-generated content (UGC) into user-generated story (UGS) will become valuable as we move to multidisciplinary, multiscreen and multiplatform content streams. Mojo digital literacies support the shift in role and responsibility of the audience from consumer to citizen contributor.

Communities

The investigation in remote Indigenous communities—Galiwinku, Lajamanu, Ramingining, Bathurst Island and Numbulwar, in the Australian outback—demonstrated that citizens without prior journalism experience could learn to create professional digital stories of a quality that can be sold to the professional media. It also confirmed that mojo training could lead to professional recognition and even local media jobs. Overall the research shows that while the technology and training program is accessible, gaining long-term traction in communities is difficult without ongoing support. Short-term training without support will not create generational change.

More specifically, the research in Indigenous communities demonstrates that:

- It is important to reject deficit theorizing and focus on positive cultural attributes;
- Care needs to be taken to treat participants with cultural respect and as partners in the mojo process and outcomes;
- Special attention is required when dealing with potential community politics and ethical issues that impact process and outcomes;
- More planning could be done with schools, local media and other bodies to facilitate long-term benefits; and
- More work is required to develop sustainable posttraining models.

The recommendation is that mojo is integrated as part of a strategic collaborative in-community communications framework through BRACS or RIBS[1] operations. This occurred in Galiwinku, where state and federal government groups used mojos to create local health messaging. While the aim is to provide ongoing encouragement and technical and peer group support with continued in-community training, sustainability will come through real partnerships with local infrastructure. The research indicated that one method of achieving sustainability is to introduce mojo through local schools, where teachers have a curricular interest in using digital literacies as a tool to elicit a more engaged student narrative. To test this hypothesis, I conducted additional workshops in community and urban schools.

Schools

The research indicates that mojo skills and praxis can form the basis for innovative literacy programs across the curriculum that work to explore cultural, social and linguistic differences in a more holistic way. Mojo acts as a key to authorize associated experiences through more reflective challenge-based learning activities. As teachers begin to use new communication technologies to deliver multimodal patterns of literacy, much broader than language alone, analogue stagnation becomes even more pronounced. New global connectedness makes it imperative to deal with technology, language and culture as a type of *multiliteracy* that is seen as central to civic life and promoting citizenship ideals (Cope and Kalantzis 2012). Mojo praxis is an innovative way of using technology and skills to engage students to think constructively and comment about their local environment, including community, school and workplace. This provides students with exposure to a broader spectrum of society that begins a lifelong civic connectedness (Clark and Monserrate 2011).

Trevor Galbraith, head of IT at Corpus Christi College in Perth, where mojo workshops were run, is already seeing this. Immediately after being trained, student mojos covered the archbishop of Perth's appeal to all the schools in Western Australia and two staff and four kids from the session then interviewed a refugee from Thailand who didn't want to speak with a big media but was happy to speak to a mojo. Mojo at school is about marrying school projects with community life to create a more holistic and connected narrative in a new dialectic between school and community. The primary and secondary workshops demonstrated the following:

- Students from age 11 can cope with the storytelling and technical aspects of mojo.
- Unlike traditional school-based video production that is restricted to class use because of associated costs, mojo uses relatively low-cost smartphone technology. Accessible outside school hours, it enables all students to participate in all phases of mojo production at school and at home.
- Students have used mojo to create stories quickly, which have won national competitions like the national ATOM[2] Awards.
- In composite classes, older students were observed helping younger students with script, and the younger ones helped the older students with the technology.
- Teachers see mojo as an accessible tool to augment and modify existing curriculum in areas including English, history, social studies, drama and even sciences.

- Schools involved in the workshops are creating their own mojo resources.[3]
- Schools involved in the workshops are discussing hyperlocal mojo networks to share ideas, teaching initiatives and mojo stories online.

One major difficulty of embedding mojo in education is scheduling. At Cairns West Primary School, teachers have developed lunchtime and after-school mojo groups to overcome these issues. Galbraith believes scheduling is a problem that is being resolved but might mean rewriting the curriculum, which is exactly what one school did after its teachers attended mojo training. Galbraith began working with schools that participated in the mojo training workshops to scope a hyperlocal network for exchanging content and ideas.

Similarly, a TAFE[4] in-community workshop for disengaged Indigenous youth resulted in students being offered work. One student was offered a contract to cover a sporting event, a commission that had previously been done by professionals. The communication skills and self-esteem of that student, who declared he could not hold a complete conversation before mojo, has grown to where he is confident enough to speak on an education panel with the Queensland Minister of Education, about the literacy benefits associated with mojo.

One of the features of the TAFE workshop was a preliminary train-the-trainer component to train teachers to plan, film, edit, write and publish and teach UGS creation. It is critical to choose potential trainers carefully, on the basis of their interest in digital storytelling, journalism, video production and participation in web-type activities and their willingness to work out of hours. TAFE in Queensland is planning to introduce mojo training to its teachers across 36 campuses.

Tertiary

I believe there is real potential for mojo to form part of a communications degree based on a pedagogy that locates it as an interdisciplinary area of study between journalism, television and other communications studies. Mojo's holistic approach suggests it could be introduced early in the journalism school curriculum (see Chapters 6 and 7). Table 9.1 lists journalism training objectives and how they intersect with mojo training.

Table 9.1 Journalism training and mojo intersect

Journalism training objective	Intersect with mojo
Obligation to truth and citizen benefit	Mojo requires face-to-face storytelling that delivers firsthand information published for citizen benefit
Advanced story research and verification skills	Mojos are trained in every facet of mobile journalism and taught to research and verify content before publication from the beginning of training

(Continued)

Journalism training objective	*Intersect with mojo*
Independence	Mojo tools enable mojos to undertake every aspect of story production from location without leaving the scene
Forum for criticism	Mojos publish online to enable widespread critique of their work

Because mojo includes production skills, a potential exists to create university campus television networks that use mojo praxis to provide students with real-world turnaround, content creation and editorial experience. At Nottingham University, in Ningbo China, students who attended these mojo workshops were inspired to set up their own television network called NUTS. Similar opportunities arose for postgraduate students at the Danish Journalism School at Aarhus University in Denmark, who are potentially able to use their newly acquired mojo skills to create multimedia stories for a new university-run online news site, Jutland Station. Campus-based, student-run networks can also use mojo praxis to produce UGS and user-generated programs (UGP) for media's content streams. In the process, students learn about short- and long-form story structure, content licensing and the extended use value of content packages. These types of online networks were once cost prohibitive; today they can exist in education linking schools nationally, even internationally. These networks provide students with a variety of real-world training experiences and an opportunity to showcase and on-sell their stories.

Professional Media

Research with professional journalists completed a triangulation study of the use value of mojo. It enabled mojo skills to be tested in the professional sphere, to, among other things, validate mojo training at the tertiary feeder level. If Poul Madsen, managing editor *of Ekstra Bladet*, is right, and things have changed so much, so quickly, that by 2016 his paper won't earn any money, journalists will need to know how to make digital content to survive. Finding the right model to keep journalists and produce strong content and make money is probably every editor's current focus.

We know media organizations realize economies of scale by having staff specialize in operational areas they are most suited to: production, editorial or post.[5] However, mojo suggests that one person can learn the skills needed to do it all across all phases of multimedia story production and become a complete mobile journalist. For example, knowing how to edit makes the mojo a much better cameraperson by teaching them what shots and sequences are needed. Knowing how to write in and out of pictures—the shots that were recorded in the field—makes the mobile journalist a better editor. These skills become vital as news organizations and media networks require more complete UGS rather than just UGC for their new web TV formats.

One question that's been asked time and again over the past few years is, how long should a mobile video story be? In this book we discuss the shape and the ideal length of UGS. In the online news environment, ideal story length is an elastic concept. At *Ekstra Bladet* it was initially thought that 30–45 seconds was the preferred length for multimedia news content. Marc Settle, from BBC College of Journalism, says the ideal online video story length is 75 seconds, because that is the standard length of a report or rant on the BBC—when someone talks to the camera and explains what is happening (cited in Burum 2014). Their view is that short-form digital equals mobile. While 30- to 75-second durations might work for a news bulletin, they may not work behind the pay wall or for web TV platforms. Indeed, we see video stories on *Wall Street Journal* and *New York Times* sites that are well over six minutes long.

Ekstra Bladet managers initially also told me that they did not want journalists to edit their own content on their mobiles. The premise being that a central hub of reporter and editor curators would edit all journalists' mobile content. Four weeks into training an email was circulated advising staff that deadline pressures and increased volume of UGC made it imperative that *all journalists* learn how to edit. The TV department's story curation team, consisting of a few desk-bound journalists, did not have time to edit field journalists' footage.

Mathew Ricketson wrote in the *Age* newspaper that because "technology and deadline pressures were encouraging journalists to stay at their desks," they were risking "losing touch with their audience." He continued that with information "available via mobile phones and computers," the need to "press the flesh had been greatly reduced" (cited in Rodrigues 2008: 120).

What this research shows is that as journalists begin to make more formed digital content, in particular UGS and UGP, they will need to *press the flesh* more, not less. Rodrigues cites Gary Hughes, former head of the investigative journalism unit at the *Age*, who says that "the investigative approach or thorough research, perseverance in reporting and the mental attitude to do in-depth reporting is being lost" (2008: 120). However, investigative journalists are still researching in-depth stories.[6] The DNA is still here and still being passed on to younger journalists. However, because senior investigative journalists are being asked to do more digital work, those interviewed for this research indicated they were worried about not having enough time to do it well. Depending on their age, some journalists may choose not to upskill and wait for retirement packages, others will need too.

The current trend of news organizations experimenting with more substantive web TV offerings suggests that producing short mojo UGS may not be enough. This raises many questions, including what gets priority on the front page, which is a breaking news page? Calling all stories on the front page "articles" causes issues as news converges from print to longer multimedia stories and more developed formats. This view is shared by *Guardian* journalists: "The article is no longer the atomic unit of news," and "we should reconsider the article and its place" (Jarvis 2011). At *Ekstra Bladet* a video editor sat alongside the front-page editor to push the importance and place of video stories in the news schedule and the front page.

Current mojo workshops with Scandinavian, Middle East and Asian news media are more complex and teach journalists to develop long-form stories and web TV formats. Unlike earlier workshops where online news editors had to be convinced to let their journalists participate, current workshops are driven by editors' needs. At some media organizations journalists, trained in mojos' neo-journalistic digital literacies, are providing ongoing in-house training for other journalists.

Alongside this neo-journalistic approach to story convergence a countervailing activity called social media is impacting journalism. Social media, like Twitter, provides a global social awareness representation of the lives and opinions of its users (Hermida 2012) and has altered how real-time news is received and created. Its own description of connecting users to the latest on what they find interesting is both its appeal and its Achilles' heel. As Kovach and Rosenstiel (2007) noted, "From the moment the 24/7 digital news was introduced, the process of verification, the beating heart of credible journalism in the public interest has been under challenge." Verification, a role the profession suggests only journalists can fulfill, bestows credibility on journalism (cited in Hermida 2012: 3). Yet as Hirst says, journalism can so often suffer from a "bias of convenience" (2012: 104), which together with gatekeeping shapes a form of journalistic truth. This so often happens with the written-by-rote method of reporting on Indigenous news. The same criticism is leveled at books, which are said to suggest completeness and truth containment (Pettitt 2013). This attitude is reflected in Shakespeare's *Winter's Tale*: "I love a ballad in print ... for then we are sure they are true" (Shakespeare 1996: 258). The reality is that local community or student media content is not quarantined from this type of bias, especially in untrained hands.

Currently journalism practices are understood as a set of literacies informed by ethics standards and routines set by print journalism. As new technology develops, we will need new literacies "that integrate, written and oral and audiovisual modalities" within "screen-based and networked electronic systems" (Prinsloo cited in Hermida 2012: 4). Hermida argues that new literacies require a shift from individual intelligence, where expertise and authority are located in individuals and institutions, to a focus on collective intelligence, where expertise and authority are distributed and networked (cited in Lankshear and Knobel 2007). I agree that the Internet can supply a collective intelligence, but this does not negate the role individual learning plays to facilitate collective reflectivity, ethical praxis and a eudemonic focus. This is even more crucial in community or schoolyard journalism, where audience and producer are known to each other.

The debate around whether new literacies value participation over publication is also relevant. New literacies like mojo enable informed online participation, especially because they lead to publication, which is pivotal to creating a functioning democratic global communications public sphere. Mojo provides skills to enable individuals to search for and embark on what Kovach and Rosentiel (2007) describe as "journalistic truth." Even in a 24/7 newsroom truth is filtered by reporter curators—up to 50 times an hour on specific stories (Ruud 2012). As more of the audience learn digital journalism literacies, journalists lose their exclusive control of the flow of meaningful checked content and become "just some of the many voices in public communication" (Deuze 2008: 12). One tension described by Westlund (2011) involves investigating how media workers make sense of this shift from the old role to the new. Indeed, how long will the reporter curator want to curate the news from tweets and other social sources and the two-way information flow? "Is this why I studied for three years ... to sit behind a desk and trawl the net?" This was a rhetorical question asked by one of *Ekstra Bladet*'s junior reporter curators. As journalists begin to embrace digital and mobile possibilities, in particular UGS and UGP creation, no longer is the old ascribed a lower value. The new fosters sense making as it forms a neo-journalistic partnership with the old: "Individuals' memories, experiences and knowledge form organisational intelligence that not only records and stores the old, but transforms and applies this knowledge into the shaping of the new" (Westlund 2011: 338).

Organizations like *Ekstra Bladet* deal with this reality by driving the marketplace realities with their shift to more formed content across a number of online platforms. While analysts predict an uncertain future for the news business, Madsen is upbeat as he plots the move from the aging notion of publication to platforms and workflows. He sees a time when *Ekstra Bladet* will split its division into news and TV. His is a two-year vision for the eb.dk portal to sit alongside eb24 news and a number of other channels. "We are combining great journalism, our tradition at EB, and for me it's a great pleasure to be head of this organization. You need content and programs where we can combine doing it on different medias, with mobile or mojo at the center of it all. Yes, there's a plan that will give us a great future" (cited in Burum 2014).

Madsen's plan is focused on commercial realities, and expansion involves trained mobile journalists and the transformation of a print news organization into a web TV news provider. On the back of growth in its digital audiences, declining print circulation and advertising revenues, and a £33 million loss in 2010, the *Guardian* also stepped up its digital first vows (Jarvis 2011). With 50 million distinct monthly users, it predicted doubling £47 million of revenue in 2011[7] to almost £100 million by 2016 (Sabbagh 2011). As of March 2015, the *Guardian*'s online digital revenue was £80 million, with losses sitting at £30 million and an online audience of more than 120 million monthly users (Durrani 2015). Unlike Madsen, the *Guardian*'s former managing editor, Alan Rusbridger, was not publically predicting the end of the print edition: "Every newspaper is on a journey into some kind of digital future. That doesn't mean getting out of print, but it does require a greater focus of attention [on] the various forms that a digital future is likely to take" (2010). This includes hybrid forms, as print will still play a role in countries like India that lack access to computing in certain rural and remote areas.

A registered trust, the *Guardian* views social justice high on its agenda. Following two years of juggling size and shape, theguardian.com is now the third largest English-language newspaper website in the world, opening new offices in the United States and Australia. CEO Andrew Miller summed it up this way: "We have to change the way that we do things, but we can never change what we are" (Robertson 2013). The *Guardian*'s DNA is such that it is embracing citizen input in a more formal way. The group's head of diversity, Yasoir Miza, is working on two interconnecting programs to ensure editorial coverage from minority groups "is more inclusive and representative[8] and moves away from stereotypes and labelling to increase the breadth and depth of minority voices within our papers and online" (Miller 2013). Miller adds that "journalism can be a powerful tool in creating dialogue understanding and cohesion, while promoting pluralism … if we open up our platform to draw in often unheard, marginalised voices [we] enrich our coverage and fulfil our commitment to social justice and open journalism values" (2013). In an effort to encourage diversity-open journalism, the *Guardian* has run a series of mobile technology workshops for people living in marginalized communities in India. Partnering with a development organization called Radar, they taught marginalized people to produce SMS texts, featuring their views of local events. Five of the citizen reporters have been given opportunities to pitch their ideas to the *Guardian*. As part of this research, six Timorese citizen reporters were taught mojo storytelling and have been producing and publishing UGS weekly for the past three years.

In summary, one aim of mojo praxis is to provide a foundation on which to realize components of the earlier discussed diversity principle. The above-described practices and commercial and government policies are based on an assumption that a diverse production source will lead to content diversity and in turn a diverse exposure of local content streams, including programs and ideas across demographics and types. But this relationship has been proven to be questionable (Napoli and Karppinen 2013). The earlier discussed introduction of 80 BRACS sites in remote Australian communities is an analogue example of communication policy driven by source diversity principles that did not always work. Issues of spectrum scarcity, license allocations and high barriers to entry are no longer immediately obstacles for Internet communications. However as Napoli points out, it would be wrong for policy makers to assume that Internet solves all diversity policy issues (2013: 4).

Internet Policy: An Overview

The Internet has maintained its current open framework since 114 countries gathered in Australia in 1988 to agree on a treaty of international telecommunications free from economic and technical regulation. But a proposal by a group of ICCIS countries[9] to restrict the use of social media could threaten its independence (Pappas 2012). Australia's legislation regarding the Internet was an amendment to the Broadcasting Services Act 1992 designed to provide a means for addressing complaints about certain content, to promote quality television to audiences throughout Australia, to make Internet technologies available to the Australian community, to encourage providers of content to respect community standards, to restrict access to certain Internet content, and to protect children from exposure to Internet content that is unsuitable for children. But much of the Internet's content is available to all children who can access the Internet. The Australian government passed an amendment bill in 1999 aimed at controlling Internet content. It can be argued that the government's view was contradictory: they wanted to improve regulation to ensure public benefit imperatives did not impose unnecessary financial and administrative burdens on Internet content hosts and Internet service providers (ISPs).[10] This view, which appears to be contrary to public benefit ideals, together with increased Internet traffic, meant the deficiencies of the 1992 Act were compounded, so recently the government initiated a number of media reviews:

- Review of Australian Government Investment in the Indigenous Broadcasting and Media Sector (IBR 2010);[11]
- Convergence Review (CR 2011);[12]
- Independent Inquiry into the Media and Media Regulation (MI 2012).[13]

In relation to online content and Internet use, the CR addressed these key concerns: that Australians should have access to *and opportunities for participation in* a diverse mix of services, voices, views and *locally generated content* that reflects and contributes to the development of national and cultural identity; that Australians should have access to a diverse range of content across platforms, services *and devices*; and that an investigation is needed into whether training can help address aspects of use, legality, ethics and editorial issues in order to meet public policy objectives (DBCDE 2012). Moreover, while the three reviews had uniquely identifiable objectives, all three identify the need to alter regulations that govern content providers and define content in the context of the new, converged media landscape.

Napoli believes one of the issues confronting Internet legislators is that often, when defining regulation, issues are "not discussed explicitly under the theme of 'diversity' but under other Internet governance terms such as free flow of information" (Napoli and Karppinen 2013: 5). One reason for this may be that instead of the established goals of source and content diversity, concerns around delivery modes, such as search engines and their providers, tend to relate more to the issue of exposure diversity, which remains less established in policy making. Yet, many of these issues, like flow, that have not been articulated in terms of diversity "would seem to be directly relevant to what's been called 'diversity by design,'" or "creating an architecture or service that helps people to make diverse choices" (Helberger cited in Napoli and Karppinen 2013: 5). So what does policy look like when, as Napoli (2013) advocates, it considers audiences in a more evolutionary context—more than just consumers of media, but rather as citizens and publics?

In its deliberations the CR concluded that policy and regulation in the following areas are justified in the public interest to facilitate a diverse media sphere:

- *Media ownership*: Concentration of services in the hands of a few can hinder the free flow of news and debate.
- *Content standards across all platforms*: Services should reflect community standards, including protecting children from inappropriate content.
- *Production and distribution of Australian and local content*: Social and cultural benefits arise from content that reflects Australian identity, character and diversity (DBCDE 2012).

The CR based its conclusions on the premise that access to diverse media creates a more democratic state and that all people "regardless of ability, must have access to information and the services in order to be an equal citizen, equal consumer, equal member of the public" (Boreham 2012). Nowhere is this more crucial than in the Indigenous media sphere, where mobile journalism practices, as described in this book, can assist in meeting the IBR's recommendations for a well-resourced and skilled Indigenous media sector. This sector will work to enhance self-esteem, self-identity and pride in communities, while providing training and employment opportunities (DBCDE 2011b). Chair of Australian Indigenous Studies at Melbourne University, Professor Marcia Langton, observes that "it's essential for Indigenous people to control the means of production [of media] for any meaningful change to occur" (Finkelstein 2011). Langton's observation applies equally to all citizens who can improve their own state of being by participating as publishers in a diverse online media space.

Language and cultural preservation was the validation for Michaels's policies and practices in participatory journalism in Yuendumu almost 40 years ago (Michaels 1986). Today, sitting at the core of Internet policy is a desire to increase "cultural and linguistic diversity" (Napoli 2013). The so-called father of the Internet, Tim Berners-Lee, sees this principle as central to the unifying ideal of "the humanity connected by technology," which, as Napoli suggests, is a facilitator in forging larger global communities and seeing a multilingual Internet "as a citizen right and a government obligation" (Berners-Lee cited in Napoli 2013).

But as Berners-Lee and others are realizing, maintaining the ideal and a level of net neutrality, to promote access and diversity within the corporate imperatives of the Internet, is a key to realizing a diverse content stream. The degrees to which government legislates media will impact diversity and hence net neutrality—the equal ability to access common opportunity and services on the Internet—a state where providers do not provide favors to strategic partners. Even before the Internet was ubiquitous, access to media was used as a tool for totalitarian propaganda. Recent examples are the Germans before and during WW2, Mugabe's control of media and economics in Zimbabwe, edited propaganda televised in Sarajevo by state-controlled networks during the Bosnian war, underground media in Kosovo in the late 1990s published to avoid state-controlled propaganda, embedding and controlling journalists in the Iraq War, the Great Firewall of China and government ISP closure during and after the Arab Spring.

The degree to which government legislates and defines the Internet within a telecommunications framework, or as a commercially available information bandwidth, will determine a level of net neutrality. For example, the Internet is a platform—email, web and streaming—where diverse competition among application developers occurs, who "are in a battle for the attention and interest of end-users"; hence it is "important that the platform be neutral to ensure the competition remains meritocratic" (Wu 2003: 146).

Moreover, in the United States the level of net neutrality is seen as a measure of the health of the First Amendment—freedom of speech. A recent ruling by the U.S. Appeals Court[14] shows that net neutrality is both an ideal and the type of control valve that impacts a level of commerciality—the availability of service and the ability to report freely—and potentially impacts diversity. The increased possibility of using the Internet to create a less marginalized voice might be possible for people who have access. But currently only 34 percent of people globally have access (de Argaez 2014), and even in Australia most homes in Indigenous communities in the remote outback do not have Internet communication terminals (ICTs) and cannot access Internet facilities. Currently the National Broadband Network (NBN) will not roll fiber into remote Indigenous communities, choosing instead to save costs and upgrade satellite services. In central Australia, "Indigenous households are 76% less likely to have Internet access than non-Indigenous metropolitan households" (Rennie et al. 2011: 9). These deficiencies, together with no plans to convert the analogue BRACS (RIBS) systems,[15] are an indication of the ineffectiveness of net neutrality policies. Providers will only deliver access where it's viable and provide supplementary arrangements where it's profitable.

Google's plans for a dumb phone that talks to its resource full smart-cloud-net, is another example where open-source Internet policies, designed to maintain net neutrality, may not work. Access to Google's smart net will require users to have a Google dumb phone. The same can be said for iOS-specific apps that are not available on Android and other OS, or Comcast's ability to promote affiliate NBC's content over ABC's to its Internet subscribers, while blocking BitTorrent.[16] As platforms become more cloud specific, platform owners, such as Google, become more powerful and are able to do deals with broadband providers—they become gatekeepers with pay walls that impact net neutrality. An Australian example is Telstra's unmetered Foxtel video downloads, which give both corporations an advantage in reaching their audiences. This type of sponsorship, which is biased in favor of the commercial partners, makes the net restrictive to some.

The U.S. Federal Appeals Court ruling in favor of providers is an indication of where the United States is heading. While it classified broadband providers as information providers, the appeals court did not impose anti-discrimination provisions against providers. The immediate rush by companies like Netflix to align with providers such as Comcast (and Google with Verizon) indicates the weight of that decision.

Professor Susan Crawford, from Harvard, put it simply: "Companies that are selling Internet access to Americans are not supposed to choose winners or losers—to decide which applications or services will be more successful in reaching subscribers" (Kafka 2014: 1). But they already are (Gmail, Hangout, iTunes). Tim Wu, who coined the term *net neutrality*, said in the *New Yorker*, "Since its creation, the FCC has had the authority to police all communications by wire in the United States. Instead, [then FCC chairman] Genachowski grounded the rules in what is called—legal jargon—the agency's 'auxiliary authority'. If the FCC were a battleship, this would be the equivalent of quieting the seventeen-inch guns and relying on the fire hoses" (Wu 2014: 1). As Wu suggests, this leaves the door open for Google and Facebook to do traffic deals with providers. This is now occurring, as one time enemies Comcast and BitTorrent partner to create what in essence is an ISP *tollbooth*. This is long-standing practice commonly referred to as *peering connection*, which is used to alleviate *Internet backbone* issues during busy traffic periods. These practices of prioritizing streams include streaming infrastructure discreetly to large paying companies like Google and Facebook. So the net neutrality issue is not really fast lanes—which are already fast—but as Tim Wu points out, it's more the number of lanes that are available (McMillan 2014). And with Comcast acquiring Time Warner Cable, the lanes are decreasing.

While the Internet is identified as a place where free speech is possible, the reality is that it's only possible for some. Even for those who have access to the Internet, one way to mitigate the impact of legislation and discriminatory practices is through education. In Australia the government has taken a more proactive approach and launched an education campaign to help users and, in particular, students and parents, understand the implications of accessing information and meeting people online (DBCDE 2011a). One of the benefits of mojo skills training is to educate citizens to deal with an increasing lack of net neutrality, to keep Internet corporate impact in check.

Net neutrality has been described as a U.S. issue. But with some Australian providers being U.S. owned and with a projected increase in Australian Internet traffic by 270 percent over the next four years, and Internet users predicted to jump 30 percent to 23 million by 2018 (Taylor 2014), who gets what and how much they pay for it is a global issue. In particular, with a predicted rise in Australian Internet speeds, citizens will be streaming more video online (Taylor 2014) and will look for fastest ISP. Given this, the opportunity arises for ISP to provide back-end deals that challenge net neutrality.

With so many smart devices hanging off networks, running rich media and full motion video, ISPs able to cope with cost, speed and reliability will have an advantage. It seems that in a capitalistic market, consumers will drive demand and governments will continue to respond by defining and corralling net neutrality based on a free market approach (Wu 2014). In Australia we'll have to wait and see how long the Australian consumer watchdog (the Australian Competition and Consumer Commission) can effectively manage net neutrality. One of the advantages of the mojo discussed here is that we mostly use 3G or 4G and local radio towers to provide connectivity. However, recent complaints against telecom giant AT&T over a decision to require specific wireless data plans to use Apple's FaceTime video chat over its 3G network are becoming more common and questioning notions of net neutrality. It is incumbent on educators to make sure that citizens are aware of net neutrality issues and ready to benefit from the net possibilities of being wired.

A Common Digital Language

My research around the development of a common digital language (CDL) leads me to conclude that legislation around Internet governance that promotes diversity of cultures and languages (in essence alternative content creation) is only one step in creating participatory content spheres. What has been discussed throughout this book is a common digital language, a literacy, which makes diverse online UGS possible across spheres of communication. This is not unlike what was required at the genesis of the Internet. Even with its foundation laid in 1969, the Internet was not effective until it had a common language scaffold, "essentially a set of rules that allows for easier communications between two parties who normally speak different languages" (Pavlik and McIntosh 2014: 212). In 1971, email enabled a more purposeful use of connected computers and demonstrated the need for a common language. This led to TCP/IP rules, and the term *Internet* was born (2014: 212). In 1991 the further development of HTML by Berners-Lee created the web page and transformed the Internet into a global publishing platform (2014: 212).

In much the same way, UGS creation requires a language and associated skills to realize its potential for enabling high-quality alternative digital journalism—schoolyard stories, grassroots community content, mainstream media news and web TV content. This language is balanced and seeks objectivity between events and personal issues. As Forde reminds us, this is important because "journalists are human beings, everything they produce is subjective" (2011: 119). The humanity Berners-Lee identifies also exists among professional journalists who, according to Forde, believe good journalism can reject neutrality (2011). A key to this conundrum is the dialectic that occurs between the audience turned journalist and the professional, or between alternative and mainstream media, regarding the emphasis on telling unbiased stories that are verified. What we need to do is to teach citizens and students the skills to tell these types of stories, and remind professional journalists that objectivity comes from being accurate, fair and balanced. It is hoped that these skills will help professional journalists cross the digital divide and develop in citizen journalists what Forde calls "a nose for news" (2011: 116). The question is, what is news value, and how does this differ across spheres of communication?

Fraser notes that the idea of an "egalitarian, multicultural society only makes sense if we suppose a plurality of public arenas in which groups with diverse values and rhetorics participate," a society with a "multiplicity of publics" (Fraser 1992: 126). Hence, it would follow that there might be multiple definitions of news value between public arenas (spheres) and their publics. However, the neo-journalistic approach of mojo, which retains the primary skill sets required in any good journalism praxis, provides a common standard while importantly enabling the personal skills and tools for citizens to speak in their own voice and participate and express their own cultural identity and style. Fraser notes that it is this commonality that distinguishes publics from enclaves and potentially unites them with "the public at large" (1992: 124) in a more purposeful interaction, which also maintains their multifaceted voice. These multiple publics, or subfields of communication, function as "spaces for withdrawal and regroupment" within an "indeterminate public" and "as training grounds for agitational activities directed toward wider publics" (1992: 124).

As this research has shown, interpublic discursive interaction is supplied through common digital tools and literacies—a common digital language (CDL). The purpose of this language is to create a nexus between and across spheres. Throughout my research, this occurred when mojo stories landed on media news bulletins and won awards in festivals, which further generated interest. Hence I believe a possibility exists for a hyperlocal meeting of these three public spheres facilitated by a common digital language (see Figure 9.1), not as one communications public, but as three diverse, discursive and transformative subfields of communication—a state where Fraser has identified "publics talk across lines of cultural diversity" (1992: 126). Like a good salad, each ingredient retains its individual flavor, but as mojos use the common digital language to spoon into the center, they begin to reveal the powerful mix of ingredients working as one.

Figure 9.1 describes a hyperlocal mechanism for a functioning content sphere. Here creation occurs in all of the three spheres: community, education and media. There are three possible curating points in each sphere: the individual—resulting in alternative recorded moments, organisational—with the potential for content creation that has more purpose, and a cross-cultural level—generating an alternative but professional type of content that intersects with all spheres through the common digital language and skills that transform content into more professional UGS or UGP. The use of a common language creates a bridge between the spheres, uniting them in a community of practice (inner circle), which is generated when like-minded people gather with technology, skills, purpose and a politicized will.

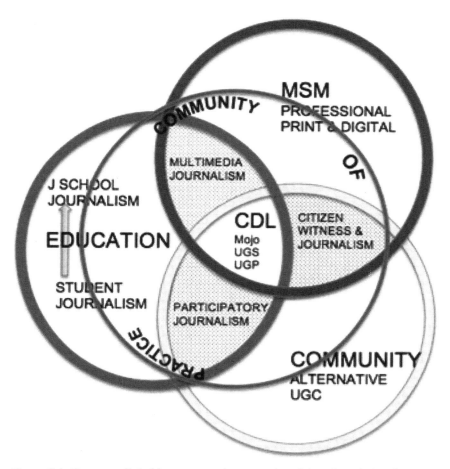

Figure 9.1 Common digital language and community of practice relationship.

One example of how the above model can be used is for schools or universities to cover events in their community and share the raw UGC and edited UGS with local media, who use it in news bulletins (as happened with Cherbourg mojo stories). Media then also establish a web page for local education and community content. This gives the community mojo project extra validation as its alternative content is legitimized online as more professional TV content. Another way is for education and community to set up their own local web TV portals, or marry with local community television[17] and broadcast their local content (UGC, UGS and UGP) first. Once community or education-based hyperlocal networks are established, their stories and formats can be licensed by media organizations who increasingly will be looking for more outsourced UGC, UGS and UGP. This may result in revenue for mojo work in the future. A third way is for media to use school or community mojos as local paid fee-for-service stringers, which also potentially works to increase sustainability. The general manager of ABC Darwin made this offer to Northern Territory mojos following their workshops. However, a lack of in-community organizational support made it difficult to capitalize on this opportunity.

One issue in this self-perpetuating model, represented in Figure 9.1, is that it requires participants in all spheres to be trained in common digital literacies if they are to create appropriate content. For example, if primary and secondary students and communities are taught to create UGS, tertiary journalism studies courses need to offer more advanced versions. It will not be enough to offer one multimedia elective in an undergraduate program. What's required is a development of mojo across tertiary journalism and communications curriculum, from UGC to UGS and UGP creation.

The other aspect of the overlapping model, described in Figure 9.1, is its impact on the labor market. Overlapping spheres of labor can initially create exclusion, in particular in new media models, where exclusion can be a result of age, ethnicity or geography (Neilson and Rossiter 2005b). Job losses can also be the result of new technology that requires shifts in techne, which may be a barrier and lead to reluctance to embrace new communications. This is evidenced in the media where, for instance, there are three levels of journalists working in a print environment. The older journalists, who are well established and credentialed, are willing to have a go, but mostly because they nearing retirement age, they are not too fussed by digital. The journalists who are midcareer, who have mortgages and children at school and need to keep working, are the most likely to want to embrace digital. The crop of younger journalists or interns who have just started on their career paths are the most interesting. While they will give digital mobile story creation a go and are quite adept at using technology, they have not had much mobile or multimedia training. Once on the news floor, they appear to be more interested in their Cecil B. DeMille moment and want to do what they call *real journalism*, with a photographer or a crew. I believe this perception will change as mobile is seen as a more professional alternative.

Where communication spheres or fields intersect, another shift in labor occurs where new digital languages form new groups of digitally skilled workers. Here a new group of almost itinerant workers exists on the margins of two fields. Good enough to become freelancers, subcontractors and occasional specialist writers, the so-called self-employed live in a state that Neilson and Rossiter (2005a) describe as "precarity," where planning is difficult due to the transient nature of labor. In their attempt to become part of a global public sphere, and driven by its notions of the digital sublime, these itinerant participants pit themselves against a more professional communications labor force, forming new working relationships that span cultural and labor markets.

Precarity is a double-edged sword in the transitional state, as digital storytellers move from one field to another. On the one hand, it describes the uncertain change to previously guaranteed employment and results in a lack of stability (Neilson and Rossiter 2005b). This environment currently describes the situation of mainstream media and print journalists. On the other hand, precarity "supplies the precondition for new forms of creative organization that seek to accept and exploit the flexibility inherent in networked modes of sociality and production" (Neilson and Rossiter 2005a: 1). Neilson describes precarity as "capital's response to the rejection of 'jobs for life' and demands for free time and flexibility by workers in the 1970s" (Neilson and Rossiter 2005a: 1), and it might also be a new state that defines a nonpermanent itinerant digital communications workforce that crosses spheres of communication.

An area that warrants further investigation is the degree to which the increased capital that comes with the CDL discussed here is successful in creating a rallying point, and the skills needed to enable mobile journalists and new digital media workers, to move across all spheres, to participate at a permanent or semipermanent level in a new, more global public sphere.

Summary

In closing, we can recall that Habermas's public sphere took shape in the period from the 15th to the 20th century and was defined by textuality, which Thomas Pettitt (2013) calls the Guttenberg parenthesis. This concept suggests mass communication was "an interruption in the broader arc of human communication" (2013: 3). Pettitt says that the current communications revolution closed the parenthesis on textuality and opened the public sphere to more arbitrary communication that includes gossip, comment and more folklore. As books and newspapers begin to lose their status as primary sources of truth, Pettit asks, "When there were no books, how did people sort out the truth? How did they decide what they would rely on and what they wouldn't rely on?" (Pettitt cited in Garber 2013). They did it through eyeballing, and on this side of the parenthesis, we do it through digital interaction.

However, with so much content being uploaded, we need to self-editorialize—a form of self-curation—at the individual level. This requires more reflectivity by content creators. We might need to throw away the rulebook developed during the period of closed parentheses, but keep the rules that make sense, a neo-journalistic view designed to help create content form. These rules need to be formulated for an open-source digital environment in order to perpetuate organic growth of style and structure. In essence, what we have outside the parentheses is many styles of digital content that need to be welded into the genre called story. This will require digital nodes of excellence that seek out and join with like nodes. But transforming the fragmented structure of network societies into communities of practice that create relevant content, including UGS and UGP, will not be easy.

This challenge might exist because participants in the current public sphere of overlapping forms of communication are, as Deuze (2009: 263) suggests, a "sceptical and self-interested citizenry," who supercharge the fragmentation of society "into countless individualised public spheres." This makes cohesiveness more difficult, but Fraser posits that it is like any other public sphere where citizens decide what is of concern to them and where there is no guarantee that they will agree (1992). Fraser envisions a public sphere where, through a process of deliberation, participants are transformed from self-seeking individuals to a "public-spirited collective" (192: 130). As argued previously, one way of achieving this is through education to ensure that "men and women deal critically and creatively with reality and discover how to participate in the transformation of their world" (Freire 1970: 16). Mojo training is one set of tools that enable skills, reflectivity and transformation possibilities through individual and collective publication of UGS and UGP.

In my working life I experienced the so-called golden age of journalism where old and young reporters went to the local pub to share war stories and advice. I think a new golden age is upon us, and what we might see in that cyber bar is a crowd from community, school and media, a cocktail of content creators calling themselves mobile journalists, or mojos. In 1990, I sat in a makeshift TV studio, in remote Yuendumu, in the Tanami Desert in central Australia, and watched Francis Jupurrula Kelly switch on his large video camera, walk a few meters to his desk and begin reading the evening news. "That's the news, bush way," said Francis, who was already an old hand at self-shot community program making, which he had been producing since 1982. But as we have seen, in Indigenous and other remote communities, early trends can either succeed or fail. If, as McChesney warns, we act as if social change is impossible, it will be, because this is our human dilemma. Although in critical junctures, he says, "our powers increase and the odds can swing dramatically" (McChesney 2007: 221). We need, as Ruud suggests, to be positive, determined and proactive about change.

> Changes come from the power of many, but only when the many come together to form that which is invincible ... the power of one.
>
> *Bryce Courtenay (1989)*

With more than 7 billion mobiles and about 2.6 billion smartphones in use in 2015, citizens have control of massive mobile communications power. The question is, how will we use it? My form of neo-journalism is an attempt to create a middle ground, a new dialectic between traditional skills and the possibilities of new technologies that impacts the relationship between alternative and mainstream media, and within alternative media itself. If the thesis of this study is correct and this approach will provide a new digital language, or bridge, between alternative and mainstream media, then the dialectic occurs in the synthesis of the relationship between the three spheres discussed here. This new ground requires not only, as Merrill (1993) notes, a realization by journalists of their responsibility, but also that all newly trained mojos, working as mobile journalists, realize this too. I contend that only when everyone wanting to produce journalism, in whatever form, understands their responsibility to the craft and to humanity, to public benefit ideals, will journalism, in all its forms, play its great role in creating a new, more diverse public sphere.

Dan Gillmor, one of the early test pilots of the "next version of journalism" (2004: 247), hopes that "the former audience" become "active users of news and not mere consumers" (2004: 238). An informed citizenry, says Gillmor, must "demand more and be part of the conversation" (2004: 238). He defines this as an input that is thoughtful and nuanced and not a "booster shot for knee-jerk reaction" (2004: 238). I hope this study adds yet another shade to the discussion about how mobile journalism skills and technology, *a next version of storytelling*, might be used to advance the conversation to help create a more democratic public sphere. Like Gillmor, I believe that given the tools to engage in the reflectivity implied in the dialectic that should exist between technology (determinist or use value), skills (professional values within alternative journalism) and the profession of journalism (ideals, meaning and business imperatives), we can change the world one story at time. I wonder what that next story will be, and what the next community, school or professional mojo will teach me.

Notes

1. The Remote Indigenous Broadcast Service is the updated version of Broadcast for Remote Aboriginal Communities Scheme.
2. The story at http://gunbalanyamojo.wordpress.com/2012/01/10/gunbalanya-meat-works/ won the Australian Teachers of Media (ATOM) Award for middle schools.
3. Mojo resource created by school (http://www.youtube.com/watch?v=_n_4op L0xBw).
4. Technical and Further Education.
5. Models like Beyond Production's style of creating content, where specialists are employed to do one specific role in the creation chain, are designed to maximize output and minimize cost.
6. See *Wall Street Journal* and *New York Times* websites for increased length of video stories.
7. Actual 2011 digital revenue was £45.7 million.

8. Miller's use of the term *representative*, to define one representing many views, is often characterized by stereotypical outcomes.
9. Russia, China, India, Brazil, South Africa, and other countries established the International Code of Conduct for Information Security (ICCIS).
10. Broadcasting Services Amendment (Online Services) Act 1999, No. 90, 1999—Schedule 1, http://www.austlii.edu.au/au/legis/cth/num_act/bsasa1999449/sch1.html.
11. Review of Australian Government Investment in the Indigenous Media Sector, http://www.dbcde.gov.au/__data/assets/pdf_file/0017/137060/Review_of_Australian_Government_Investment_in_the_Indigenous_Broadcasting_and_Media_Sector_2010_PDF,_752_KB.pdf.
12. G. Boreham, http://www.dbcde.gov.au/__data/assets/pdf_file/0007/147733/Convergence_Review_Final_Report.pdf.
13. R. Finkelstein, Report of the Independent Inquiry into the Media and Media Regulation, February 2012, www.dbcde.gov.au/digital_economy/independent_media_inquiry.
14. The U.S. Appeals Court rejects federal rules that Internet providers need to treat all web traffic equally and rules that the Federal Communications Commission (FCC) cannot impose antidiscrimination laws on broadband providers.
15. Analogue switch off happened in December 2013, leaving all RIBS.
16. A protocol supporting the practice of peer-to-peer file sharing that is used to distribute large amounts of data over the Internet.
17. See the relationship between University of Western Sydney and TV5.

Appendices

Appendix A: Link to *Mojo: The Mobile Journalism Handbook*

This book (https://www.routledge.com/products/9781138824904) describes the praxis based on the work in this book. It includes 13 how-to videos to assist people wishing to participate in mojo praxis. It also includes a detailed explanation of story, character, resolution, actuality (SCRAP) and associated digital storytelling tools.

Appendix B: Links to Documentaries

A number of documentaries were produced by Ivo Burum using a mixture of professionally shot videos and the mojos' own iPhone footage. Both of the below documentaries were screened to the respective mojos and their community representatives before being published. The documentaries provide an overview of the mojo process in two Indigenous case studies.

Mojo Working

This documentary describes the development stages of the mojo workshops: selection and training, filming and the edit phase of the NT Mojo case study workshop. Shot at Batchelor Institute for Indigenous Training and Education (BIITE) and in remote mojo communities in the Northern Territory, the program showcases mojo footage while providing candid comments from mojos on what they thought about the project. The documentary depicts the filming, editing, writing and publishing phases. The documentary is designed to be used as an introduction to mojo and as a promotional tool for communities and schools wishing to embark on mojo programs. The documentary was screened in community and broadcast on SBS and can be found at http://www.youtube.com/watch?v=jRmGACFJdJo.

Cherbourg Mojo Out Loud

This documentary describes the introduction of mojo into one community to assist with engagement of youth who had left school. The comments from participants are powerful reflections on the benefits of mojo praxis. The documentary will be used to create awareness in Queensland and Australia about mojo possibilities within the education sphere. Queensland Technical and Further Education (TAFE) intends to use the documentary at literacy conferences and across their campuses to introduce mojo praxis. The documentary can be viewed at http://www.youtube.com/watch?v=-_ol8Kg7mj0.

Appendix C: Safeguards Document

This document is provided to Indigenous communities or schools to describe the safeguard protocols. Safeguards are tabled for community members to discuss and agree on. They demonstrate that we have thought about safety issues, such as the potential of mojos misusing their technology to download restricted and prohibited material and uploading their own unplanned and restricted filming activities.

It is important to state to communities that mojos will not have "unfettered" access through the network to use network capacity for illegal or other purposes, including the production and distribution of user-generated content outside the project scope. It is important to assure community members that the safeguard protocols, together with inbuilt iPhone restriction technology, guidelines, and our chosen app's onboard upload management facility, will not allow the use of the iPhone to download or upload restricted material, outside the scope of the project guidelines.

Safeguard Levels

Choice of participants: This project is about empowering people to take more control of their lives through participation in media to create stories for them and about them. So choosing the right participants is crucial.

Community leaders working at [insert community name] will nominate candidates aged between 15 and 18 and be selected on the basis of their desire to be in the program and their trustworthiness as indicated by community elders (or school teachers).

Community elders [staff or teachers] and trainers will mentor and support participants during training, without impacting the fidelity of the research.

Guidelines: These were prepared from lessons learned on previous programs and include an agreement not to access or produce prohibited material and also to reinforce ethical imperatives and issues of defamation. Participants need to agree and sign these. A Los Angeles–based participatory storytelling collective called Voz Mob also "reinforces agreed upon core values," which guide their work, to their affiliates. We suspect these values—transparency, integrity, honesty, community decision making, and equitable resource distribution—also apply to participant storytellers.

Training: The ability to download content from the Internet and upload videos is not a new mobile concept and can be done on many types of mobiles using readily available data packages. We have chosen to teach a group of people how to use mobile technology constructively, and our training reinforces ethical behavior and explains defamation and the need for respect of all involved. Stories are not published unless participants follow guidelines.

Consent: Mojos are taught about the importance of only filming with proper consent.

Production: In this context, we reaffirm lessons learned during training. We implement these during the shoot phase and fix anything that needs fixing during the shoot and the edit.

Moderation: Participants upload to a private site and we moderate before going live.

Upload capacity: Mojo requires participants to have an upload capacity. The exact amount of data is determined during the training and setup phase to correspond to the number of expected videos. Participants need all their data allowance to upload their project videos and are made aware of this. All phones have a capped call and data allowance, and this prevents massive cost blowouts. A monitoring policy warns if a participant is making excessive calls and organizers act on this.

Production cycle: Careful planning is the key to creating an environment where participants feel empowered to excel within project parameters while allowing the creative freedom for participants to grow their skills and confidence. The production cycle is summarized as follows:

- Develop a project proposal based on appropriate ideals and assumptions that is supported by research parameters.
- Choose the right participants.
- Provide on-the-ground mentoring and support.
- Provide effective training via the specific training manual.
- Provide flexible technology that can deliver outcomes within project parameters.
- Establish a set of proven production guidelines that spell out every phase of production.
- Establish protocols to obtain appropriate filming approvals and access.
- Monitor the filming process while providing participants with the creative freedom to deliver according to research parameters.
- Provide on-the-ground support during the production phase.
- Provide a vehicle for publishing the work (website) to inspire participants to continue the work.
- Provide feedback during and after the project.
- Report on the project to assist with the development of future models.

References

ABI [Allied Business Intelligence]. 2013. The mobile app market will be worth $27 billion in 2013 as tablet revenue grows. London: ABI.

Alcoff, Linda. 1991. The problem of speaking for others. *Cultural Critique* 20 (Winter):5–32.

Allan, Stuart. 2013. *Citizen Witnessing Revisioning Journalism in Times of Crisis.* Malden, MA: Polity Press.

Anfara, Vincent, and Norman Mertz. 2006. *Theoretical Frameworks in Qualitative Research.* Thousand Oaks, CA: Sage.

Apperley, Thomas. 2011. Regulation in the digital economy: Convergent regulation for the digital economy. Parkville, Australia: Institute for a Broadband-Enabled Society.

Archer, Margaret. 2007. *Making Our Way through the World.* Cambridge: University of Cambridge Press.

Atkinson, P., and D. Silverman. 1997. Kunderas immortality: The interview society and the invention of self. *Qualitative Inquiry* 3 (3):304–25.

Atton, Chris, and James Frederick Hamilton. 2008. *Alternative Journalism.* London: Sage.

Attran, Scott, Douglas Medin, and Norbert Ross. 2005. The cultural mind: Environmental decision making and cultural modelling within and across populations. *Psychological Review* 112 (4):744–76.

Barker, Chris. 2008. *Cultural Studies (Theory and Practice).* London: Sage.

Batty, Phillip. 2012. Interview.

Bauder, Harald. 2010. Dialectics of media practice. *Canadian Journal of Media Studeis* 6 (1).

Beaumont, Claudine. 2009. New York plane crash: Twitter breaks the news, again. *Telegraph.* http://www.telegraph.co.uk/technology/twitter/4269765/New-York-plane-crash-Twitter-breaks-the-news-again.html (accessed 20 January 2014).

Bell, Wendy. 2008. *A Remote Possibility.* Alice Springs, Australia: IAD Press.

Benhabib, Seyla. 1992. Models of public space: Hannah Arendt, the liberal tradition, and Jurgen Habermas. In *Habermas and the Public Sphere*, edited by Craig Calhoun, 73–98. Cambridge: Massachusetts Institute of Technology Press.

Bennett, W. 2008. Civic learning in changing democracies: Challenges for citizenship and civic education. In *Young Citizens and New Media: Learning and Democratic Engagement*, edited by Peter Dahlgren, 59–78. New York: Routledge.

Benson, Rodney. 2003. Commercialism and critique. In *Contesting Media Power: Alternative Media in a Networked World*, edited by Nick Couldry and James Curran, 111–27. Lanham, MD: Rowman and Littlefield.

Benson, Rodney. 2006. News media as a "journalistic field": What Bourdieu adds to new institutionalism, and vice versa. *Political Communication* 23:187–202.

Benson, Rodney. 2009. Shaping the public sphere: Habermas and beyond. *American Sociologist* 40 (Fall):175–92.

Benson, Rodney, and Erik Neveu. 2005. *Bourdieu and the Journalistic Field.* Cambridge, UK: Polity Press.

Berger, John. 1972. *Ways of Seeing.* London: BBC.

Bishop, Rusell, Mere Berryman, Tom Cavanagh, and Lani Teddy. 2009. Te Kotahitanga: Addressing educational disparities facing Māori students in New Zealand. *Teaching and Teacher Education* 25 (5):734–42.

Bloom, Benjamin, and Davi Krathwohl. 1984. *Taxonomy of Educational Objectives, The Classification of Educational Goals, Handbook I: Cognitive Domain.* New York: Longman.

Blumenkranz, Carla, Keith Gessen, and Nikil Sava. 2013. Too Much Sociology. nplusonemag.com.

Boczkowski, Pablo. 2004. *Digitizing the News: Innovation in Online Newspapers.* 1st ed. Cambridge: Massachusetts Institute of Technology Press.

Boreham, Glen. 2012. Convergence review final report. Canberra: Australian Government.

Bourdieu, Pierre. 1984. *Distinction: A Social Critique of the Judgement of Taste.* London: Routledge.

Bourdieu, Pierre. 1985. The social space and the genesis of groups. *Theory and Society* 14 (6):723–44.

Bourdieu, Pierre. 1986. The forms of capital. In *Handbook of Theory and Research for the Sociology of Education,* edited by J. Richardson, 241–58. New York: Greenwood.

Bourdieu, Pierre. 1989. Social space and symbolic power. *Sociological Theory* 7 (1):14–25.

Bourdieu, Pierre. 1990. *The Logic of Practice.* Stanford, CA: Stanford University Press.

Bourdieu, Pierre. 1998. *On Television.* New York: New Press.

Bourdieu, Pierre. 2005. The political field, the social science field and the journalistic field. In *Bourdieu and the Journalistic Field,* edited by Rodney Benson. Malden, MA: Polity Press.

Bourdieu, Pierre, and Jean-Claude Passeron. 1994. *Academic Discourse: Linguistic Misunderstanding and Professorial Power.* Cambridge, UK: Polity Press.

Bourdieu, Pierre, and Loic Wacquant. 1992. *An Invitation to Reflexive Sociology.* Chicago and Cambridge, UK: Chicago Press and Polity.

Bowman, Shayne, and Chris Willis. 2003. We media: How audiences are shaping the future of news and information. http://wemedia.com/2004/02/01/we-media-how-audiences-are-shaping-the-future-of-news-and-information/.

Brook, Stephen. 2009. Half UK local and regional papers could shut by 2014, MPs are told. *Guardian,* 16 June. http://www.theguardian.com/media/2009/jun/16/half-local-papers-could-shut-2014.

Bruns, Axel. 2005. *Gatewatching: Collaborative Online News Production.* New York: Peter Lang Publishing.

Bruns, Axel. 2008. Life beyond the public sphere: Towards a networked model for political deliberation. *Information Polity* 13 (1–2):71–85.

Bruns, Axel, and Tim Highfield. 2012. Blogs, Twitter, and breaking news: The pro-
    dusage of citizen journalism. In *Produsing Theory in a Digital World: The Inter-
    section of Audiences and Production*, edited by Rebecca Ann Lind. New York:
    Peter Lange.
Bruns, Axel, and Jan-Hinrik Schmidt. 2011. Produsage: A closer look at continuing
    developments. *New Review of Hypermedia and Multimedia* 17 (1):3–7.
Buck-Morss, Susan 2001. A global public sphere? *Radical Philosphy* (December):
    10–19.
Bulkley, Kate. 2012. The rise of citizen journalism. *Guardian*, 11 June. http://www.
    guardian.co.uk/media/2012/jun/11/rise-of-citizen-journalism.
Bürén, Kristina. 2012. World press trends report 2012. Paris: World Association of
    Newspapers and News Publishers.
Burum, Ivo, ed. 1991. *Satellite Dreaming*. Australia: Ronin, ABC TV.
Burum, Ivo. 1994. Birth and single parents. In *Home Truths*, edited by Ivo Burum.
    Australia: ABC TV.
Burum, Ivo, ed. 1999. *Race around Oz*. Australia: ABC TV.
Burum, Ivo, ed. 2003. *After the Fires*. Australia: ABC TV.
Burum, Ivo, and Martin Hirst. 2011. Title. *Go2News*.
Burum, Ivo. 2012a. *Mojo Working*. Australia: NITV.
Burum, Ivo. 2012b. Using mobile media to create a more diverse public sphere in
    marginalised communities: How to mojo. *International Journal of Community
    Diversity* 12 (1):11–22.
Burum, Ivo. 2013. *Cherbourg Mojo Out Loud*. Melbourne: SBS/NITV.
Burum, Ivo. 2014. Perfect digital. *Channel* (1).
Calhoun, Craig. 1992. Introduction. In *Habermas and the Public Sphere*, edited by
    Craig Calhoun. Cambridge: Massachusetts Institute of Technology Press.
Carey, James. 1987. The press and public discourse. *Center Magazine* 20 (2):4–16.
Carr, Wilfred, and Stephen Kemmis. 2004. *Becoming Critical: Education Knowledge
    and Action Research*. London: Routledge.
Castells, Manuel. 2001. *The Internet Galaxy: Reflections of the Internet, Business
    and Society*. New York: Oxford University Press.
Castells, Manuel. 2008. The new public sphere: Global civil society, communication
    networks, and global governance. *Annals of the American Academy of Political
    and Social Sciences* 616 (78):78–91.
Castells, Manuel. 2009. *Communications Power*. New York: Oxford University
    Press.
Clark, Lynn Schofield, and Rachel Monserrate. 2011. High school journalism and
    the making of young citizens. *Journalism* 12 (4):417–32.
Clough, Peter, and Cathy Nutbrown. 2006. *A Students Guide to Methedology*.
    London: Sage.
Cole, Jeffrey. 2011. Highlights: The 2011 Digital Future Project—Year ten. In *Digital
    Futures Report*, edited by Jeffrey Cole. Los Angeles: University of Southern
    California.
Cole, Jeffrey. 2013. The Digital Future Project 2013. In *World Internet Project*,
    edited by Jeffrey Cole. Los Angeles: University of Southern California.
Constanza-Chock, Sasha. 2011. Digital popular communication lessons on infor-
    mation and communication technologies for social change from the immigrant
    rights movement. *National Civic Review* 100 (3):29–35.

Constine, Josh. 2014. Facebook Climbs To 1.59 Billion Users And Crushes Q4 Estimates With $5.8B Revenue. http://techcrunch.com/2016/01/27/facebook-earnings-q4-2015/.

Cope, Bill, and Mary Kalantzis. 2012. *Literacies*. New York: Cambridge University Press.

Coscarelli, Joe. 2012. The New York *Times* is now supported by readers, not advertisers. *New York Magazine*, 26 July. http://nymag.com/daily/intel/2012/07/new-york-times-supported-by-readers-not-advertisers.html.

Crossley, Nick. 2004. On systematically distorted communication: Bourdieu and the socio-analysis of publics. *Sociological Review* 52 (s1):88–112.

Crotty, M. 2003. *The Foundations of Social Research: Meaning and Perspective in the Research Process*. London: Sage.

Curran, James. 1991. Rethinking the media and the public sphere. In *Communication and Citizenship: Journalism and the Public Sphere*, edited by Peter Sparks and Colin Dahlgren. London: Routledge.

Curran, James. 2007. Introduction. In *The Alternative Media Handbook*, edited by Kate Coyer, Tony Dowmunt, and Alan Faountain. New York: Routledge.

Dahlgren, Peter. 1995. *Television and the Public Sphere: Citizenship, Democracy, and the Media*. Thousand Oaks, CA: Sage.

Dahlgren, Peter, and Colin Sparks. 1991. *Communication and Citizenship: Journalism and the Public Sphere*. London: Routledge.

DBCDE [Department of Broadband, Communications and the Digital Economy]. 2011a. Advancing Australia as a digital economy: An update of the national digital economy strategy. Canberra: DBCDE.

DBCDE [Department of Broadband, Communications and the Digital Economy]. 2011b. Convergence review emerging issues paper. Canberra: Australian Government.

DBCDE [Department of Broadband, Communications and the Digital Economy]. 2012. Convergence review executive summary. In *Department of Broadband Communicatuion and Digital Economy*. Canberra: Australian Government.

de Argaez, Enrique. 2014. Internet world stat. Mniwatts Marketing Group. http://www.internetworldstats.com/emarketing.htm.

Deuze, Mark. 2003. The web and its journalisms: Considering the consequences of different types of news media online. *New Media and Society* 5 (2):203–30.

Deuze, Mark. 2005. What is journalism? Professional identity and ideology of journalists reconsidered. *Journalism* 6 (4):442–64.

Deuze, Mark. 2006. Participation, remediation, bricolage: Considering principal components of a digital culture. *Information Society* 22 (2):63–75.

Deuze, Mark. 2007. *Media Work, Digital Media and Society Series*. Cambridge, UK: Polity.

Deuze, Mark. 2008. Understanding journalism as newswork: How it changes, and how it remains the same. *Westminster Papers in Communication and Culture* 5 (2):4–23.

Deuze, Mark. 2009. The future of citizen journalism. In *Citizen Journalism: Global Perspectives*, edited by Stuart Allan and Einar Thorsen, 255–64. New York: Peter Lang.

Deuze, Mark. 2012. *Media Life*. Cambridge, UK: Polity Press.

Dewey, John. 2012. *The Public and Its Problems*, edited by Melvin Rodgers. University Park, PA: Penn State University.

Dick, Bob. 2000. Postgraduate programs using action research. *Learning Organization* 9 (4):159–70.

Dodge, Toby. 2012. From the 'Arab awakening' to the Arab Spring; the post colonial state in the Middle East. In *After the Arab Spring: Power Shift in the Middle East?* edited by Nicholas Kitchen, 5–11. London: London School of Economics.

Dole, Chris. 2012. *Healing Secular Life: Loss and Devotion in Modern Turkey.* Philadelphia: University of Pennsylvania Press.

Dopfner, Mathias. 2013. The best is yet to come. In *Innovations in Newspapers World Report 2013*, edited by Claude Erbsen. Paris: World Association of Newspapers and News Publishers.

Duffield, Lee. 2011. Media skills for daily life: Designing a journalism programme for graduates of all disciplines. *Pacific Journalism Review* 17 (1):141–55.

Duffield, Lee, and John Cockley. 2006. *I Journalist.* Sydney: Pearson Education.

Dumpala, Preethi. 2009. The year the newspaper died. *Business Insider Australia*, 4 July. http://www.businessinsider.com/the-death-of-the-american-newspaper-2009-7.

Durrani, Arif. 2015. Guardian's digital revenues hit £80m but losses remain around £30m. *Campaign Magazine*, 9 March. http://www.campaignlive.co.uk/article/guardians-digital-revenues-hit-80m-losses-remain-around-30m/1337224.

Dutton, Jane. 2012. Was the revolution lost in Tunisia and Egypt? Al Jazeera. http://www.aljazeera.com/programmes/insidestory/2012/09/20129584729858732.html.

Economist. 2012. Breaking up news corp: Murdoch does the splits. *Economist*, 19 November.

El-Ghobashy, Mona. 2012. The praxis of the Egyptian revolution. In *The Journey to Tahrir: Revolution, Protest, and Social Change in Egypt*, edited by Jeannie Sowers and Chris Toensing, 21–40. London: Verso.

Elia, Ilicco. 2012. Interview. London.

Ellis, Justin. 2012. Alan Rusbridger on *The Guardian*'s open journalism, paywalls, and why they're pre-planning more of the newspaper. Cambridge, MA: Nieman Journalism Lab. http://www.niemanlab.org/2012/05/alan-rusbridger-on-the-guardians-open-journalism-paywalls-and-why-theyre-pre-planning-more-of-the-newspaper/.

Entwistle, George. 2012. George Entwistle: Speech to BBC staff. BBC. http://www.bbc.co.uk/mediacentre/speeches/2012/george-entwistle-to-staff.html (accessed 18 September 2012).

Ewart, Jacquie, Susan Forde, Kerrie Foxwell, and Michael Meadows. 2007. Community media and the public sphere in Australia. In *New Media Worlds: Challenges for Convergence*, edited by Virginia Nightingale and Tim Dwyer. Melbourne: Oxford University Press.

Favell, Andy. 2013. Mobi thinking. http://mobithinking.com/mobile-marketing-tools/latest-mobile-stats (accessed 19 September 2011).

Feldman, Charles. 2008. *No Time to Think: The Menace of Media Speed.* New York: Continumum International.

Ferree, Myra, William Gamson, Jurgen Gerhards, and Dieter Rucht. 2002. Four models of the public sphere in modern democracies. *Theory and Society* 31 (3):289–324.

Finkelstein, R. 2011. Report of the Independent Inquiry into the Media and Media Regulation. Canberra: Australian Government Department of Broadband.

Fontana, Andrea, and James Frey. 2000. The interview: From structured questions to negotiated text. In *Handbook of Qualitative Research*, edited by N. Denzin and Y. Lincoln, 645–72. Thousand Oaks, CA: Sage.

Forde, Susan. 2011. *Challenging the News: The Journalism of Alternative and Community Media.* London: Palgrave Macmillan.

Fraser, Nancy. 1992. Rethinking the public sphere: A contribution to the critique of actually existing democracy. In *Habermas and the Public Sphere*, edited by Craig Calhoun, 109–42. Cambridge: Massachusetts Institute of Technology Press.

Freire, Paulo. 1970. *Pedagogy of the Oppressed*. London: Continuum International.

Funk, Carolyn. 1998. Practicing what we preach? The influence of a societal interest value on civic engagement. *Political Psychology* 19 (3):601–14.

Gahran, Amy. 2013. Patch.com announces closure of 400 hyperlocal sites. Knight Dogitla Media Center. http://www.knightdigitalmediacenter.org/blogs/agahran/2013/08/patchcom-announces-closure-400-hyperlocal-sites.

Galbraith, Trevor. 2013. Interview.

Gant, Sott. 2007. *We're All Journalists Now*. New York: Free Press.

Garber, Megan. 2013. The Gutenberg parenthesis: Thomas Pettitt on parallels between the pre-print era and our own Internet age. Cambridge, MA: Neiman Journalism Lab.

Garnham, Nicholas. 1986. The media and the public sphere. In *Communicating Politics*, edited by P. Golding, Graham Murdock, and P. Schlesinger, 45–53. Leicester, UK: Leicester University Press.

Garnham, Nicholas. 1992. The media and the public sphere. In *Habermas and the Public Sphere*, edited by Craig Calhoun. Cambridge: Massachusetts Institute of Technology Press.

Garvin, Andy. 2013. #ISOJ Keynote: Can social media help us create a more informed public? PBS Media Shift. http://www.pbs.org/mediashift/2013/04/isoj-keynote-can-social-media-help-us-create-a-more-informed-public111.

Gaventa, John. 2002. Introduction: Exploring citizenship, participation and accountability. *IDS Bulletin* 33 (2).

Gaventa, John, and Jethro Pettit. 2012. Bourdieu and 'habitus'. Institute of Development Studies, University of Sussex. http://www.powercube.net/other-forms-of-power/bourdieu-and-habitus/ (accessed 15 October 2013).

Gawenda, Michael. 2008. Do newspapers have a future? And how long is that future? AN Smith Lecture in Journalism, University of Melbourne.

Gentikow, Barbara. 2007. The role of media in developing literacies and cultural techniques. *Nordic Joronal of Digital Literacies* 2:78–96.

Ghonim, Wael. 2012. *Revolution 2.0: The Power of the People Is Greater Than the People in Power, a Memoir*. New York: Houghton Miflin Harcourt.

Gilgun, J. 2010. The power of the case. *Current Issues in Qualitative Research* 1 (1–8):13.

Gillmor, Dan. 2006. *We the Media: Grassroots Journalism by the People, for the People*. Sebastopol, CA: O'Reilly Media.

Gillmor, Dan. 2010. Mediactive. San Francisco. Mediactive.com.

Goode, Luke. 2009. Social news, citizen journalism and democracy. *New Media Society* 11 (8).

Goodrich, Ron. 2010. Hide, hiding, hidden: Narrative as concealment and revelation. *Double Dialogues* 12 (Winter).

Greenslade, Roy. 2010. Rupert Murdoch: Rusbridger is talking bullshit. *Greenslade Blog*, 12 February. http://www.guardian.co.uk/media/greenslade/2010/feb/03/rupert-murdoch-rusbridger-bs.

Gripsrud, Jostein, Moe Hallvard, Anders Molander, and Graham Murdock. 2010. *The Idea of the Public Sphere*. Lanham, MD: Lexington Books.

Habermas, Jurgen. 1989. *The Structural Transformation of the Public Sphere. An Inquiry into a Category of Bourgeois Society*. Cambridge: Massachusetts Institute of Technology Press.

Habermas, Jurgen. 1996. *Between Facts and Norms: Contributions to a Discourse Theory of Law and Democracy.* Cambridge: Massachusetts Institute of Technology Press.

Habermas, Jurgen. 2006. Political communication in media society: Does democracy still enjoy an epistemic dimension? The impact of normative theory on empirical research. *Communication Theory* 16 (4):411–26.

Habermas, Jurgen, and Thomas McCarthy. 1987. *The Theory of Communicative Action*, vol. 2: *Lifeworld and System*. Boston: Beacon Press.

Hadland, Adrian. 2008. Shooting the messenger: Mediating the public and the role of the media in South Africa's xenophobic violence. Cameroun: Council for the Development of Social Science Research in Africa.

Hallin, Daniel, and Paolo Mancinin 2004. *Comparing Media Systems: Three Models of Media Politics.* 1st ed. Cambridge: Cambridge University Press.

Hanrahan, Michael, and Deborah Madsen. 2006. From literacy to e-literacy. In *Teaching Technology, Texuality: Approaches to New Media*, edited by Michael Hanrahan and Deborah Madsen. New York: Palgrave Macmillan.

Harcup, Tony. 2011. Alternative journalism as active citizenship. *Journalism* 12 (15): 15–31.

Harrison, John, Martin Hirst, and Michael de Wall. 2004. Newspace: A place, not just a platform, for a critical pedagogy of journalism. University of Queensland, School of Journalism and Communication, Brisbane.

Hart, Chris. 2005. *Doing Your Masters Dissertation.* London: Sage.

Hartley, J., and Alan McKee. 2000. *The Indigenous Public Sphere: The Reporting and Reception of Aboriginal Issues in the Australian Media.* 1st ed. New York: Oxford University Press.

Hartley, John. 2009. *The Uses of Digital Literacy.* Piscataway, NJ: Transaction Publishers.

Haseman, Brad. 2006. A manifesto for performative research. *Media International Australia Incorporating Culture and Policy Practice-Led Research* (118):98–106.

Hassenzahl, Marc. 2003. The thing and I: Understanding the reflationship between user and product. In *Funology: From Usability to Enjoyment*, edited M. Blythe, C. Overbleeke, A. Monk, and P.C. Wright, 31–42. Dordrecht: Kluwer Academic.

Haughney, Christine. 2013. *Time Magazine* branches out into documentary films. http://www.nytimes.com/2013/08/12/business/media/time-magazine-ventures-into-documentary-films.html?_r=0.

Hawkins, J., and R. Catalano. 1992. Risk and protective factors for alcohol and other drug problems in adolescence and early adulthood: Implications for substance abuse prevention. *Psychlogical Bulletin* 112 (1):64–105.

Hedman, Ulrika, and Monika Djerf-Pierre. 2013. The social journalist: Embracing the social media life or creating a new digital divide? *Digital Journalism* 1 (3): 1–18.

Hermida, Alfred. 2010a. From TV to Twitter: How ambient news became ambient journalism. *Media Culture* 13 (2).

Hermida, Alfred. 2010b. How to teach social media in journalism schools. PBS Media Shift. http://www.pbs.org/mediashift/2010/08/how-to-teach-social-media-in-journalism-schools242.html.

Hermida, Alfred. 2011. The active recipient: Participatory journalism through the lens of the Dewey-Lippmann debate. Presented at the International Symposium in Online Journalism, Austin, TX.

Hermida, Alfred. 2012. Tweets and truth: Journalism as a discipline of collaborative verification. *Journalism Practice* 6 (5–6):1–10.

Herr, Kathryn, and Gary Anderson. 2005. *The Action Research Dissertation: A Guide for Students and Faculty*, edited by Lisa Shaw. London: Sage.

Hirst, Martin. 2009. What is alternative journalism? *Global Media Journal* 3 (1):1–6.

Hirst, Martin. 2011. *News 2.0: Can Journalism Survive the Internet?* 1st ed. Sydney: Allen and Unwin.

Hirst, Martin. 2012. One tweet does not a revolution make: Technological determinism, media and social change. http://www.academia.edu/1789051/One_tweet_does_not_a_revolution_make_Technological_determinism_media_and_social_change.

Hirst, Martin, and John Harrison. 2007. *Communication and New Media: From Broadcast to Narrowcast*. Melbourne: Oxford University Press.

Hirst, Martin, and Greg Treadwell. 2011. Blogs bother me. Presented at World Journalism Education Congress, Grahamstown, South Africa.

Hitchens, Lesley. 2006. *Broadcasting Pluralism and Diversity: A Comparative Study of Policy and Regulation*. Portland, OR: Hart.

Horwitz, Robert. 2005. On media concentration and the diversity question. *Information Society* 21 (3):81–204.

Huffington, Arianna. 2011. When HuffPost Met AOL: "A merger of visions." *Huff-Post*, 6 February.

Husson, Thomas. 2013. Despite impressive growth, Facebook is facing mobile ad challenges. *Forbes*, 25 July.

Jakubowicz, Andrew, Heather Goodall, and Martin Jeannie. 1994. *Racism, Ethnicity, and the Media*. Sydney: Allen & Unwin.

Jarvis, Jeff. 2011. Digital first: What it means for journalism. *Guardian*, 26 June. http://www.theguardian.com/media/2011/jun/26/digital-first-what-means-journalism (accessed 12 January 2014).

Jenkins, Henry. 2008. *Convergence Culture: Where Old and New Media Collide*. New York: New York University Press.

Jensen, Klaus Bruhn, ed. 2012. *A Handbook of Media and Communication Research: Qualitative and Quantitative Methodologies*. 2nd ed. New York: Routledge.

Jolkovski, Anton. 2013. Interview with Ole Mølgaard, Program Director, CBS Executive, Denmark. Paris: World Association of Newspapers and News Publishers.

Jones, Bryony. 2011. What will AOL-Huff Post merger mean? CNN.

Judge, Simon. 2016. Global smartphone shipments hit a record 1.4 billion units in 2015. Smartphone Market Research. http://www.smartphonemarketresearch.com/global-smartphone-shipments-hit-a-record-1-4-billion-units-in-2015/.

Kafka, Peter. 2014. What's net neutrality? What happened to net neutrality yesterday? What happens next? ReCode. http://recode.net/2014/01/15/whats-net-neutrality-what-happened-to-net-neutrality-yesterday-what-happens-next-a-qa-for-the-rest-of-us/ (accessed 15 June 2014).

Kaku, Michio. 2011. *Physics of the Future: How Science Will Shape Our Daily Lives by 2010*. New York: Doubleday.

Keen, Andrew. 2006. *The Cult of the Amateur: User Generated Media Are Killing Our Culture and Economy*. 5th ed. London: Nicholas Brealey.

Kern, Eliza. 2013. Facebook beats expectations with $1.81 billion in revenue, shows gains on mobile. Gigaom. https://gigaom.com/2013/07/24/facebook-beats-expectations-announces-second-quarter-revenue-of-1-81-billion/.

Kovach, Bill, and Tom Rosenstiel. 2007. *The Elements of Journalism: What Newspeople Should Know and the Public Should Expect*. 1st rev. ed. New York: Three Rivers Press.

Kuhn, Raymond. 2011. Historical Devlopment of the Media in France. In *The Media in Contemporary France*, 5–8. McGraw Hill. http://www.mcgraw-hill. co.uk/openup/chapters/9780335236220.pdf.

Kwek, Glenda, and C. Kruger. 2012. New Ltd hit by $476 million loss as revenues decline. *Sydney Morning Herald*, 19 December. http://www.smh.com.au/business/ news-ltd-hit-by-476m-loss-as-revenues-decline-20121218-2bl2j.html.

Langton, Marcia. 1993. *Well, I Heard It on the Radio and I Saw It on the Television.* Sydney: Australian Film Commission.

Lankshear, Colin, Michele Knobel, Chris Bigum, and Michael Peters. 2007. *A New Literacy Sampler*, edited by Colin Lankshear and Michele Knobel. New York: Peter Lang.

Lasica, Joseph 2003. What is participatory journalism? Online Journalism Review. http://www.ojr.org/ojr/workplace/1060217106.php.

Lasswell, Harold. 1948. The structure and function of communication in society. *Communication Theory and Research Magazine* 2007 (24):215–28.

Lawson, George. 2012. The Arab uprisings: Revolution or protests? In *After the Arab Spring: Power Shift in the Middle East?* edited by Nicholas Kitchen, 12–16. London: London School of Economics.

Leffert, Nancy, Peter Benson, Peter Scales, Anu Sharma, Dyanne Drake, and Dale Blyth. 1998. Development assets: Measurement and prediction of risk behaviors among adolescents. *Applied Development Science* 2 (4):209–30.

Leveson, Brian. 2012. An inquiry into the culture, practices and ethics of the press. London: The Stationary Office. http://www.official-documents.gov.uk/document/ hc1213/hc07/0779/0779.pdf, http://www.levesoninquiry.org.uk/about/the-report/.

Lewis, Justin, Andrew Williams, and Bob Franklin. 2008. A compromised Fourth Estate? *Journalism Studies* 9 (1):1–20.

Lippmann, Walter. 2008. *Liberty and the News.* Paperback ed. Princeton, NJ: Princeton University Press. Original edition, 1920.

Little, Mark. 2013. When everyone is an eye-witness, what is a journalist? http://blog. storyful.com/2013/04/21/when-everyone-is-an-eye-witness-what-is-a-journalist/#. Vqoti4S4aLE.

Lottridge, Danielle, and Gale Moore. 2009. Designng for human emotion. *New Review of Hypermedia and Multimedia* 15 (2):147–72.

Mahlke, Sascha. 2008. User experience of interaction with technical systems. PhD Research, Ingenieurwissenschaften, Berlin (D83).

Mansour, Sherif. 2013. *On the Divide: Press Freedom at Risk in Egypt.* New York: Committee to Protect Journalists.

Marchetti, Dominique. 2005. Subfields of specialised journalism. In *The Journalistic Field*, edited by Rodney Benson. Cambridge, MA: Polity Press.

Marzano, Robert. 2007. The need for a revision of Bloom's taxonomy. In *The New Taxonomy of Educational Objectives*, edited by Robert Marzano and John Kendall, 1–19. London: Sage.

Mason, Mark. 2010. Sample size and saturation in PhD studies using qualitative interview. *Forum: Qualitative Social Research* 11 (3):Article 8.

Mason, Paul. 2012a. The new revolutionaries: Experts in messing up hierarchies. In *The Arab Spring: Rebellion, Revolution and a New World Order*, edited by Toby Manhire, 280–3. London: Guardian.

Mason, Paul. 2012b. *Why It's Kicking Off Everywhere: The New Global Revolutions.* London: Verso.

McChesney, Robert. 2001. Global media, neoliberalism and imperialism. *International Socialist Review* 52 (10).

McChesney, Robert. 2007. *Communication Revolution: Critical Junctures and New Media*. 1st ed. New York: New York Press.

McChesney, Robert, and V. Pickard, eds. 2011. *Will the Last Reporter Please Turn Out the Lights*. New York: New Press.

McDonald, Steve. 2014. Introduction to location sound recording. AFTRS. http://www.aftrs.edu.au/short-courses/introduction-to-location-sound-recording/U537.

McKee, Alan. 2005. *The Public Sphere: An Introduction*. New York: Cambridge University Press.

McKendrick, Joseph. 2013. OTT video: Coming to a paid channel near you. New Providence, NJ: Unisphere Research.

McKernan, Jim. 1988. Teacher as Reseracher: paradigm and praxis. *Contemprary Education* LIX (3):173–200.

McKinnon, Colin. 2012. Interview.

McLuhan, Marshall. 1951. *The Mechanical Bride: Folklore of Industrial Man*. Toronto: Copp Clark Company.

McLuhan, Marshall. 1964. *Understanding Media: The Extensions of Man*. Paperback ed. New York: Penguin.

McLuhan, Marshall. 1969. The *Playboy* interview. *Playboy*, March.

McMillan, Robert. 2014. What everyone gets wrong in the debate over net neutrality. *Wired*. http://www.wired.com/2014/06/net_neutrality_missing/.

McNiff, Jean, and Jack Whitehead. 2006. *All You Need to Know about Action Research*. London: Sage.

Meadows, Michael. 2005. Journalism and the indigenous public sphere. *Pacific Journalism Review* 11 (1):36–41.

Meadows, Michael. 2013. Putting the citizen back into journalism. *Journalism* 14 (1):43–60.

Meadows, Michael, Susan Forde, Jacquie Ewart, and Kerrie Foxwell. 2009. Making good sense: Transformative processes in community journalism. *Journalism* 10 (2):155–70.

Meadows, Michael, Susan Forde, Jacquie Ewart, and Kerrie Foxwell-Norton. 2010. Making spaces: Community media and formation of the democratic public sphere in Australia. In *Making Our Media: Global Initiatives toward a Democratic Public Sphere*, edited by Clemencia Rodriguez, Dorothy Kidd, and Laura Stein, 163–81. Kreswell, NJ: Hampton Press.

Meadows, Michael, and Kerrie Foxwell. 2011. Community broadcasting and mental health: The role of local radio and television in enhancing emotional and social well-being. *Radio Journal: International Studies in Broadcast and Audio Media* 9 (2):89–106.

Merrill, John. 1993. *The Dialectic in Journalism*. 2nd ed. Baton Rouge: Louisiana University Press.

Meyrowitz, Joshua. 1998. Multiple media literacies. *Journal of Communication* 48 (1):96–108.

Michaels, Eric. 1986. The aboriginal invention of television in Central Australia 1982–1986. Institute Report Series. Canberra: Australian Institute of Aboriginal Studies.

Michaels, Eric. 1989. *For a Cultural Future: Francis Jupurrurla Makes TV at Yuendumu*, vol. 3: *Art and Criticism Monograph*. Malvern, Australia: Art and Text Publications.

Michaels, Eric. 1994. *Bad Aboriginal Art and Other Essays: Tradition, Media, and Technological Horizons*. Minneapolis: University of Minnesota Press.

Miller, Andrew. 2013. Pursuing diversity among our colleagues and in our coverage. *Guardian*, 20 November. http://www.theguardian.com/sustainability/sustainability-report-2013-people-diversity.

Morris, Simon. 2012. Interview.

Mosco, Vincent. 2004. *The Digital Sublime*. 1st ed. Cambridge: Massachusetts Institute of Technology Press.

Mosco, Vincent. 2009. Review article: Approaching digital democracy. *New Media Society* 11 (8):1394–400.

Mosireen. 2012. About Mosireen. Mosireen Collective. http://www.mosireen.org.

Muhlmann, Geraldine. 2010. *Journalism for Democracy*. Malden, MA: Polity Press.

Napoli, Philip. 1999. Deconstructing the diversity principle. *Journal of Communication* 49 (4):7–34.

Napoli, Philip. 2011. *Audience Evolution: New Technologies and the Transformation of Media Audiences*. New York: Columbia University Press.

Napoli, Philip. 2013. Audiences as consumers, audiences as citizens. University of Southern California, Annenberg. https://www.youtube.com/watch?v=afL11eOBTZE.

Napoli, Philip, and Kari Karppinen. 2013. Translating diversity to Internet governance. *First Monday* 18 (12).

Navarro, Zander. 2006. In search of a cultural interpretation of power: The contribution of Pierre Bourdieu. *IDS Bulletin* 37 (6):11–22.

Neilson, Brett, and Ned Rossiter. 2005a. From precarity to precariousness and back again: Labour, life and unstable networks. *Fibreculture Journal* 5.

Neilson, Brett, and Ned Rossiter. 2005b. Multitudes, creative organisation and the precarious condition of new media labour. *Fibreculture Journal* 5.

Newman, Marc, and Juyong Park. 2003. Why social networks are different from other types of networks. *Physical Review E* 68:036122.

Newman, Nic. 2015. Executive summary and key findings of the 2015 report. *Digital News Report 2015*.

O'Donnell, Penny, David McKnight, and Jonathan Este. 2012. Journalism at the speed of bytes. University of New South Wales, Sydney, Walkley Foundation.

Palmer, Shelly, and Raffensperger, Mike. 2011. *Overcoming the Digital Divide*. New York: York House Press.

Pappas, A. 2012. Developer economics: App market forecasts 2013–2016. Developer Economics. https://www.developereconomics.com/reports/app-economy-forecasts-2013-2016/.

Pastuovic, Sonja. 2013. Interview.

Patching, Roger. 1996. 900 into 300 won't go: Are Australia's journalism courses producing too many graduates? *Australian Journalism Review* 18 (1):53–64.

Patching, Roger, and Martin Hirst. 2013. *Journalism Ethics: Arguments and Cases for the Twenty-First Century*. London: Routledge.

Pavlik, John. 2000. The impact of technology on journalism. *Journalism Studies* 1 (2): 229–37.

Pavlik, John, and Shawn McIntosh. 2014. *Convergence Media: A New Introduction to Mass Media*. New York: Oxford University Press.

Peters, Jeremy, and V. Kopytoff. 2011. Betting on news, AOL is buying the Huffington Post. *New York Times*, 7 February. http://www.nytimes.com/2011/02/07/business/media/07aol.html?_r=1.

Pettitt, Thomas. 2013. Closing the journalism parenthesis: News mediation in a post-Gutenberg environment. Entrepreneurial Journalism and Media Meetup, University of New York, Graduate School of Journalism, New York, 17 October.

Phelan, Sean. 2011. The media as the neolibralized sediment: Articulating Laclau's discourse theory and Bourdieu's field theory. In *Discourse Theory and Critical Media Politics*, edited by Lincoln Dahlberg and Sean Phelan, 128–53. New York: Palgrave Macmillan.

Puentedura, Ruben. 2012. The SAMR model: Background and exemplars. http://www.hippasus.com/rrpweblog/archives/2012/08/23/SAMR_BackgroundExemplars.pdf.

Puentedura, Ruben. 2013. Technology in education: A brief introduction. https://www.youtube.com/watch?v=rMazGEAiZ9c.

Quinn, Stephen. 2005. *Convergent Journalism: The Fundamentals of Multimedia reporting*. New York: P. Lang.

Quinn, Stephen. 2012. *MoJo—Mobile Journalism in the Asian Region*. Singapore: Konrad-Adenauer-Stiftung.

Quinn, Stephen. 2013. *Asia's Media Innovators*, vol. 3: *Crowdsourcing in Asian Journalism*. Singapore: Konrad-Adenauer-Stiftung.

Quinn, Stephen, and Vincent F. Filak. 2005. *Convergent Journalism: An Introduction: Writing and Producing across Media*. Burlington, MA: Focal Press.

Radoll, Peter. 2002. Information and communication technology, 16. National Aboriginal and Torres Strait Islander Social Survey. Canberra: Australian Government.

Rashed, Fawaz. 2011. Twitpoper. Twitter. http://twitter.com/FawazRashed/status/48882406010257408 (accessed June 2012).

Reid, Alaster. 2013. How microvideo is playing an increasing role in the newsroom. https://www.journalism.co.uk/news/how-microvideo-is-playing-an-increasing-role-in-the-newsroom/s2/a553423/.

Rennie, E. 2001. Community television and the transition to digial broadcasting. *Australian Journal of Communication* 28 (1):57–68.

Rennie, E., A. Crouch, A. Wright, and J. Thomas. 2011. Home Internet for remote indigenous communities. Sydney: Australian Communications Consumer Action Network.

Ressa, Maria. 2014. Challenge to a free press. Presented at East-West International Media Conference, Yangon, Myanmar, 10 March.

Rheingold, Howard. 1994. *The Virtual Community: Homestealing on the Electronic Frontier*. 2nd ed. New York: HarperCollins.

Rheingold, Howard. 2002. *Smart Mobs*. Cambridge, MA: Perseus Books.

Rheingold, Howard, ed. 2012. *Net Smart*. Cambridge: Massachusetts Institute of Technology Press.

Ritchie, Jane, Jane Lewis, and Gillian Elam. 2003. Designing and selecting samples. In *Qualitative Research Practice: A Guide for Social Science Students and Researchers*, edited by Jane Ritchie and Jane Lewis, 77–108. Thousand Oaks, CA: Sage.

Robertson, Graeme. 2013. Staff rise to the demands of digital-first strategy. *Guardian*, 20 November. http://www.theguardian.com/sustainability/sustainability-report-2013-people-overview (accessed 1 December 2014).

Robertson, Mark. 2014. 400+ hours of video uploaded to YouTube every minute. http://www.reelseo.com/youtube-300-hours/ (accessed 7 February 2016).

Rodrigues, Uscha. 2008. Changing newsrooms: A survey of journalists in Victoria, Australia. *Australian Journalism Review* 30 (1):113–22.

Rogaway, Phillip. 1994. Marshall McLuhan interview from *Playboy*, 1969. ECS 188: Ethics in the Age of Technology, University of California, Davis. http://web.cs.ucdavis.edu/~rogaway/classes/188/spring07/mcluhan.pdf.

Rogers, Everett. 2003. *Diffusion of Innovations*. 5th ed. New York: Free Press.

Rosen, Jay. 1999. *What Are Journalists For?* New Haven, CT: Yale University Press.

Rosen, Jay. 2006. The People Formerly Known as the Audience. *PressThink*, 27 June. http://archive.pressthink.org/2006/06/27/ppl_frmr.html.

Rosenberg, Scott. 2011. Huffington is to AOL as AOL was to Time Warner. http://www.wordyard.com/2011/02/07/huffington-is-to-aol-as-aol-was-to-timewarner/ (accessed 7 February 2016).

Rosenberry, Jack. 2010. Roots of civic and citizen journalism. In *Public Journalism 2.0: The Promise and the Reality of Citizen Engaged Press*, edited by Jack Rosenberry and Burton St. John III, 9–12. New York: Routledge.

Rosensteil, Tom. 2013. Why we need a better conversation about the future of journalism education. http://www.poynter.org/2013/why-we-need-a-better-conversation-about-the-future-of-journalism-education/210196/.

Rusbridger, A. 2010. Does journalism exist? Annual Hugh Cudlipp Lecture. http://www.theguardian.com/media/2010/jan/25/cudlipp-lecture-alan-rusbridger.

Ruud, Geir. 2012. Interview.

Ryan, Ricahard, and Edward Deci. 2001. On happiness and human potentials: A review of research on hedonic and eudaimonic well-being. *Annual Review of Psychology* 52:141–66.

Sabadello, Markus. 2012. The Arab revolutions: Reflections on the role of civil society, human rights and new media in the transformation processes, edited by Zsolt Sereghy, Sarah Bunk, and Bert Preiss. Stadtschlaining, Austria: Austrian Study Center for Peace and Conflict Resolution.

Sabbagh, Dan. 2011. *Guardian* and *Observer* to adopt 'digital-first' strategy. *Guardian*, 16 June. http://www.theguardian.com/media/2011/jun/16/guardian-observer-digital-first-strategy.

SalahEldeen, Hany, and Michael Nelson. 2012. Losing my revolution: How many resources shared on social media have been lost? In *Proceedings of the Second International Conference on Theory and Practice of Digital Libraries*, Paphos, Cyprus, September 23–27, 2012, 125–37.

Salt, Jeremy. 2011. The great Arab revolution. *Arena*, 111.

Schmidt, Eric. 2011. Preparing for the big mobile revolution. *Harvard Business Review*, 24 January.

Schön, D. 1983. *The Reflective Practitioner*. London: Temple Smith.

Schramm, W. 1974. The nature of communication between humans. In *The Process and Effects of Mass Communication*, edited by Wilbur Schramm and Donald F. Roberts. Urbana: University of Illinois Press.

Schultz, Julianne. 1998. *Reviving the Fourth Estate: Democracy, Accountability, and the Media*. Cambridge: University of Cambridge Press.

Schwandt, Thomas. 1997. *Qualitative Inquiry: A Dictionary of Terms*. Thousand Oaks, CA: Sage.

Shakespeare, William. 1996. *The Winter's Tale*, edited by Stephen Orgel. New York: Oxford University Press.

Shihab-Eldin, Ahmed. 2012. WTF happened to Egypt's revolution? *Huffington Post*, 19 June. http://www.huffingtonpost.com/ahmed-shihabeldin/wtf-egypt-revolution_b_1610189.html.

Shirky, Clay. 2008. *Here Comes Everybody: The Power of Organisation without Organisations*. London: Allen Lane.

Shoemaker, Pamela. 2009. *Gatekeeping Theory*. New York: Routledge.

Shortell, Timothy. 2012. Division of labor and social integration. In Durkheim's theory of social class. http://www.brooklynsoc.org/courses/43.1/durkheim.html.

Singer, Jane, David Domingo, Alfred Hermida, and Steve Paulussen. 2011. *Participatory Journalism in Online Newspapers: Guarding the Internet's Open Gates*. Chichester, UK: Wiley.

Small, Stephen, and Marina Memmo. 2004. Contemporary models of youth development and problem prevention: Toward an integration of terms, concepts and models. *Family Relations* 53 (1):3–11.

Smith, Aron. 2013. Smartphone ownership—2013. Washington, DC: Pew Research Center.

Spencer, Lloyd, and Andrzej Krauze. 2012. *Introducing Hegel: A Graphic Guide*. London: Icon Books.

Standage, Tom. 1998. *The Victorian Internet*. New York: Walker Publishing Company.

Starkey, G., and A. Crisell. 2009. The traveller who came calling: A short history of radio journalism. In *Radio Journalism, Journalism Studies: Key Texts*, 1–22. London: Sage.

Stein, Ewan. 2012. Revolutionary Egypt: Promises or perils. In *After the Arab Spring: Power Shift in the Middle East?* edited by Nicholas Kitchen, 23–27. London: London School of Economics.

Stevens, Neville. 2010. Review of Australia government investment in the indigenous broadcasting and media Sector, edited by Department of Broadband, Communications and the Digital Economy. Canberra: Australian Government.

Stevens, Neville. 2011. Indigenous broadcasting review report. Canberra: Department of Broadband, Communications and the Digital Economy.

Stubbs, Liz. 2002. D. A. Pennebaker and Chris Hegedus—Engineering nonfiction cinema. In *Documentary Filmmakers Speak*, 41–67. New York: Allworth Press.

Surowiecki, J. 2009. *The Wisdom of Crowds*. London: Abacus.

Sustein, C. 1993. *Democracy and the Problem of Free Speech*. New York: Free Press.

Swartz, David. 1997. *Culture and Power: The Sociology of Poerre Bourdieu*. Chicago: University of Chicago Press.

Swartz, David. 2002. The sociology of habit: The perspective of Pierre Bourdieu. *Occupational Therapy Journal of Research* 22 (Suppl.):61s–69s.

Taylor, Colleen. 2013. TechCrunch disrupt Berlin backstage with Tim Armstrong. Berlin: AOL.

Taylor, Josh. 2014. Australian competition watchdog will help net neutrality: Cisco. ZDNet. http://www.zdnet.com/article/australian-competition-watchdog-will-help-net-neutrality-cisco/#!.

Tunney, Sean, and Garrett Monaghan, eds. 2010. *Web Journalism: A New Form of Citizenship*. Thronbill, Ontario: Sussex.

Turner, Graeme. 1988. *Film as Social Practice*. London: Routledge.

Vargas, Jose. 2012. Spring awakening [Book review]. *New York Times*, 17 February. http://www.nytimes.com/2012/02/19/books/review/how-an-egyptian-revolution-began-on-facebook.html?_r=1.

Volkmer, Ingrid. 2012. International communication theory in transition: Parameters of the new global public sphere. Massachusetts Institute of Technology Communications Forum, August. http://web.mit.edu/comm-forum/papers/volkmer.html.

Wadsworth, Yoland. 2011. *Everyday Evaluation on the Run*. 3rd ed. Crows Nest, Australia: Allen and Unwin.

Waller, Lisa. 2010. Indigenous research ethics: New modes of information gathering and storytelling in journalism. *Australia Journalism Review* 32 (2):19–31.

Walsh, Maureen. 2011. *Multimodal Literacy*. Newtown, Australia: Lingare Pty Ltd.

Weerakkody, N. 2009. *Research Methods for Media and Communicaion*. South Melbourne: Oxford University Press.

Wenger, Etienne. 2007. Communities in practice: A brief introduction. Eugene: University of Oregon. https://scholarsbank.uoregon.edu/xmlui/handle/1794/11736 (accessed 18 September 2011).

Westlund, Oscar. 2011. *Cross Media News Work—Sensemaking of the Mobile Media Revolution*. Gothenburg: University of Gothenburg.

Westlund, Oscar, and H. Arne Krumsvik. 2012. On the shaping of new digital media: A tale on intra-organizational interplay in old news media [Peer review]. Presented at 10th World Media Economics and Management Conference, Thessaloniki, Greece, 23–27 May.

Westlund, Oscar. 2013. Mobile news. *Digital Journalism* 1 (1):6–26.

Wilhelm, Alex. 2013. Leaked revenue figures illustrate need for hundreds of Patch layoffs. *Tech Crunch*, 19 August. http://techcrunch.com/2013/08/19/leaked-revenue-figures-illustrate-need-for-hundreds-of-patch-layoffs/.

Williams, Kim. 2012. The SA Press Club. Adelaide, Australia. http://www.sapressclub.com.au/forms/invitation-williams2.pdf.

Williams, Raymond. 2000. Culture is ordinary. In *Schooling the Symbolic Animal: Social and Cultural Dimensions of Education*, edited by Bradley Levinson, 31–35. Lanham, MD: Rowman and Littlefield.

Willmot, Eric. 1984. Out of the silent land: Report of the Task Force on Aboriginal and Islander Broadcasting and Communications. Canberra: Australian Government Publishing Service.

Wilson, Ernest. 2005. Engaged scholars and thoughtful practitioners: Enhancing their dialogue in the knowledge society. *Information Technologies and International Development* 2 (4):89–92.

Wilson, Ernest, and S. Costanza-Chock. 2009. Digital public media: New diversity of same old boys network. Presented at Public Media Corps, New York.

Womack, Brian. 2012. Google chairman says Android winning mobile war with Apple: Tech. Bloomberg. http://www.bloomberg.com/news/2012-12-12/google-chairman-says-android-winning-mobile-war-with-apple-tech.html (accessed 12 December 2012).

Woo, W. 2005. Defining a journalist's function. *Nineman Reports*, Winter.

Worth, Sol, and John Adair. 1972. *Through Navjo Eyes: An Exploration in Film Communication and Anthropology*. Bloomington: Indiana University Press.

Wu, Tim. 2003. Network neutrality, broadband discrimination. *Journal of Telecommunications and High Technology Law* 2:141.

Wu, Tim. 2014. Closing time for the open Internet. *New Yorker*, 15 January. http://www.newyorker.com/tech/elements/closing-time-for-the-open-internet (accessed 15 July 2014).

Yin, Robert. 2003. *Case Study Research: Design and Method*. Thousand Oaks, CA: Sage.

Zaponne, Chris. 2012. Fairfax to shed 1900 staff, erect paywalls. *Sydney Morning Herald*, 18 June. http://www.smh.com.au/business/fairfax-to-shed-1900-staff-erect-paywalls-20120617-20ix1.html.

Zuber-Skerritt, Ortrun, and Chad Perry. 2002. Action research within organisations and university thesis writing. *Learning Organization* 9 (4):171–79.

Zuckerman, Ethan. 2014. Challenge to a free press. Presented at East-West International Media Conference, Yangon, Myanmar, 10 March.

Index